Cambridge Imperial and Post-Colonial Studies

Series Editors
Richard Drayton, Department of History, King's College London,
London, UK
Saul Dubow, Magdalene College, University of Cambridge,
Cambridge, UK

The Cambridge Imperial and Post-Colonial Studies series is a well-established collection of over 100 volumes focussing on empires in world history and on the societies and cultures that emerged from, and challenged, colonial rule. The collection includes transnational, comparative and connective studies, as well as works addressing the ways in which particular regions or nations interact with global forces. In its formative years, the series focused on the British Empire and Commonwealth, but there is now no imperial system, period of human history or part of the world that lies outside of its compass. While we particularly welcome the first monographs of young researchers, we also seek major studies by more senior scholars, and welcome collections of essays with a strong thematic focus that help to set new research agendas. As well as history, the series includes work on politics, economics, culture, archaeology, literature, science, art, medicine, and war. Our aim is to collect the most exciting new scholarship on world history and to make this available to a broad scholarly readership in a timely manner.

Mariusz Lukasiewicz

Gold, Finance and Imperialism in South Africa, 1887–1902

A View from the Stock Exchange

palgrave
macmillan

Mariusz Lukasiewicz
Institute of African Studies
Leipzig University
Leipzig, Germany

ISSN 2635-1633   ISSN 2635-1641   (electronic)
Cambridge Imperial and Post-Colonial Studies
ISBN 978-3-031-51946-8   ISBN 978-3-031-51947-5   (eBook)
https://doi.org/10.1007/978-3-031-51947-5

Cover credit: Clu

This Palgrave Macmillan imprint is published by the registered company Springer Nature Switzerland AG
The registered company address is: Gewerbestrasse 11, 6330 Cham, Switzerland

Paper in this product is recyclable.

For Rosy and Ellie

PREFACE

Since its establishment in November 1887, the Johannesburg Stock Exchange (JSE) has served as something of a mirror to South Africa's multifaceted political economy, reflecting its industrialisation, settler colonialism, global economic integration, racial capitalism and political transformation from apartheid to an inclusive constitutional democracy. From its origins in the canvas tents on the dusty goldfields of Johannesburg to the architectural grandeur of its current location in the city's new central business district, Sandton, the JSE has connected South Africa's mineral resource industries with international financial and human capital for over 135 years. This book, however, is *not* a corporate history of the formative years of the JSE and should not be read as such. The book's analytical framework is beyond the organisational and operational scope of a financial intermediary that specialises in the sale of public stocks and government securities. Its global historical perspective highlights the dynamic nature of institutional narratives, which must be examined through diverse and competing sociopolitical lenses. Most importantly, the book does not reflect the views of JSE Limited and its employees, nor has it been endorsed by them.

My aim is to provide a historical reflection on the larger role and early global politics of financial intermediaries in South Africa's minerals-energy complex and trace the formative stages of what has come to be known as 'white monopoly capital.[1]' The popular (and increasingly populist) view of 'white monopoly capital' actively marginalising South Africa's Black majority in the private sector remains a dominant theme in critical discussions on socioeconomic inequality and serves as a convenient distraction from the fiscal unsustainability of state-owned or state-captured enterprises. South Africa's neoliberal agenda of the 1990s allowed large financial and mining houses to quickly overcome decades of corporate isolation through, among other strategies, joint ventures with foreign corporations and offshore listings.[2] Despite a slight contraction of the mining sector in recent years, gold, platinum and coal still make up the backbone of the South African primary sector in terms of value, production and employment, accounting for around 35% of total employment in industry and manufacturing.[3]

The internal contradictions of South Africa's industrial economy are most visible when mining interests are at stake. Despite heightened tensions over changing political alliances in South Africa's trade union landscape, the African National Congress (ANC) depends heavily on partisan lobbying and entrenchment in the mining sector's organised labour. Given its size and economic importance, as well as its strong position as a catalyst for international trade, the mining industry, largely represented by the newly rebranded Minerals Council of South Africa (South African Chamber of Mines until 2018), continues to maintain a strategic alliance with the JSE. This is intended to protect its public reputation by upholding 'socially responsible practices' and, most importantly, maximising shareholder value, while leaving labour unionism behind.[4]

The political significance of the entanglements between the key organisations of South African industrial capitalism, which served as the premise for this book project, was reaffirmed when on 27 October 2011, when the

---

[1] See: Van der Walt, L., 2015. Beyond white monopoly capital. *South African Labour Bulletin, 39*(3), pp. 29–42.

[2] Bond, Patrick. *Elite transition: From apartheid to neoliberalism in South Africa.* London: Pluto Press, 2014.
Marais, Hein. *South Africa: Limits to change: The political economy of transition.* Palgrave Macmillan. 2001. p. 128.

[3] Facts and Figures Pocket Book 2022. Minerals Council South Africa. https://www.mineralscouncil.org.za/industry-news/publications/facts-and-figures.

[4] Frankel, Philip. *Between the Rainbows and the Rain: Marikana, Migration, Mining and the Crisis of Modern South Africa.* African Books Collective, 2013. pp. 145–147.

ANC Youth League held the '*March for Economic Freedom in Our Life-time.*' Embodying the ANC Youth League's demands for nationalisation of the mines and expropriation of white-owned land without compensation, the march targeted three strategic institutions: the Chamber of Mines, the Johannesburg Stock Exchange and the Union Buildings in Pretoria. The final memorandum of grievances was presented at the JSE amidst cheers of 'down with white capital economy.'[5]

South Africa's disparities in the allocation of mining capital, land and labour were even instrumentalised by Thomas Piketty in his *Capital in the Twenty-First Century* and 2015 Nelson Mandela lecture, to illustrate how 'abnormal' rates of return on competing factors of production can lead to outbreaks of physical violence.[6] The asymmetric conflict between South Africa's land, labour and political power tragically culminated in the Marikana massacre on 16 August 2012 when 34 people, mostly unionised workers from the Lonmin platinum mine were brutally shot by police. Insofar as the victims were demanding higher wages and greater job security, the massacre exposed the violent inclinations of South Africa's industrial relations and raised new questions on the political stamina of the Tripartite Alliance between COSATU, the ANC and the South African Communist Party. In the post-Marikana political landscape, labour activism became more strategic, paving the way for the rise of the Economic Freedom Fighters under the leadership of Julius Malema, the expelled ANC Youth League Leader. This development intensified the populist critique of South Africa's racialised capitalism, further redirecting it towards the international operations of the JSE.[7]

The subjects of the book are, therefore, ultimately also a reflection of my own experiences in critically discussing colonial and apartheid era

[5] Bauer, Nickolaus. "Malema arrives to lead Young Lions into history books." Mail & Guardian. 27 October 2011. http://mg.co.za/article/2011-10-27-let-the-long-walk-to-economic-freedom-and-pretoria-begin.

[6] Piketty, Thomas. *Capital in the twenty-first century*. Harvard University Press, 2014. PP. 39–41.
Transcript of Nelson Mandela Annual Lecture 2015. Nelson Mandela Foundation. https://www.nelsonmandela.org/news/entry/transcript-of-nelson-mandela-annual-lecture-2015.

[7] Nicolson, Greg. "EFF marches: 'This isn't a Mickey Mouse organisation'."Daily Maverick. 28 October 2015. https://www.dailymaverick.co.za/article/2015-10-28-eff-marches-this-isnt-a-mickey-mouse-organisation/.

economic institutions and economic geography in South Africa. Through growing up and witnessing the political transition in the country between 1991 and 1994, albeit through the narrow outlook of an immigrant family navigating identity and belonging in rural Limpopo, I was made conscious of how economic participation is still hindered by the country's divisive history. My childhood in Phalaborwa exposed me to the interplay between international capital, industrial mining, and a racialised labour force during the Palabora Mining Company's transition to deep-level mining. My academic interest in South Africa's omnipresent socioeconomic inequalities was, however, sparked during my studies at the University of Cape Town.

When I attended the UCT's orientation week in February 2003, the official opening of the academic year took place in the central building that was then still known as Jameson Hall (Today's Sarah Baartman Hall). After a short but very energetic lecture by the Student Representative Council, we were led out of the hall and down the 'Jammie Stairs' towards the now infamous Cecil John Rhodes statue, where we took a short break before being divided into smaller groups to view the Smuts and Fuller Halls. These overlook the Cape Flats, where the apartheid government forcibly moved the city's non-white population, a stark reminder of South Africa's troubled past. For many of my more privileged fellow first-year students, that first day of exploring the Upper Campus ended with an uphill walk to the Rhodes' Memorial, where many had parked their private cars.

Although I completed the great majority of my formal education in government schools, at that stage of my intellectual development and academic interests, I was still rather ignorant of what Cecil John Rhodes, Leander Starr Jameson and Jan Smuts had meant for UCT, Southern Africa and postcolonialism more generally. However I was not the only first-year student from Cape Town's Southern Suburbs who failed to identify the symbolism and historicity. As though just to underscore how ignorant UCT's student body and management were about these colonial personalities and their postcolonial significance, the Orientation Week finished with an official SRC 'rave' in Cape Town's premier club, the Rhodes House! I often cringe at how I and many of my socially conscious, and indeed politically active, fellow students of all ethnic backgrounds remained oblivious to these divisive symbols for such a long time. Although my student experiences cannot be compared to the activist spirit and academic rigour of the 'liberal-radical' debates in the 1970s and

1980s, I was fortunate enough to witness the political mobilisation and agenda-setting of the first generation of post-apartheid students in the lecture halls and seminar rooms of numerous Rhodes Scholars(!).

In the years following my graduation, UCT had become a noticeably different place. Three years into my Ph.D. programme in Geneva, and having personally witnessed the manifestation of the Rhodes Must Fall Movement (RMFM) during an Easter visit to Cape Town in March 2015, I became a participant in the revitalised debates on decolonisation and the legacy of British imperialism and apartheid in South Africa. From this point onwards, the RMFM spread across international academic communities and transformed the way in which we explore and seek to overcome the legacies of colonialism and apartheid. Social and political debates in South Africa and, increasingly, in Britain and the USA, demonstrate just how the postcolonial moment is never fully beyond the colonial.[8]

This book, therefore, applies an empirical approach to addressing crucial historical and historiographical questions on the institutional origins of socioeconomic inequality and political conflict in South Africa. The mobilisation, provision and sustainability of finance for colonial South Africa's industrial transformation sit firmly at the core of 'the cult of Rhodes' and colonial nostalgias in Southern Africa. As the JSE currently expands its services and products across Africa, the financial intermediary remains a living symbol of colonial and apartheid history. With the National Treasury of South Africa acknowledging that the nature and extent of financial exclusion for most South Africans poses a significant socioeconomic challenge and political risk,[9] the stock market's historical and institutional legacies need to be linked to wider postcolonial discourses. In consonance with this view, this book's critical engagement with the power and embeddedness of imperial finance, as well as the agency and legacy of Cecil John Rhodes himself, offers a theoretical foundation and expands the empirical applications of the stock exchange with

---

[8] Knudsen, B.T. and Andersen, C., 2019. Affective politics and colonial heritage, Rhodes Must Fall at UCT and Oxford. *International Journal of Heritage Studies*, 25(3), pp.239–258.

[9] An Inclusive Financial Sector For All. National Treasury of South Africa. November 2023. https://www.treasury.gov.za/comm_media/press/2023/2023112701%20An%20I nclusive%20Financial%20Sector%20for%20all%202023.pdf

a view to fostering a deeper understanding of (post-)colonial social and economic institutions in South Africa.

Leipzig, Germany   Mariusz Lukasiewicz
November 2023

ACKNOWLEDGEMENTS

The bulk of the research for this book was conducted as part of my doctoral studies, but the manuscript was subsequently significantly expanded, restructured and rewritten. First, I sincerely thank Gareth Austin, Gopolan Balachandran, Marc Flandreau and Aidan Russell for investing much time, patience and effort in guiding me along the bumpy academic road, during my time in Geneva. A special acknowledgment must go to Gretjie Verhoef at the University of Johannesburg, who helped me access a number of archival collections in Johannesburg and encouraged me to present the initial ideas for this book in Johannesburg, Kyoto and Boston. In Leipzig, I thank Dmitri van den Bersselaar and my wonderful colleagues at the Institute of African Studies for expanding my intellectual horizons beyond the Zambezi. In South Africa, I would also like to express my sincere thanks for the intellectual support received from colleagues and friends at the Wits Institute for Social and Economic Research, Stellenbosch University, the International Studies Group at the University of the Free State, and the Department of Historical Studies at the University of Cape Town. Participation in the African Economic History Network was instrumental in shaping my research interests and professional development.

I have been fortunate enough to benefit from excellent support and professional assistance from a number of archives, libraries and research collections in South Africa and Europe. This project was initially made possible by unrestricted access to the Johannesburg Stock Exchange's historical archive in Sandton. I would also like to thank the archive, library and administrative staff at the British Library, London; WITS Historical Papers, Johannesburg; the UNISA Library, Pretoria; the Brenthurst Foundation Library, Johannesburg; Barlow World Archives, Johannesburg; the Standard Bank Archives, Johannesburg; the University of Stellenbosch Library; the University of Cape Town Archival Services; Western Cape Archives and Records Services, Cape Town; Basler Afrika Bibliographien, Basel; Archives diplomatiques du ministère des Affaires étrangères, Paris; Archives historique de Paribas, Paris; the Guildhall Library, London; the Bodleian Library, University of Oxford and the Capital Markets of the World Special Collection at The Graduate Institute of International and Development Studies.

Several preliminary ideas and results from Chapters 2, 3 and 5 were published in part in three journal articles. Here I would like to thank Taylor & Francis for granting me permission to reproduce amended sections of my articles. Some results in Chapters 2 and 3 appeared in a different form in 'From diamonds to gold: The making of the Johannesburg Stock Exchange, 1880–1890.' *Journal of Southern African Studies* 43, no. 4 (2017): 715–732, and 'Early regulation and social organisation on the Johannesburg Stock Exchange, 1887–1892.' *Business History* 63, no. 4 (2021): 686–704. A small part of the arguments presented in Chapter 5 were previously published in 'Bourses, banks, and Boers: Johannesburg's French connections and the Paris Krach of 1895.' *Economic History of Developing Regions* 36, no. 2 (2021): 124–148.

At Palgrave Macmillan, I would like to thank the series editors, Richard Drayton and Saul Dubow, for welcoming the project and their feedback on the book's contents, presentation and marketing. Various comments and corrections suggested by the series' anonymous reviewers were invaluable in improving the manuscript. I would also like to acknowledge the clear and timely guidance received from the publishing and editorial teams, and thank, in particular, Lucy Kidwell, Agila Muruganandam and Birke Dalia. Eleanor Cruickshank and Benedict Flett presided over most proofreading with great accuracy. The responsibility for any errors and omissions, however, remains my own.

Most importantly, I thank my family for putting up with me while researching and writing this book. This project could not have been completed without the loving support that I always receive from my parents, Irena and Marek. My brother Greg, sister-in-law Rebecca, and nieces Ava and Sienna, were wonderful hosts and tolerant listeners during numerous research trips to initially Johannesburg and then later London. Finally, I thank Rosy and Ellie for unconditionally supporting my writing every step of the way. It is to them that I dedicate this book and remain forever grateful.

Praise for Gold, Finance and Imperialism in South Africa, 1887–1902

"Weaving together previous literature with novel research in a number of historical archives, Mariusz Lukasiewicz contributes with a richly detailed narrative of the role that the Johannesburg Stock Exchange played in the early formation of capitalism in South Africa, until and including the outbreak of the South African War."

—Klas Rönnbäck, *Professor in Economic History, Department of Economy and Society, University of Gothenburg*

"Lukasiewicz's engaging and deeply researched early history of the Johannesburg Stock Exchange (JSE) employs the tools of a business historian to unpack the wider history of the industrialisation and internationalisation of the South African economy in the context of colonialism, mining finance and the racial organization of the economy. By using business records from archives in four different countries to unpack the many complex connections between business, government, domestic elites, and international stakeholders, he presents a new perspective on key historical events in nineteenth-century South African historiography through the lens of the JSE's involvement. He addresses the role that the exchange played, together with the Chamber of Mines, in the creation and maintenance of a racialised system of labour in the mines that sought to control the physical and social mobility of African miners. The substantial growth of South African gold mining also meant that mining companies were not solely capitalised through the JSE, with South African shares traded at European stock exchanges. As mining finance rapidly internationalised in the 1890s, the JSE became increasingly exposed to international capitalism. The book also highlights that the role of the JSE in some key political events of the period has been largely overlooked, and carefully establishes its role in the origins of the failed Jameson Raid. These imperial connections of a very elite organizations continued into the South African war that ended with Johannesburg's surrender in 1900, positioning the JSE as the main capital market in the emerging colonial economy. Lukasiewicz's book is a deeply researched study of a financial organization and its intimate links with British imperialism and South Africa's settler colonialism."

—Stephanie Decker, *Professor in Strategy, Department of Strategy and International Business, Birmingham Business School, University of Birmingham*

"Lukasiewicz presents a fresh perspective on the Johannesburg Stock Exchange's (JSE) formative role in shaping the financial and political contours of colonial South Africa and its interface with global markets. By providing new revelations about the JSE's strategic adaptations in an era of international market exclusions, the work signals a revival of academic interest in South African financial history. This is important because of the enduring influence of these historical financial structures and the many lessons that remain relevant to contemporary market challenges."

—Johan Fourie, *Professor of Economic History, Stellenbosch University*

"Gold, Finance and Imperialism in South Africa, 1887–1902 is a diligently researched and well-crafted case study in "the nexus between finance and imperialism" (p.17). Deploying the skills of the eclectic economic historian, Dr. Lukasiewicz provides an in-depth (re)examination of the key role assigned to the Johannesburg Stock Exchange—and finance capital as such—in late Victorian British imperialism by J.A. Hobson. Based on an impressive array of primary source material from the archives of financial institutions in Johannesburg, Cape Town, London and Paris, and the leading financial newspapers of the period, the book underscores the role of international finance capital in the spread of British imperialism. It sheds light on the complex interplay of local and global finance capital, British-Afrikaner politics in South Africa (centred on the ZAR) and imperial politics. Consequently, this volume is much more than a study of the JSE as an institution, though it highlights its internal politics and, especially its significant but neglected role in the Jameson Raid. Indeed, this book highlights the role of the JSE in the clash between British imperialism and Afrikaner republicanism, culminating in the South African War of 1899–1902. It situates the JSE (and Johannesburg, which developed into a cosmopolitan Victorian outpost and the financial and industrial hub of ZAR) within various webs, networks and layers of professional, commercial, and political entanglements involving bankers, miners, chartered accountants, insurers, financiers, and merchants, as well as politicians in South Africa and Britain. Dr. Lukasiewicz deserves commendation for producing this illuminating study of actors and institutions at the intersection of trans-imperial and global finance and politics."

—Ayodeji Olukoju, *Professor of History, University of Lagos*

"The idea of Capital is important in South Africa, but it has not attracted very much serious investigation since Herbert Frankel's work in the 1960s. In this book, Mariusz Lukasiewicz maps the local political and international financial connections that created South African mining capital in the Johannesburg Stock Exchange. His story places the dusty mining camp in the crosshairs of investment flows from London and Paris and a network of stock exchanges across Europe before the start of the twentieth century."

—Keith Breckenridge, *Professor and acting Co-Director, Wits Institute for Social and Economic Research (WISER), Johannesburg*

NOTE ON ETHNONYMS, POLITICAL GEOGRAPHY AND CURRENCIES

All writers of South African history are faced with many problems when applying ethnonyms to past periods and run the risk of reproducing colonial and apartheid era racial categorisation. This remains a constant challenge and highlights the necessity of thinking more carefully about the relationship between context, historicity and scientific practice. What is 'common currency' for academics is not always appropriate for most readers. Having spent the majority of my life in South Africa, I am very well aware of these political and social constructs and attempt to stay away from any terminology that may be offensive, disrespectful, derogatory or historically inaccurate towards any racial and ethnic groups in South Africa. I therefore use the term *African* when referring to all Black people who did not consider themselves European settlers. Any other terms used when referring to African people or peoples are conceptualised and used in the context being addressed.

How race and racism infiltrated the trading floors of international stock exchanges is evident in the terminology given to South African mining stocks. The 'k-word,' which already in the late nineteenth century was the most derogatory and humiliating name given to Africans in Southern Africa,[1] entered the jargon of international financial markets, referring

---

[1] Anievas, Alexander, Nivi Manchanda, and Robbie Robbie Shilliam, eds. *Race and racism in international relations: confronting the global colour line*. Abingdon: Routledge. 2014. p. 145.

to portfolios of South African gold and diamond mining securities. This highly offensive term is not used in the text and is only cited in the reference documents as per original historical source. The racial term is never used in connection or reference to any person or group of people.

The term *White* is used for all people of European descent who came to South Africa. These 'Europeans' represented different interest groups with varying objectives in politics, commerce and religion. More importantly for studies of extra-European settler societies in southern Africa, the growing white population had unequal and conflicting relationships with Africans' land, labour and capital. The term *Afrikaners* is reserved for African-born (or at least—raised) people of European descent, mainly of Dutch, German and French Huguenot descent, who identified themselves with the *Afrikaans* language, which still is a member of the West Germanic group of languages. The term *Boer (Dutch = Farmer)*, which has over the years been used as a generic term for all Afrikaans speakers in southern Africa throughput the twentieth century, will be used strictly for Afrikaners living in rural parts of the South African Republic and engaging in mostly agricultural professions.

The term Southern Africa is a political rather than geographic description. Currently, the United Nations Geoscheme defines Southern Africa as a sub-region consisting of Botswana, Eswatini, Lesotho, Namibia and South Africa, corresponding to the members of the Southern African Customs Union, established in 1910. As is the scholarly practice for studies of nineteenth and early twentieth century Africa, the term will not be capitalised, emphasising the pre-state formation identity of the region. The term southern Africa will therefore be used for the entire Southern African region, including the territories of modern Zambia, Zimbabwe, and Mozambique. The term South Africa (used in the pre-1899 context, unless stated otherwise) is strictly reserved for the territory consisting of the Cape Colony, Natal, the Orange Free State, and the South African Republic (ZAR). A special differentiation needs to be made between the Transvaal (Dutch: across the Vaal river) and the South African Republic. Although the term Transvaal was widely used in Afrikaner-British diplomatic relations since the early 19th century, Afrikaners officially adopted the name of the South African Republic for the territory of the Transvaal in the constitution (*Grondwet*) of 1858.[2] It was only after the *first* Anglo-Boer War (1880–1881) that the new name was officially recognised by the British government with the signing of the London Convention in 1884. Although the name was accepted by the British, many official and unofficial sources still used the term Transvaal up until the formation of the Union of South Africa in 1910. The book therefore uses the South African Republic (ZAR) to refer to the political territory of the current Gauteng, Mpumalanga, Limpopo and (parts of) the North West provinces. Many place names have also changed since 1980 in Zimbabwe and 1994 in South Africa. The book uses pre-1899 geographical designation and town/city names, always respecting the historicity within the political context in which they were used.

The South African Rand was introduced as South Africa's official currency in 1961, the same year South Africa left the British Commonwealth and became a republic. Between 1825 and 1961 the territories making up modern South Africa used (and at times even issued) some denominations of the pound sterling (£). Even the ZAR issued of British sovereign gold coins after 1880 as a response to the financial dominance of the Cape Colony and Natal.[3] The independent republic also issued some of its own notes (ponds instead of pounds) from 1867 to 1902 and coins from 1892 to 1902.[4] More importantly for monetary policy and politics, between 1825 and December 1932,[5] the pound sterling in circulation in all the territories of southern Africa operated on a *de facto* gold standard. Unless stated otherwise, all the prices and wages in this book are given in the pre-decimal denominations of *£ s d* (pounds, shillings, and pence). Share prices for South African securities on the *Bourse de Paris*

---

[2] See: Alonford J Robinson. 'Transvaal.' In : Appiah, Anthony, and Henry Louis Gates. *Encyclopedia of Africa*. Vol. 1. Oxford University Press. 2010. pp. 493–494.

[3] See: Breckenridge, Keith. 'Money with Dignity': Migrants, Minelords and the Cultural Politics of the South African Gold Standard Crisis, 1920–33.' *The Journal of African History* 36. 2 (1995). pp. 271304.

[4] See: Feingold, Ellen, Johan Fourie, and Leigh Gardner. "A tale of paper and gold: The material history of money in South Africa." *Economic History of Developing Regions* 36, no. 2 (2021): 264–281.

[5] See: *The special features of gold in South Africa*. In: Feinstein, Charles Hilliard. *An economic history of South Africa: conquest, discrimination, and development*. Cambridge: Cambridge University Press. 2005. pp. 93–99.

were quoted in French francs. Additionally, some sections of Paris' unofficial mining market quoted prices in the currency of the country where the security was issued. The book uses an exchange rate of 1 pound sterling to 25 French francs as a simplification for the period under investigation based on the nineteenth-century gold standard which expired in 1914.[6]

[6] For exact rates see: Table DB 18. In: Flandreau, Marc and Zumer Frédéric. *Development Centre Studies The Making of Global Finance 1880–1913*. Paris: OECD Publishing. 2009. p. 127.

CONTENTS

ABBREVIATIONS

BFAS	*Banque française d'Afrique du Sud*
BLA	Brenthurst Library Archives
BSAC	British South Africa Company
BSE	Bulawayo Stock Exchange
BWA	Barloworld Archives
CO	Colonial Office in London
CT	Cape Town
DEIC	Dutch East India Company
GFA	Graduate Institute Financial History Collection
GLA	Guildhall Library (London Metropolitan Archives)
JCE	Johannesburg Consolidated Estate
JECC	Johannesburg Exchange & Chambers Company
JHB	Johannesburg
JSE	Johannesburg Stock Exchange
JSEA	Johannesburg Stock Exchange Archives
KSE	Kimberley Stock Exchange
LSE	London Stock Exchange
NASA	National Archives of South Africa
PBA	*Archive de la Banque de Paris et des Pays-Bas*
PTA	Pretoria
SA	South Africa
SBA	Standard Bank of South Africa Archives
SACMA	South African Chamber of Mines
USL	University of Stellenbosch Library
WHP	Wits Historical Papers
ZAR	South African Republic (*Zuid-Afrikaansche Republiek*)

LIST OF FIGURES

LIST OF TABLES

CHAPTER 1

Introduction: Colonial South Africa, Mineral Revolutions and Finance

According to the Ghanaian historian Albert Adu Boahen, by as late as 1880, as much as 80% of the continent of 'Africa was ruled by her own kings, queens, clan and lineage heads, in empires, kingdoms, communities and polities in various sizes and shapes.'[1] The European conquest of Africa was, however, already well underway and it was in southern Africa where colonial forces and settler societies consolidated their power over the greatest stretches of land, capitalising recently discovered mineral wealth. Diamonds, along with the growing wool sector, were the commodities that transformed the basis of southern Africa's settler economy, much like wool did for Australia, wool and meat production for New Zealand, and fishing, fur, timber and wheat for Canada.[2] Unexpectedly, and fortuitously, as profitable, crass and exploitive the discovery of diamonds was, it would be gold that took South Africa from the British Empire's periphery to the centre of imperial political strategy at the close of the Victorian era. South Africa's gold discoveries would coincide with

---

[1] Boahen, Albert Adu. "Africa and the Colonial Challenge." In: Boahen, Albert Adu, ed. *General History of Africa: Vol. VII Africa Under Colonialism 1880–1935*. Paris: UNESCO. 1985. p. 1.

[2] De Kiewiet, Cornelius William. *A History of South Africa: Social & Economic*. Oxford: The Clarendon Press. 1941. p. 89.

M. Lukasiewicz, *Gold, Finance and Imperialism in South Africa, 1887–1902*, Cambridge Imperial and Post-Colonial Studies, https://doi.org/10.1007/978-3-031-51947-5_1

the transition to a global financial system based on the availability of gold and the 'spirit of Victorian Expansion.'[3]

By the mid-nineteenth century, South Africa was a complicated patchwork of British colonies, Boer settler republics and African states. Southern Africa still offered limited economic prospects for European imperialist powers and the increasingly racialised nature of settler colonialism created a violent landscape of socioeconomic inequality, wars of territorial conquest and forced population displacements. Divisive colonial policies and continued settler expansion between the Cape Colony and the Limpopo River left most of the African population with limited and inadequate access to land. The period of the *Mfecane*, between 1815 and 1840, resulted in the death and forced migrations of thousands of Africans.[4] It was during these violent years that the formal establishment of the two largest Boer settler republics, the Orange Free State (OFS) and the South African Republic (ZAR), added a further colonial dimension to an already volatile political geography.

The Cape Colony and Natal evolved into established British colonies with settlers lobbying for greater political autonomy and agricultural market reforms. The growth and development of the diamond mining sector in and around Kimberley from the 1870s provided the fiscal impetus for a gradual transfer of power from the metropole to 'responsible settler governments.' The independent extra-colonial territories of the ORF and the ZAR, however, experienced a very different sociopolitical climate. Pacified by the conferral of a knighthood by Queen Victoria, and a new source of revenue from coal, President Johannes Henricus Brand was enjoying renewed political stability. As such, he called confidently for greater political engagement between the two British colonies and the *Afrikanerbond (Dutch:* Afrikaner Union*).*[5] Of the two Boer

---

[3] Ronald, Robinson, James Gallagher and Alice Denny. *Africa and the Victorians: The Official Mind of Imperialism.* London: Macmillan. 1981. pp. 1–26.

See Table 29. In: Stone, Irving. *The Global Export of Capital from Great Britain, 1865–1914: A Statistical Survey.* London: Macmillan. 1999. pp. 322–331.

[4] See: Eldredge, Elizabeth A. "Sources of Conflict in Southern Africa, c. 1800–30: The 'Mfecane' Reconsidered." *The Journal of African History* 33, no. 1 (1992): 1–35.

Etherington, Norman. "A Tempest in a Teapot? Nineteenth-century Contests for Land in South Africa's Caledon Valley and the Invention of the Mfecane." *The Journal of African History* 45, no. 2 (2004): 203–219.

[5] Tamarkin, Mordechai. *Cecil Rhodes and the Cape Afrikaners: The Imperial Colossus and the Colonial Parish Pump.* London: Frank Cass and Co. 1996. pp. 6–12.

settler republics, however, the ZAR's independence was more divisive and fragile. Since its establishment after the Great Trek in 1852 as part of the Sand River Convention, the ZAR had a very tense relationship with Britain and her territorial possessions in southern Africa.[6] Having been granted independence, albeit not complete sovereignty, in the London Conventions of 1881 and 1884, the *Zuid-Afrikaansche Republiek*—incorrectly referred to as the Transvaal by most British colonialists still bitter at the outcome of the First Boer War[7]—was on the verge of bankruptcy.[8] President Kruger became a trusted and respected leader for the Boer settlers across the Vaal River, seeking to integrate Afrikaner nationalism into his economic policies, believing a strong, centralised, Afrikaner-led settler state could act as a counter to British imperialism in southern Africa.[9] Although Kruger's policies were able to expand and tax the lucrative agricultural market, state finances remained in deep crisis. The ZAR managed to maintain its independence but at huge economic and social costs.[10]

The 1886 discovery of significant gold reef deposits on the range of hills known as the Witwatersrand,[11] would change the course of southern African history. As summarised by John Illife, the discovery of gold on the Witwatersrand set South Africa on a different colonial trajectory from the rest of the African continent, gradually transitioning towards an industrialising economy, the consolidation of European settler authority, and

---

[6] Cain and Hopkins, *British Imperialism: 1688–2015.* pp. 344–345.

[7] See: Laband, John. *The Transvaal Rebellion: The First Boer War, 1880–1881.* London: Routledge. 2014.

[8] Giliomee, Hermann Buhr and Bernard Mbenga. *New History of South Africa.* Cape Town: Tafelberg. 2007. p. 194.

[9] Ross, Robert. *A Concise History of South Africa* (2nd Ed.). Cambridge: Cambridge University Press. 2008. p. 65.

[10] See: De Kiewet, C. W. *A History of South Africa: Social and Economic.* 1941. p. 114.
Trapido, Stanley. "The South African Republic: Class Formation and the State, 1850–1900." *Collected Seminar Papers. Institute of Commonwealth Studies.* Vol. 16. London: Institute of Commonwealth Studies. 1973.

[11] Witwatersrand (Dutch: White water's ridge) refers to the low-lying hills in today's Gauteng province. The name was also often used to refer to Greater Johannesburg, the centre of the South African gold mining industry.

the development of an unique system of racial repression, making colonial South Africa 'as distinct from the continent as Pharaonic Egypt.'[12]
As much as narratives of colonial South Africa's exceptionalism have
often contributed to oversimplifications and intellectual parochialism in
historical studies of Africa's colonial legacies, the gold discoveries greatly
affected the development of Anglo-Afrikaner-African relations and forged
a new republican Afrikaner identity. Viewed from a global economic
perspective, the mineral discoveries on the Witwatersrand in the early
1880s, transformed the ZAR from a small agricultural economy into
an independent Boer republic on the brink of an economic and financial revolution. Almost overnight, Johannesburg was transformed from a
small mining settlement into one of the most dynamic and volatile cities
in the world.[13] The ZAR's economic potential went from the verge of
bankruptcy in 1886 to a fiscal output equal to the Cape Colony's by the
end of 1888.[14]

Yet, it was not until 1887, a year after the main discoveries of gold, that
the real economic impetus was provided by Johannesburg's burgeoning
financial industry. The city experienced a surge of commercial enterprise,
with mining, utilities, construction and financial services the dominating
sectors. After a visit to Johannesburg in May 1887, the Standard Bank
General Manager from the Cape Colony reported seeing a small town
of 3 000 people, with new foundations of many buildings and a hive
of financial activity that, to him, could hardly be justified as no gold in
any significant quantity had yet been produced.[15] The Standard Bank of
South Africa had already opened its first Johannesburg branch (a small
tent with a piece of paper indicating the opening hours) in October 1886,
and additional banks soon followed as small prospectors searched desper-
ately for venture capital before the large colonial banks from Kimberley

---

[12] Iliffe, John. *Africans: The History of a Continent* (2nd Ed.). Cambridge: Cambridge
University Press. 2007. p. 272.
    See also: Iliffe, John. "The South African Economy, 1652–1997." *The Economic
History Review* 52, no. 1 (1999): 87–103.

[13] Giliomee, Hermann Buhr and Bernard Mbenga. *New History of South Africa*. 2007.
p. 200.

[14] Meredith, Martin. *Diamonds, Gold, and War: The Making of South Africa*. London:
Simon & Schuster. 2008. p. 201.

[15] Henry, James A. *The First Hundred Years of the Standard Bank*. 1963. p. 94.

and the Cape bought out all the claims.[16] Towards the end of 1887, the Standard Bank's Johannesburg and Cape Town management was convinced that the ZAR had become, and would continue to grow, as the financial centre of southern Africa.[17] Even with the Standard Bank taking the greater majority of early mining finance, the Natal Bank, the Cape of Good Hope Bank and the Bank of Africa opened their doors (or tent flaps) before the end of the year. All the banks were soon doing brisk business, showing confidence and foresight in actively developing the financial infrastructure of a mining town that was still not able to prove its weight in gold.[18]

The main financial products and services provided by the young financial industry were related to the purchase and issue of mining equity. Joint-stock companies quickly became the vehicle for combining wealth and spreading risk in the ZAR's developing mining sector. From the first days of its existence as a financial hub, Johannesburg was linked to mining shares and share market speculation.[19] The first share transactions on the Rand took place in a rustic canvas tent, with trade taking place on Sundays owing to a strictly enforced regulation that prohibited the entry of African workers to the gold reefs on this day. With only the 'day of rest' available for financial speculation, initial trading was done in such a hasty and rudimentary manner that most colonial banks issued an official warning to prevent their Johannesburg bank managers from using internal funds to fuel the share mania.[20]

The rise of the Johannesburg Stock Exchange (JSE) is inextricably linked to this early capital market and the political history of the ZAR. Established in late 1887, the JSE became the financial intermediary that epitomised South Africa's industrialisation, global economic entanglements, colonialism, anti-apartheid sanctions and the neoliberal financial order. It was the JSE where regulatory simplification and limited financial barriers of entry created a favoured financial climate for a young and capital-hungry mining industry. Drawing lessons from the economic and

---

[16] Ibid. pp. 91–93.

[17] SBA. GMO 3/1/21, 8 August 1887. p. 616.

[18] Ibid.

[19] 'Speculation.' *The Diggers' News*, 23 November 1889. p. 3.

[20] SBA. GMO 3/1/20. *Special Report*, 2 August 1886. p. 151.

financial experiences in Kimberley and Barberton, the growth of Johannesburg's capital market was the defining shift in the shaping of a new financial system in ZAR. From its early beginnings in a canvas tent on the dusty goldfields of Johannesburg, the JSE has served as a vital link and intermediary, connecting South Africa's natural resource industries with international finance and politics for over 135 years.

At first glance, the JSE's early history might appear parochial and disconnected from historiographical advances. Despite acknowledging the importance of sound financial systems for financial globalisation throughout the nineteenth century,[21] historians have preferred to study large 'global financial centres' within service-oriented economies, focusing their research on clustering and specialisation, mainly in the City of London, New York and Paris. The specific intermediaries scrutinised include banks and the capital market, with stock exchanges and insurance companies receiving comparatively less attention.[22] However, stock exchanges are always much more than mere marketplaces for stocks and securities. They ultimately act as agents for the economy, providing critical insights into the evolution of political, legal and social institutions.[23] As such, they are increasingly becoming recognised as important objects of sociopolitical study.[24] Following Douglas North's definition that institutions encompass the (formal and informal) 'rules of the game,' with organisations and entrepreneurs as the players,[25] this work demonstrates that the JSE's early history illuminates the interactions between local, regional and global institutional arrangements that emerged in the context of nineteenth-century financial globalisation.

At the imperial level of analysis, the early history of Johannesburg's capital market, with the JSE's expanding financial networks, contributes

---

[21] For nineteenth century financial globalisation, see: Flandreau, Marc, and Frederic Zumer. *The Making of Global Finance*. Paris: OEcD. 2004.

[22] Cassis, Youssef. *Capitals of Capital: The Rise and Fall of International Financial Centres 1780–2009*. Cambridge: Cambridge University Press. 2010. p. 2.

[23] See: Preda, A. The Sociological Approach to Financial Markets. *Journal of Economic Surveys* 21, no. 3 (2007): 506–533.

[24] See: Poitras, Geoffrey, ed. *Handbook of Research on Stock Market Globalization*. Edward Elgar Publishing. 2012.

[25] Quoted in: Hodgson, Geoffrey M. "What are institutions?" *Journal of Economic Issues* 40, no. 1 (2006): p. 9.

to a better understanding of how financial capitalism shaped the divisive political identity of colonial South Africa and amplified the British imperial project in southern Africa. Despite its central role in Johannesburg's growing financial sector, the Exchange was only important to a small, but well organised community of international financiers. Africans and Afrikaners did not invest with the JSE and only a small minority of mostly European miners participated in the speculative trade. The town's African migrant workers viewed the JSE with great suspicion and regarded the daily trade as an extension of the foreigners' mining activities.[26] Although President Kruger's government in Pretoria tolerated Johannesburg's financial industry, it became increasingly concerned about how its cosmopolitan society and growing links to international finance could disrupt Boer authority within the Republic.

Britain and the Cape Colony kept a close watch on the ZAR's industrial and financial growth. British imperial expansion into Africa followed, to a large extent, the metropolitan demands of finance. The main concerns lay in Egypt and southern Africa, where the City of London's interests were most prominently represented.[27] The Bank of England's leadership of the international gold standard, coupled with the City's reliance on gold in its financial market, saw South Africa's gold producers become integral participants in London's bullion market almost from the beginning of mining operations in Johannesburg.[28] Although British governments of the 1880s could not direct the output and export of South African gold, they could reasonably hope that the ZAR's dependence on London's gold market would create favourable economic and political relations between the two countries. Despite its critique and empirical limitations, Cain and Hopkins' concept of 'gentlemanly capitalism' has frequently been deployed to trace the consistently renegotiated social and political values that connected London's financial institutions to formal and informal

[26] Tsa Lichaba Johannesburg. *Leselinyana La Lesutho*, 15 January 1896. pp. 1–2.

[27] Cain, Peter J. and Anthony G. Hopkins. *British Imperialism: 1688–2000*. London: Pearson Education. 2002. p. 337.

[28] Ally, Russell. 1994. p. 14.

empire-building efforts.[29] As summarised by Bowen, gentlemanly capitalists were positioned at the heart of Victorian expansionism, and firmly entrenched in the City of London's international financial sector, from where they strategically marshalled economic resources, moulded public opinion and exerted significant political influence over decision-making processes in the metropole and at the imperial frontiers.[30] It was however when gentlemanly capitalism clashed with the aspirations of settler colonialists at the fringes of the empire that the concept became contested and interpreted in contrasting ways.[31] Nowhere is this more clear than in southern Africa where the City of London's interests in the ZAR's economy expose the antagonistic relationship between economic imperialism, informal empire and territorial colonialism.[32] As Cain and Hopkins describe, the ZAR's new mining frontier was populated by financial entrepreneurs whose business activities were distant from the gentlemanly norms and conduct of Victorian Britain, forcing British foreign policy to shift away from cultural idealism and towards political realism.[33] The strategy it adopted from the 1880s onwards would mobilise British finance to further Britain's influence in the ZAR, as well as colonial politicians, above all Cecil John Rhodes, to isolate Kruger's Republic

---

[29] See: Dumett, Raymond E. "Introduction: Exploring the Cain/Hopkins Paradigm: Issues for Debate; Critique and Topics for New Research." In: Dumett, Raymond E. *Gentlemanly Capitalism and British Imperialism: The New Debate on Empire.* Routledge, 2014. pp. 1–43.

Porter, A. "'Gentlemanly Capitalism' and Empire: The British Experience Since 1750?" *The Journal of Imperial and Commonwealth History* 18, no. 3 (1990): 265–295.

[30] Bowen, H. V. "Gentlemanly Capitalism and the Making of a Global British Empire: Some Connections and Contexts, 1688–1815." In: Akita, Shigeru, ed. *Gentlemanly Capitalism, Imperialism and Global History.* Springer, 2002. p. 20.

[31] See: Dilley, Andrew. "'The Rules of the Game': London Finance, Australia, and Canada, c. 1900–14." *The Economic History Review* 63, no. 4 (2010): 1003–1031.

Attard, Bernard. "From Free-Trade Imperialism to Structural Power: New Zealand and the Capital Market, 1856–68." *The Journal of Imperial and Commonwealth History* 35, no. 4 (2007): 505–527.

Hopkins, A. G. "Gentlemanly Capitalism in New Zealand." *Australian Economic History Review* 43, no. 3 (2003): 287–297.

[32] Phimister, Ian. "Empire, Imperialism and the Partition of Africa." In: Akita, Shigeru, ed. *Gentlemanly Capitalism, Imperialism and Global History.* Springer. 2002. p. 79.

[33] Cain, Peter J., and Anthony G. Hopkins. *British Imperialism: 1688–2000.* 2002. p. 325.

within its frontiers.[34] As this book argues, Johannesburg's financial capitalists, though diverging from 'gentlemanly' values and objectives, would much like their contemporaries in London, leverage the stock exchange's nodal status to interfere in the local, regional and imperial politics of late nineteenth century southern Africa.

This book provides a historical assessment of the JSE's foundation, rise and interaction with South Africa's mineral revolution and British imperialism during the final stage of the 'Scramble for southern Africa.'[35] Discussing the combined effects of Johannesburg's financialisation and political mobilisation, the book focuses on the period between the JSE's establishment in 1887 and the end of the South African War in 1902. Using original documentation from Johannesburg's banking sector, the JSE, its landlord the Johannesburg Estate Company, the Witwatersrand Chamber of Mines, and many other local and foreign financial intermediaries, this book investigates the institutional design and organisational characteristics of a local capital market with global ambitions in an international financial system committed to gold. As emphasised in earlier works by Kubicek, Phimister and Jeeves, the sociopolitical organisation of Johannesburg's early mining and financial sectors has significant implications for the study of British imperialism and its links to the Jameson Raid of 1895, as well as the outbreak of the South African War in 1899.[36] Despite attempting to balance British financial interests with loyalty to Pretoria's republicanism before the war, the JSE clearly sided with British commercial, political and legal interests once its legitimacy among foreign investors began to be challenged. This contribution adds a novel argument and new empirical evidence to the historiographical debates on the role of global finance and its links to British imperialism in South Africa.

---

[34] Cain, Peter J. and Hopkins, Anthony G. *British Imperialism: 1688–2000.* 2002. p. 325.

[35] See: Schreuder, D. M. *The Scramble for Southern Africa, 1877–1895: The Politics of Partition Reappraised.* 1980.

[36] See, for example:

Phimister, Ian. "Markets, Mines, and Magnates: Finance and the Coming of War in South Africa, 1894–1899." *Africa: Rivista semestrale di studi e ricerche* 2, no. 2 (2020): 5–22.

Kubicek, Robert V. *Economic Imperialism in theory And Practice: The Case of South African Gold Mining Finance 1886–1914.* Durham. Duke University Press. 1979.

Jeeves, Alan. "Aftermath of Rebellion—The Randlords and Kruger's Republic after the Jameson Raid." *South African Historical Journal* 10, no. 1 (1978): 102–116.

THE MINERAL REVOLUTION AND MINING
FINANCE AT THE STOCK EXCHANGE

The significance of what historians of South Africa have come to call the 'mineral revolution' dominates all perceptions of radical economic and social change from the 1880s onward.[37] Although the suitability of the term 'revolution' to describe the combined socioeconomic effects of diamond and gold mining on South Africa as a whole remains a matter of historical and historiographical debate, the growth of the mining industry was certainly revolutionary enough in its impact on the ZAR's finances and political confidence. The development of the gold mining industry ensured that the ZAR, and before too long the whole of southern Africa, experienced a socioeconomic revolution which would come to be dominated by financial capitalism.[38]

The historiography of the ZAR's concurrent mineral and financial revolutions provides the source material to reflect on many issues of financial development, globalisation, and European imperialism in southern Africa. It was precisely in the final quarter of the nineteenth century that European capital and enterprise were exported in unprecedented quantities to develop mining in North and South America, Australia, Russia, and southern Africa.[39] First in the eastern parts of the ZAR and then on the Witwatersrand, southern African settler economies became a prime destination for international mining prospectors, diggers and financiers.[40] Johannesburg quickly grew from a mining camp to a financial centre with numerous local, colonial and international financial intermediaries channelling the flow of capital to and from the ZAR's industrialising economy. By establishing a new market for local, regional and international mining finance, the JSE emerged as the gold mining industry's primary financial

---

[37] Feinstein, Charles. *An Economic History of South Africa: Conquest, Discrimination, and Development.* 2005. pp. 91–97.

[38] Richardson, Peter and Jean-Jacques Van-Helten. "The Gold Mining Industry in the Transvaal 1886–99." In: Warwick, Peter. *The South African War: The Anglo-Boer War 1899–1902.* Longman. 1980 p. 20.

[39] Burt, R. The London Mining Exchange 1850–1900. *Business History* 14, no. 2 (1972): 124–143.

[40] See: Rönnbäck, K. and O. Broberg. *Capital and Colonialism: The Return on British Investments in Africa 1869–1969.* Springer. 2019.

intermediary. It played a critical role in raising capital and forging international networks that strongly shaped the ZAR's early industrialisation process.

The capital market's contribution to the capital-intensification of the ZAR's mining industry naturally raises the standard economic history questions about the interplay between the cost of capital, land and labour utilised in the gold industry's production processes. The investigation deliberately uses the agency of the JSE to explain some early aspects of racial segregation and labour coercion on the Rand. As will be demonstrated with multiple references to the cooperation between the JSE and the Witwatersrand Chamber of Mines, mining labour costs were initially relatively disproportionately high, but the price of unskilled labour was driven down in the early 1890s by a combination of measures taken by Johannesburg's industrialists and the Pretoria government. A natural question that arises in this context is whether, given the ready, and relatively cheaply available financial capital to the mines through the JSE, was there eventually a tendency to substitute labour for capital over time? Although this putative substitution effect has loosely been referred to as the 'economic rationalisation' of the mining industry, the evidence provided in this book focuses on exposing the capital market's organisational and regulatory responses, and not its position with respect to major structural shifts in the gold industry's factors of production.[41]

Stock exchanges, primarily in London, and from 1887 Johannesburg, would be where financial and human capital determined the future of South Africa's gold-driven economy. Although Africa has a long history of trade in securities,[42] the development of organised stock exchanges on the continent coincided with the first age of financial globalisation and European colonisation in the nineteenth century.[43] The expansion of financial services in southern Africa played a key role in the settler

---

[41] Farnie, Douglas Anthony. "The mineral revolution in South Africa." *South African Journal of Economics* 24, no. 2 (1956): 128.

[42] See: Rosenthal, Eric. *On change through the Years; a History of Share Dealing in South Africa.* Cape Town: Flesch Financial Publications. 1968.

[43] For First Era of Financial Globalisation, see: Bordo, Michael and Marc Flandreau. "Core, Periphery, Exchange Rate Regimes, and Globalization." In: Bordo, Michael D., Alan M. Taylor, and Jeffrey G. Williamson, eds. *Globalization in Historical Perspective.* Chicago: University of Chicago Press. 2007. pp. 417–472.

societies' capital accumulation.[44] British colonial influence ensured that initially shareholding, and later stock trading, became integral to the economy of settler societies. By the end of nineteenth-century Egypt, the Cape Colony, Natal and Rhodesia had well-developed stock markets and complementary financial infrastructure. Although several stock exchanges were already in operation on the African continent in the final quarter of the nineteenth century, the JSE emerged as a financial industry leader in what soon became the wealthiest city in southern Africa.

FINANCE AND IMPERIALISM IN SOUTH AFRICA: REVISITING HOBSON'S JOHANNESBURG

The predominant theoretical theme that develops throughout this book is the nexus between finance and imperialism. Although there is no definitive theory linking greater financialisation and territorial imperialism,[45] the ideological battles that shaped the study of political economy throughout the twentieth century have given rise to voluminous works on the subject.[46] It was the Egyptian financial crisis of the 1880s that expanded the theorisation of British economic imperialism and it would be southern Africa where the theories were originally applied.[47] The concurrent development of gold mining and finance in Johannesburg turned South Africa into an epistemic testing ground for various economic theories advanced to explain the imperial expansion of Europe (and particularly Britain) in the three decades before the outbreak of WWI.

---

[44] Magee, Gary B., Lorraine Greyling and Grietjie Verhoef. "South Africa in the Australian Mirror: Per Capita Real GDP in the Cape Colony, Natal, Victoria, and New South Wales, 1861–1909." *The Economic History Review* 69, no. 3 (2016): 900.

[45] Orhangazi, Özgür. "Finance, Finance Capital, Financialisation." In: Ness, Immanuel, and Zak Cope, eds. *The Palgrave Encyclopedia of Imperialism and Anti-Imperialism.* Vol. 1. New York: Palgrave Macmillan. 2016. pp. 103–107.

[46] For excellent review of literature, see: Mommsen, Wolfgang J. *Theories of Imperialism.* Chicago: University of Chicago Press. 1980.

[47] Cain, Peter. "JA Hobson, financial capitalism and imperialism in late Victorian and Edwardian England." *The Journal of Imperial and Commonwealth History* 13, no. 3 (1985): 1–27.

See also: Landes, David S. *Bankers and Pashas: International Finance and Economic Imperialism in Egypt.* Cambridge: Harvard University Press. 1958.

From Hobson to Hobsbawm,[48] the South African War was significant in revealing the economic roots of British empire-building and the historical development of capitalism.[49] In Johannesburg, the way in which early financial aspirations were transformed into imperial territorial interests by powerful mine owners and investors, would rapidly shape the political identity of the Rand and, indeed colonial settler societies across the whole region. For the British social theorist John Atkinson Hobson, the outbreak of the South African War in October 1899 was a clear and dramatic shift in the operations of worldwide forces of international finance.[50] Victorian Britain's financial hegemony and London's dominance over the international monetary market was intended to secure a stable economic environment on the Rand.[51] Furthermore, according to Hobson, the way financial capital linked to the demand for labour, and President Kruger's inability to provide administrative reforms for cheaper African labour, was the tipping point that spurred British efforts to intervene militarily in the ZAR.[52]

Although theoretical reasoning in defining the imperial agency in the development of Johannesburg's financial sector is used sparingly in this book, the JSE was indeed central to Hobson's understanding of the ZAR's financial and social structures on the eve of the war. According to Hobson, the greatest gambling instrument in Johannesburg was the stock exchange and it was mostly in stocks, and not land, where the foreign capitalists had invested.[53] Hobson argued that if ownership of land was a prerequisite for a franchise in the ZAR, then all the European settlers holding considerable amounts of stocks in Rand mines

[48] Hobsbawm, Eric. *The Age of Empire: 1875–1914.* London: Abacus (Time Warner Books UK). 1987. p. 168.

[49] Porter, Andrew. "The South African War and the Historians." *African Affairs* 99, no. 397 (2000): 633–648.

[50] Kynaston, David. *City of London: The History.* London: Random House. 2011. p. 181.

[51] Katz, Elaine. "Outcrop and Deep Level Mining in South Africa Before the Anglo-Boer War: Re-examining the Blainey Thesis." *The Economic History Review* 48, no. 2 (1995): 304.

[52] Jeeves, Alan. "The Rand Capitalists and the Coming of the South African War 1896–1899." *South African Journal of Economic History* 11, no. 2 (1996): 60.

[53] Hobson, John Atkinson. *Capitalism and Imperialism in South Africa.* London: Tucker Publishing Company. 1900.

would have claimed the franchise.[54] With securities and their value being their only material attachment to the ZAR, Hobson saw the JSE's members as a microcosm of capitalism's entanglement with the political economy of southern Africa and the global forces of financial speculation.[55] Although Hobson's view that the British war effort was represented by a small group of capitalists fighting for the control of the South African economy has rightly been assessed as over-simplified and coupled with unsubstantiated conspiracy theories,[56] his first-hand observations of Johannesburg's financial community as a news correspondent for the *Manchester Guardian*, led to the publication of *Capitalism and Imperialism in South Africa* and *Imperialism*, two standard works for historians of nineteenth-century imperialism.[57] More critically and disturbingly, it is also in his social analysis of Johannesburg's financial community where Hobson's antisemitism became even more explicit and, indeed, inseparable from his political thought.[58]

It is however Hobson's observations of the international capital market where his theoretical conceptions on the 'investing and speculative classes' were applied to the share trade between Johannesburg and London that this book takes up the issues of market influence, manipulations and financial hazard.[59] Hobson and his radical contemporaries like Rudolf

---

[54] Ibid. pp. 69–70.

[55] Ibid. p. 70.

[56] Jeeves, Alan. "Hobson's the War in South Africa: A Reassessment." In: Cuthbertson, G., Grundlingh, A. M. and Suttie, M. L., eds. *Writing a Wider War: Rethinking Gender, Race, and Identity in the South African War, 1899–1902.* 2002. p. 233.

See, also: Etherington, Norman. "Theories of Imperialism in Southern Africa Revisited." *African Affairs* 81, no. 324 (1982): 385–407.

[57] Hobson, John Atkinson. *Capitalism and Imperialism in South Africa.* 1900. Hobson, John Atkinson. *Imperialism: A Study.* London: J. Pott. 1902.

[58] Jeeves, Alan. "Hobson's the War in South Africa: A Reassessment." In: Cuthbertson, G., Grundlingh, A. M. and Suttie, M. L., eds. *Writing a Wider War: Rethinking Gender, Race, and Identity in the South African War, 1899–1902.* 2002. pp. 233–234.

Cowen, Michael, and Robert W. Shenton. *Doctrines of development.* Taylor & Francis, 1996. pp. 259–261.

See, also: Coleman, William Oliver. "Anti-semitism in Anti-economics." *History of Political Economy* 35, no. 4 (2003): 759–777.

Lowry, Donal. "'The Play of Forces World-Wide in their Scope and Revolutionary in their Operation [JA Hobson]': The South African War as an International Event." *South African Historical Journal* 41, no. 1 (1999): 83–105.

[59] Hobson, John Atkinson. *Imperialism: A Study.* London: J. Pott. 1902. p. 63.

Hilferding and Vladimir Lenin emphasised financial capitalists' growing political power and economic specialisation in financial operations such as speculation throughout the late nineteenth century in their theoretical understanding of imperialism.[60] Financial speculation, as defined throughout this book encompasses coordinated profiteering activities from the purchasing, hoarding or selling of shares in an attempt to anticipate or directly influence short-term price fluctuations ahead of the general investing public. It is treated here as the vital function of the stock exchange modality, a framework developed by Flandreau to describe the strategic interactions between the capital market's commodification of information and empire-shaping.[61] As frequently argued by Phimister, it was the specialisation and professionalisation of financial speculation on London's Southern African mining market, rather than actual mineral production on the ZAR goldfields, that normalised white-collar crime and financial embezzlement in what some contemporaries already referred to as 'stock jobbing imperialism.'[62]

Although this book establishes multiple direct connections made to Johannesburg's financial sector immediately before the outbreak of the South African War, it would be naïve to directly implicate the JSE in a complex plot to convince the British Empire to go to war with Kruger's ZAR. Nevertheless, using extensive original documentation from stock exchanges and banks in Johannesburg, Cape Town, London, Paris and a broad selection of Victorian era financial press (another critical aspect of

---

For conceptual history of white-collar crime, see: Berghoff, Hartmut, and Uwe Spiekermann. "Shady Business: On the History of White-collar Crime." *Business History* 60, no. 3 (2018): 289–304.

[60] Karatasli, Sahan Savas, and Sefika Kumral. "Financialization and International (Dis) Order: A Comparative Analysis of the Perspectives of Karl Polanyi and John Hobson." *Berkeley Journal of Sociology* (2013): 43.

[61] Flandreau, Marc. *Anthropologists in the Stock Exchange.* 2016. p. 9.

[62] Phimister, Ian. "Late Nineteenth-Century globalization: London and Lomagundi Perspectives on Mining Speculation in Southern Africa, 1894–1904." *Journal of Global History* 10, no. 1 (2015): 27–28.
See, also: Phimister, Ian. "Markets, Mines, and Magnates: Finance and the Coming of War in South Africa, 1894–1899." *Africa: Rivista Semestrale Di Studi e Ricerche* 2, no. 2 (2020): 5–22.
Phimister, I. Speculation and Exploitation: The Southern Rhodesian Mining Industry in the Company Era. *Historia* 48, no. 2 (2003): 88–97.

Hobson's studies of financial capitalism),[63] this book indirectly revisits Hobson's claim that the JSE was the central financial organisation of Johannesburg's financial capitalists and imperial loyalists.

SOURCES

This book uses qualitative and quantitative data collected from contemporary business records. As with any historical study of a specific financial intermediary, original internal documentation is the key to illuminating the organisation's structural, operational and administrative capacity. Business records and financial documents bring to light a different dimension compared to government publications and colonial reporting by providing isolated perspectives on the relationships between the colonial state and the private economy.[64] Using public or private archival sources does nonetheless come with its share of scientific pitfalls and it clearly needs to be analysed if the 'information' found in these sources, is intended to represent fact, fiction, or in many specific cases in this book, speculation. Most of the primary sources used in this book date from a period when Britain and the ZAR's institutions were oriented towards the exploitation of Africa's resources and people. By treating archival documents as the link between what is recognised as knowledge and who is in power to record their version, scholars need to move away from treating the archive as a pure data-collecting exercise to approaching it in a quasi-ethnographic manner.[65] The political and ideological nuances inherent in all the primary documents used in this book, their past interpretations and complex (post-)colonial interrelations, are therefore analysed and critically applied though the analytical lens of a democratic and socially inclusive South Africa.

The primary materials for this book were consulted in numerous private and public repositories in four different countries through a

[63] Jeeves, Alan. "Hobson's the War in South Africa: A Reassessment." In: Cuthbertson, G., Grundlingh, A. M. and Suttie, M. L., eds. *Writing a Wider War: Rethinking Gender, Race, and Identity in the South African War, 1899–1902.* 2002. pp. 234–236.

[64] Van den Bersselaar, Dmitri. "Business records as sources for African history." In: Thomas Spear, ed. *The Oxford Encyclopedia of African Historiography: Methods and Sources.* Vol. 1. New York: Oxford University Press. 2019.

[65] Stoler, Ann Laura. *Along the Archival Grain: Epistemic Anxieties and Colonial Common Sense.* Princeton: Princeton University Press, 2010. p. 27.

mapping process that followed the global issuance and distribution of South African mining stocks. In South Africa, records on Johannesburg's early financial history were collected at the Johannesburg Stock Exchange, the Standard Bank Historical Archive, the South African Chamber of Mines, Brenthurst Library, Barlow World Archives, Western Cape Archives and Records Services, and the WITS Historical Papers. Although the JSE's Meeting Minutes Books constitute the archival core of this investigation, the Member's Roll Books are also worth their weight in gold. The members' ledgers recorded the names of all new members, as well as the type of membership subscriptions and their payment details. These ledgers read like the 'who's who' of southern African and international finance of the late nineteenth century, offering previously unexplored evidence on the involvement of specific individuals and social networks in Johannesburg. Additionally in Britain, records located at the Guildhall Library, the British National Archives and the Bodleian Library were consulted to establish Johannesburg's financial and imperial relationships in the City of London. In France, the *Archives historique de Paribas* and the *Archives diplomatiques du ministère des Affaires étrangères* were instrumental in tracing the formation of international financial networks for the trade in ZAR securities in Paris. In Switzerland, Geneva's Capital Markets of the World Archive and the Basler Afrika Bibliographien provided fascinating insights into Johannesburg's financial and labour history.

Apart from the most significant archival collections mentioned above, the book employs a wide range of southern African, British, French, and German newspapers to illustrate the global interest in Johannesburg's financial industry and its products. These newspapers provide a broad overview of financial and political journalism for the period 1886 to 1902, emphasising the crucial role of the press in nineteenth-century financial globalisation. The analysis of Johannesburg's earliest newspapers shows how the local press collaborated with the growing financial community in their efforts to control the collection, publication and distribution of the gold mines' industrial information. More importantly for the market in South African mining shares, the changing editorial bias of the international selection of newspapers used in this study shows very different opinions on southern Africa's Anglo-African-Afrikaner relations and Johannesburg's role as a financial centre and political hotspot.

Given the range of primary and secondary sources consulted during research, this study provides novel insights into the global understanding of Johannesburg's early financial and political history. Despite focusing on the institutional framework of the JSE for the majority of the explanatory variables, the book does not develop a corporate narrative but seeks instead to critically deconstruct the Exchange's organisational structures. It does so by using archival sources to form connections and comparisons across complementary financial intermediaries and political organisations. The study is not conceived as an institutional reference work, but rather, a dynamic investigation into the origins of Johannesburg's capital market in the highly contested political space of nineteenth-century southern Africa and global finance.

Scope, Approach and Book Structure

The development of specialised financial services and techniques in various global financial hubs towards the end of the nineteenth century forged new social links between different groups of financial professionals such as bankers, merchants, financiers, insurers, arbitragers, brokers, chartered accountants and most importantly for this study, British colonial and ZAR politicians.[66] These and other layers of social organisational are here operationalised as part of the analysis of Johannesburg's financial and political microstructures, while in the process, providing a deeper understanding of the underlying imperial expansion in South Africa.[67]

As with most stock exchanges around the world at the time, the JSE was much more than just a market for securities. Stock exchanges of the nineteenth century were considered part of the 'Big Society,' in which social norms and ideological convictions were combined with intrinsic motivations such as social prestige and political influence. Far from the metropolitan capitals of European empires, Johannesburg's settler society consisted of hundreds of diggers, miners, traders, adventurers, agents

[66] See: Cassis, Youssef. *Capitals of Capital: The Rise and Fall of International Financial Centres 1780–2009*. 2010. pp. 83–84.

[67] See: O'Sullivan, Mary A. "Yankee Doodle Went to London: Anglo-American Breweries and the London Securities Market, 1888–92." *The Economic History Review* 64, no. 8 (2015): 1366.

Knorr-Cetina, Karin and Urs Bruegger. "Global Microstructures: The Virtual Societies of Financial Markets." *American Journal of Sociology* 107, no. 4 (2002): 905–950.

Davis, Lance and Larry Neal. "Micro Rules and Macro Outcomes: The Impact of Micro Structure on the Efficiency of Security Exchanges, London, New York, and Paris, 1800–1914." *The American Economic Review* 88, no. 2 (1998): 40–45.

and speculators, all congregating in a mining town loosely centred on the Market Square. The JSE was where financial aspirations and buccaneering clashed with imperial and republican divisions. Most of the earliest members had very little experience and knowledge of finance. Despite their non-gentlemanly backgrounds, these rugged 'financiers' shared the same stock exchange modality as their Victorian counterparts in London and *fin-de-siècle* Paris, namely using the 'art of the puff', a complex technique of company promotions, to inflate financial bubbles.[68] The early speculative character of Johannesburg's gold and finance industries serves as an important analytical tool in studying the settlers' compulsive gambling on anything from stocks, horse racing and football, to dog fighting, boxing and various games of dice.

The contribution of foreign financiers to the commercial expansion of Johannesburg's goldfields has long been a topic for investigation and debate for radical historians of South Africa.[69] The development of Johannesburg's mining industry led to the rise of influential mining magnates and financiers who are often collectively referred to as the Randlords. Although much has been written about the Randlords' varying connections to British imperialism in southern Africa,[70] very little is known about their interactions with the JSE, the central financial intermediary of their engagement with the ZAR's economy. By using the JSE to restructure who owned and controlled the means of production in deep-level mining, the group system's initiators, the Randlords, were able to establish and entrench themselves in an increasingly international market for South African mining securities. As much as the Randlords were hated by the opponents of Empire for their political manipulation of a fragile imperial system in southern Africa, the City of London supported their

[68] Flandreau, Marc. *Anthropologists in the Stock Exchange.* 2016. p. 8.

[69] See: Kubicek, Robert V. "The Randlords in 1895: A Reassessment." *The Journal of British Studies* 11, no. 2 (1972): 84–86.

[70] See: Wheatcroft, Geoffrey. *The Randlords.* 1987.
    Denoon, Donald. "Capital and Capitalists in the Transvaal in the 1890s and 1900s." *The Historical Journal* 23, no. 1 (1980): 111–132.
    Kubicek, Robert V. "The Randlords in 1895: A Reassessment." *The Journal of British Studies* 11, no. 2 (1972): 84–103.
    Emden, Paul Herman. *Randlords.* 1935.

financial endeavours and tolerated their political aspirations.[71] The analysis of this emergent social order and its interaction with the JSE exposes new evidence of the Randlords' imperial ambitions. More importantly for the relationship between finance and imperialism in Africa, the book's approach is to use the stock exchange as the nodal point of the financial connections between Johannesburg, London and Paris to expose direct links to the 'Scramble for southern Africa.' The book's argument thereby revolves around the JSE as a central lens for the examination of Johannesburg's financial connections to political networks in the ZAR, Cape Colony, Natal, Bechuanaland, Rhodesia, France and, most critically, Britain. From a quantitative perspective, given the methodological challenges associated with evaluating the performance of any nineteenth-century capital market,[72] it is not the objective of this study to measure how much financial capital was raised for the ZAR's mining industry in Johannesburg, London and Paris. Although excellent sources detailing the official price lists of ZAR mining stocks in various markets are utilised, a rigorous quantitative analysis of the convergence of South African stock prices in a global perspective is beyond the scope and argument of this investigation.

This book follows a mostly chronological order with some overlaps allowing for the consolidation of arguments presented. After documenting the genesis of Johannesburg's financial sector, Chapter 2 begins with the historical assessment of the JSE's institutional foundations, its rise, and interaction with southern Africa's diamond and gold mining industries. Chapter 3 then analyses the early growth and development of the social organisation on the JSE, concluding the first stage of Johannesburg's financialisation with the 'Golden Boom', which brought about an era of wild financial speculation, which by the close of 1889, nearly resulted in the closure of multiple gold mines when the inevitable crash finally arrived. Chapter 4 traces the early common history and overlapping organisational structures of the JSE and the Witwatersrand Chamber of Mines. This reveals their initial economic entanglements and subsequent political interdependence, showcasing their joint role in contributing to

---

[71] See: Kubicek, Robert V. "The Randlords in 1895: A Reassessment." *The Journal of British Studies* 11, no. 2 (1972): 84–103.

[72] For methodological concerns, see for example: Stone. Irving. *The Global Export of Capital from Great Britain, 1865–1914: A Statistical Survey.* 1999. pp. 3–4.

the racialisation of mining labour and the production of financial intelligence. Chapter 5 investigates the industrial development of deep-level mining through the lens of the capital market, documenting how stock exchanges in Johannesburg, London and Paris supported the industrial transition and contributed to the globalisation of South African gold mining shares. Chapter 6 implicates the JSE and many of its leading members in the planning and execution of the Cecil Rhodes-sponsored Jameson Raid against President Kruger's government. Chapter 7 consolidates the argument and revises the much-overlooked role and position of the JSE immediately before, during and after the South African War of 1899–1902. The book's conclusions validate and advance existing scholarly work on the disproportionately influential role played by Johannesburg's financial sector in South Africa's mineral revolution and the Anglo-African-Afrikaner conflict of the late nineteenth century.

CHAPTER 2

From Diamonds to Gold: The Rise of Share Dealing in South Africa

The JSE was not the first stock market in sub-Saharan Africa. Public and private financial intermediaries had become a key aspect of settler colonialism in southern Africa since the establishment of the Cape Colony in 1652.[1] Trading securities at informal markets became a common occurrence in the merchant circles of the Cape following the introduction of a number of financial intermediaries to the Cape Colony by the Dutch East India Company in the eighteenth century.[2] The active capital and credit market soon provided the majority of private financial resources needed for the expansion of the colonial agricultural and land markets. With the British takeover of the Cape between 1795 and 1820, and especially after the abolition of slavery in 1834, speculation on colonial debt and securities became a widespread practice in Cape Town's growing banking sector.[3] By the mid-nineteenth century, colonial banking was flourishing,

---

[1] See: Fourie, J. and Swanepoel, C. "'Impending Ruin' or 'Remarkable Wealth'? The Role of Private Credit Markets in the 18th-Century Cape Colony." *Journal of Southern African Studies* 44, no. 1 (2018): 7–25.

[2] Rosenthal, Eric. *On 'Change Through the Years; a History of Share Dealing in South Africa.* 1968. p. 17.

[3] See: Gwaindepi, A. *State Building in the Colonial Era: Public Revenue, Expenditure and Borrowing Patterns in the Cape Colony, 1820–1910.* Doctoral dissertation, Stellenbosch: Stellenbosch University. 2018.

M. Lukasiewicz, *Gold, Finance and Imperialism in South Africa, 1887–1902*, Cambridge Imperial and Post-Colonial Studies, https://doi.org/10.1007/978-3-031-51947-5_2

with Cape banks paying regular dividends and their shares being quoted at high premiums.[4] Although the Cape's capital market remained relatively small and limited to colonial merchants, wealthy settler farmers and British capital prior to the mineral discoveries of the 1860s, the proliferation of limited liability and joint-stock companies became an indispensable legal institution of the eastward-expanding colonial frontier.

In a similar, albeit much smaller, process of colonial commercialisation, the growth in the availability of financial products and services in Natal opened new avenues of capital mobilisation in Britain's second settler colony in South Africa. The British conquest of Natal in 1843 exposed the changing nature of settler capitalism and the dispossession of Africans' land east of the Great Kai River. The Boer's disillusion with the short-lived Natalia Republic was compounded by the Cape colonial government's land policies and its initial unwillingness to force African farmers into an exploitative wage-labour market and cash economy.[5] Many Boer settlers disposed of their large land claims cheaply before their departure from the newly annexed British colony, either directly to Cape land speculators, or to other more capitalised European settlers and some African merchants.[6] Land speculators, particularly amalgamated land companies, secured the largest share of this expanding land market with some companies holding as much as a 1000 000 acres of farming land.[7] This rapid commodification and marketisation of land with the extension of trade in agricultural products stimulated the emergence of new financial intermediaries and instruments that served the growing settler population. For example, the unregulated Pietermaritzburg Commercial Exchange, established in 1852, was able to host the growing land claim market and facilitate the share floatation of the Natal Cotton Company, the Colonial Bank of Natal, the Commercial and Agricultural Bank of Durban, the Natal Land and Colonisation Company, and the Natal Railway Company.[8]

---

[4] Arndt, Ernst Heinrich Daniel. *Banking and Currency Development in South Africa (1652–1927)*. Cape Town: Juta. 1928. pp. 253–254.

[5] Slater, H. "Land, Labour and Capital in Natal: The Natal Land and Colonisation Company 1860–1948." *The Journal of African History* 16, no. 2 (1975): 257–259.

[6] Ibid.

[7] Bundy, C. "The Emergence and Decline of a South African Peasantry." *African Affairs* 71, no. 285 (1972): 375.

[8] Rosenthal, E. *On 'change Through the Years: A History of Share Dealing in South Africa*. 1968. pp. 38–39.

Although securities were traded at informal markets in coastal areas of the Cape and Natal throughout the eighteenth and nineteenth century, it was only with the discovery of diamonds and the expansion of British colonial rule into Griqualand West in 1871 that unregulated and decentralised share markets transformed into regulated exchanges.[9] The first record of a regulated stock exchange on the African continent was the Kimberley Stock Exchange. This financial intermediary opened on 21 August 1880 and operated during the Cape Colony's diamond boom between 1880 and 1892 with fewer than 60 registered members. The growth and development of diamond mining and complementary financial services in and around Kimberley transformed the Cape Colony from an agricultural settler colony into an industrialising region with a steadily increasing public and private economy.[10] This was where the necessary financial, human and social capital was accumulated, the capital that would be required to get to the heart of southern Africa's mineral wealth and intensify the colonial appropriation of African resources.

Compared to the growing colonial export markets and the gradual accumulation of public and private capital in the Cape and Natal, the ZAR's economy experienced a very different development trajectory and financial climate in the final quarter of the nineteenth century. Despite a few minor and isolated discoveries of gold in the 1870s and early 1880s, the ZAR's economy was still largely agricultural, rural and pastoral.[11] Having regained its independence—but not complete sovereignty—in the London Conventions of 1881 and 1884 largely as a measure to limit imperial defence spending, the ZAR (incorrectly referred to as the Transvaal by most British colonialists still bitter at the outcome of the First Boer War) was on the verge of bankruptcy.[12] Despite President Kruger's diplomatic efforts to expand the borders and grant more land to the Boers, the ZAR's economy remained too dependent on British

[9] Ibid. pp. 57–59.

[10] See: Herranz-Loncán, A. and Fourie, J. "For the Public Benefit"? Railways in the British Cape Colony. *European Review of Economic History* 22, no. 1 (2018): 73–100.

[11] Richardson, Peter and J. J van Helten. "Labour in the South African Gold Mining Industry, 1886–1914." In: Marks, Shula and R. Rathbone, eds. *Industrialisation and Social Change in South Africa: African Class Formation, Culture, and Consciousness, 1870–1930.* 1982. pp. 79–80.

[12] Parsons, *King Khama, Emperor Joe, and the Great White Queen: Victorian Britain Through African Eyes,* 22.

colonial investments to unite Afrikaner settlers within the self-governing republican state.[13] State revenue (coming mostly from import duties and 'hut tax') and expenditure were minimal. In 1884 the entire state revenue of the ZAR was less than £ 200 000(compared to £ 2 985 984 in the Cape Colony), rising gradually to £ 218 500 in 1885 and £ 308 000 in 1886.[14] The importance and consequence of this economic reality was that with a low degree of public and private capital accumulation on the eve of the most significant Witwatersrand gold discoveries, hundreds of newly arrived European diggers were initially far more interested in the quick speculative gains that could be made from the buying and selling of small land claims than they were in investments in labour (and later capital) intensive open-surface mining.[15] Either way, if South African gold mining exploration and production was ever to take off, large amounts of financial capital were needed quickly.

This chapter provides a historical assessment of the JSE's institutional foundations, rise, and interaction with southern Africa's mineral industries and international finance. The South African mining market's imperial entanglements are examined through the initial opportunities and challenges of the European capital market. Following the early financial developments in Kimberley, Barberton, London, Paris and finally Johannesburg, this chapter investigates the political and economic connections between the rise of South Africa's gold mining industry and its foremost financial intermediary. As conducive as the London Stock Exchange and the Paris Bourse were to test the financial capacity of the diamond and gold mining industry, it was the JSE where regulatory simplification and limited financial barriers to entry created a favourable financial climate for a young and capital-hungry mining industry.

[13] Giliomee, *The Afrikaners: Bibliography of a People*, 179.

[14] Jeppe, F. *Jeppe's Transvaal Almanac and Directory for 1889*. Cape Town: The Argus Printing and Publishing Company. 1889. p. 51.

For Cape Colony See: Gwaindepi, A. *State Building in the Colonial Era: Public Revenue, Expenditure and Borrowing Patterns in the Cape Colony, 1820–1910*. Doctoral dissertation, Stellenbosch: Stellenbosch University. 2018. pp. 221–222.

[15] Van Onselen, Charles. *Studies in the Social and Economic History of the Witwatersrand, 1886–1914: 1. New Babylon*. 1982. p. 3.

MINING FINANCE AND EARLY STOCK MARKET INTERMEDIARIES IN COLONIAL SOUTH AFRICA

Following the discovery of diamonds in the late 1860s, South Africa became a full participant in the extended phase of global economic growth, trade and most importantly, capital inflows.[16] Diamonds, along with the growing wool sector, were the commodities that transformed the basis of southern Africa's settler economy, much like wool did for Australia, wool and meat production for New Zealand, and fishing, fur, timber and wheat for Canada.[17] The industrial exploitation of the diamond fields brought together investments of financial capital, the application and development of technology, and a mobilisation of labour at a scale never seen before in South Africa.[18] Throughout the 1870s industrial and financial capitalism spread into South Africa's interior, facilitating the rapid expansion of banking, insurance and financial institutions that would supply the risk-sharing services to a growing class of colonial investors.

In October 1880, The Cape Colony fully annexed Griqualand West from the Orange Free State. The new commercial legislation of the Cape Colony proved to be the major legal impetus for diamond companies and smallholdings in Kimberley to transition into joint-stock mining companies.[19] The formation of joint-stock companies that would intensify the process of corporate amalgamation marked the most significant financial innovation in the evolution of the diamond industry in South Africa.[20] The following month a group of largely unknown entrepreneurs founded the first *Kimberley Royal Share Exchange*.[21] The Exchange was established

[16] Feinstein, C. H. *An Economic History of South Africa: Conquest, Discrimination, and Development*. 2005. p. 5.

[17] De Kiewiet, Cornelius William. *A History of South Africa: Social & Economic*. Oxford: The Clarendon Press. 1941. p. 89.

[18] Kubicek, Robert. "Mining: Patterns of Dependence and Development 1870–1930." In: Konczacki, Zbigniew/Parpart, Jane/Shaw Timothy, eds. *Studies in the Economic History of South Africa: Volume II: South Africa, Lesotho and Swaziland*. 1991. p. 64.

[19] Turrell, Robert Vicat. *Capital and Labour on the Kimberley Diamond Fields, 1871–1890*. Cambridge: Cambridge University Press. 1987. p. 105.

[20] Frankel, S. Herbert. *Capital Investment in Africa*. 1938. p. 60.

[21] Rosenthal, E. *On 'change Through the Years: A History of Share Dealing in South Africa*. 1968. p. 58.

so that brokers and other financial intermediaries could meet for business at a physical market with the necessary telegraph technology without the trouble of going around the mining camps to enquire about the availability of shares and securities.[22] With regional offices in Cape Town, Port Elizabeth and Grahamstown, the Cape Colony was ready for its first official stock exchange mania.

The early local and international successes of Kimberley's diamond extraction and trade, which was underwritten by the expanding colonial state, inspired greater investor confidence and speculation on the future of the mining town and growing regional economy. The *Standard Bank of South Africa Ltd.*, by then well established in Kimberley, reported on the unprecedented borrowing and compulsive speculation that took place throughout 1881.[23] According to the Kimberley branch manager, out of 74 companies quoted on the local share list, 40 had been formed recently and the 'colonial public [had] strained [its] credit, in some cases unduly to provide the required funds.'[24] The total share capital of these newly floated companies rose to £ 8 000 000 with most of the shares subscribed by the Cape colonial public. As shown in the first quantitative studies of mining capital formation in South Africa by Frankel, at least half of this venture capital represented vendors' and promoters' scrip, and only a small proportion of the working capital was subscribed.[25]

Kimberley's first share mania exposed the dominance of institutional investors over individual mining speculators. The boom was fuelled by the colonial banks' advances against the scrip, with the Cape of Good Hope Bank taking the majority of the business despite itself being financed by the Standard Bank.[26] Individual investors mostly traded scrip directly with the mining companies. The Kimberley offices of the newly floated companies were stormed by mining prospectors and those investors who could not get in through the front door, threw in their share applications, along

[22] Turrell, Robert Vicat. *Capital and Labour on the Kimberley Diamond Fields, 1871–1890*. Cambridge: Cambridge University Press. 1987. p. 107.

[23] Henry, James A. *The First Hundred Years of the Standard Bank*. 1963. pp. 68–70.

[24] SBA. GMO 3/1/11, No. 68/81, General Remarks of Annual Report. Kimberley Branch, 19 August 1881. p. 945.

[25] Frankel, S. Herbert. Capital Investment in Africa. 1938. pp. 59–60.

[26] Turrell, Robert Vicat. *Capital and Labour on the Kimberley Diamond Fields, 1871–1890*. 1987. p. 107.

with cheques and bank notes, in through the windows.[27] The daily trade in stocks on the Royal Exchange throughout the early 1880s dominated Kimberley's social and economic life to such an extent that many mining prospectors, miners and local farmers abandoned their professions to fully focus on the Cape's growing share market.[28] Kimberley stockbrokers took advantage of these enthusiastic and largely financially illiterate investors to amass significant profits through the arbitrage on stocks of mostly worthless mining, construction and transport companies. To numerous international journalists covering the share mania, the great majority of the hastily incorporated mining companies were nothing but financial scams with no operational prospects and were in fact endangering the capital formation of the Cape Colony's most productive economic sector.

Just as the stock markets of London and New York of the early 1880s, the organisational evolution of the Kimberley Stock Exchange was defined by personal connections and intimate knowledge of financial speculation in a highly competitive economic environment. Management disputes, manipulative members, and a lack of intent to reform the poorly organised, self-regulatory mechanism of the Exchange, quickly led to the emergence of competing financial intermediaries.[29] A new body of the Kimberley Stock and Share Brokers Protective Association was formed in April 1881 with the most influential mining speculator and diamond trader in the city, Barney Barnato, deliberately being left out of the directorate. Since his arrival in Kimberley in 1873, Barnato was involved in the trade in uncut and unpolished stolen diamonds and was rumoured to be the single biggest diamond buyer in the mining camps of the 1870s and 1880s.[30] Despite the illegal nature of the trade in stolen or unaccounted for diamonds, Barney Barnato and his brother Harry were credited with igniting Kimberley's first financial boom when their *Barnato Brothers* holding company floated five separate companies in the first half of 1881 with the combined nominal capital of £493 000 on

[27] Henry, James A. *The First Hundred Years of the Standard Bank.* 1963. pp. 68–69.

[28] Rosenthal, E. *On 'Change Through The Years: A History of Share Dealing in South Africa.* 1968. p. 65.

[29] Turrell, Robert Vicat. *Capital and Labour on the Kimberley Diamond Fields, 1871–1890.* 1987. pp. 110–115.

[30] Turrell, Robert Vicat. "Sir Frederic Philipson Stow: The Unknown Diamond Magnate." In: Davenport-Hines, Richard and Peter Treadwell, eds. *Speculators and Patriots: Essays in Business Biography.* London: Routledge. 2005. p. 65.

the Exchange.[31] In spite of the Barnato brothers' financial foresight and willingness to take on heavy risk in floating new issues of mining shares, the new colonial administration of Griqualand West distanced itself from questionable financers with no established political connections in Cape Town. Convinced that these political and financial antagonisms were the doing of Cecil Rhodes' amalgamation scheme of mining companies he had developed with Alfred Beit (something that was also to happen in later years in Johannesburg), Barney Barnato decided to set up a rival financial organisation on 12 July 1881 to compete with the Kimberley Stock Exchange.[32] Barnato's exclusion from Kimberley's first exchange intensified his resentment of Rhodes's growing political influence and prompted him to establish a new stock market where he would take on a new financial role in an increasingly politicised Kimberley.[33] Having made the transition from investor to operator, Barnato set out on a new financial path of institutional rent-seeking and financial regulation.

Not much is known about Barnato's stock exchange, but contemporary archival evidence suggests that Barnato was able to make the most of his new financial institution and invited the Standard Bank of South Africa to invest extensively in his venture. According to the Standard Bank's Kimberley branch manager, James Dell, Barnato's Exchange was in existence for a short time and was flooded with new buyers looking to take advantage of the growing international demand for Kimberley's mining shares that was bound to increase further with the expansion of working capital and diamond production capacity.[34] However, and perhaps as a sign for Barnato's future engagement with stock markets and the share trade in South Africa, the efforts in the new financial organisation did not result in any improvement in his social status—Barnato was excluded from

[31] Turrell, Robert Vicat. *Capital and Labour on the Kimberley Diamond Fields, 1871–1890.* 1987. p. 118.
See also: Cleveland, Todd. *Stones of Contention: A History of Africa's Diamonds.* Athens: Ohio University Press. 2014. pp. 40–45.

[32] Rosenthal, Eric. *On 'Change Through the Years: A History of Share Dealing in South Africa.* 1968. pp. 62–63.

[33] Leasor, J. *Rhodes & Barnato: The Premier and the Prancer.* Trans-Atlantic Publications Incorporated. 1997. pp. 125–126.

[34] SBA. GMO 3/1/11, No. 68/81, General Remarks of Annual Report. Kimberley Branch, 19 August 1881. p. 924.

joining the town's new social epicentre, the Kimberley Club, in August 1881.

As if two stock exchanges in Kimberley were not enough, Rhodes used his growing political power in Cape Town and London to launch the Mutual Share and Claim Exchange with a capital of £25 000—just three days after Barnato's exchange went into operation—on 15 July 1881. Rhodes' exchange was able to boast an impressive board of international directors headed by Francis Baring-Gould, a member of the famous financial firm in the City of London, auctioneer Alfred Rothschild and the prominent Cape shipping merchant, Frank de Pass.[35] Rhodes was well aware of his comparative advantage through established European financial networks and contracted his financial partners Julius Wernher and Jules Porges to market South African diamond shares in London, Paris and Vienna.[36] Together the three Kimberley stock exchanges drove diamond mining to the first great South African share boom of 1881. By mid-1881, fewer than 15 companies were listed on the Kimberley exchanges, but these made up a total capital of £ 2 500 000.[37] By the end of the same year, there were 71 companies listed, with a total nominal capital of £9 658 960.[38]

Disappointingly, and yet predictably, Kimberley diamond shares never really made a significant long-term impression on investors in London or on the European continent.[39] Kimberley financial magnates were able to secure the necessary British and French capital to float their companies in Kimberley, but, apart from a few isolated cases, such as the Kimberley Central Company, which was able to pay up to 30 per cent dividends on its shares between 1881 and 1883, returns on most shares were minimal, even when considering the hype around shares such as De Beers', which were able to yield a dividend of 8.5 per cent for the years 1882–86.[40]

[35] Rosenthal, Eric. On 'Change Through the Years: A History of Share Dealing in South Africa. 1968. pp. 62–63.

[36] Wheatcroft, Geoffrey. The Randlords. 1987. pp. 69–72.

[37] SBA. GMO 3/1/11, No. 68/81, General Remarks of Annual Report. Kimberley Branch, 19 August 1881. p. 924.

[38] Turrell, Robert Vicat. Capital and Labour on the Kimberley Diamond Fields, 1871–1890. 1987. p. 105.

[39] Ibid. p. 111.

[40] "South African Diamond Shares." The Economist, 10 March 1888. pp. 309–310.

The low European confidence in diamonds resulted in nearly all the original flotations taking place in Kimberley, with only the most powerful Kimberley conglomerates, such as the Anglo-African Company and De Beers, being able to secure the primary markets of London or Paris for a listing.[41] It was this lack of stock market support for smaller company flotations in London and Paris that forced Kimberley magnates to adopt the most dubious stock market practices to promote, sell and inflate the value of diamond shares.[42] As reported by the General Manager of the Standard Bank branch in Kimberley regarding the progress of the first boom in 1881:

> The advance in value of all descriptions of mining property which took place at the end of last year grew in intensity, so that speculation bore the appearance of gambling. New companies were floated daily and, and for the shares the public scrambled; the object in most cases being to sell out at a good premium. Speculators made large profits, and the desire to speculate in mining stock became widespread throughout the country. We are perhaps somewhat overdone by mining shares, but the existing prosperity will probably continue, and may even increase through the introduction of European capital.[43]

Kimberley's diamond sector put South Africa on the global financial map and introduced European financial networks to new share markets along the expanding colonial frontier. The financial markets inside the ZAR were however experiencing a very different business climate. With peace and sovereignty resolved after the first Anglo-Boer War of 1881/2,[44] the significant political concessions made by Britain persuaded European investors to risk their capital and financial reputations in the poor settler economy across the Vall River.[45] Although small gold discoveries in the

---

[41] Rosenthal, Eric. *On 'Change Through the Years: A History of Share Dealing in South Africa*. 1968. pp. 62–63.

[42] Turrell, Robert Vicat. *Capital and Labour on the Kimberley Diamond Fields, 1871–1890*. 1987. pp. 111–118.

[43] SBA. GMO 3/1/11, No. 68/81, General Remarks of Annual Report. Kimberley Branch, 19 August 1881. p. 958.

[44] See: Laband, John. *The Transvaal Rebellion: The First Boer War, 1880–1881*. London: Routledge. 2014.

[45] Arndt, Ernst Heinrich Daniel. *Banking and Currency Development in South Africa (1652–1927)*. Cape Town: Juta. 1928. p. 336.

ZAR date back to the 1850s, it was not until several geological confirma-
tions of alluvial deposits in the north-eastern ZAR in the early 1870s that
experienced international miners, engineers and prospectors, chiefly from
Australia and California, were attracted to the settler republic in increasing
numbers.[46] By the end of the 1870s, the establishment of mining camps
in the Zoutpansberg district in Lydenburg, Pilgrim's Rest and the De
Kaap Valley set off South Africa's first gold rush. However, it was not until
the discovery and rapid exploitation of deeper reefs in the mining camp
that in 1885 was officially named Barberton that the De Kaap goldfields
put ZAR on the international gold producer's map. The town's financial
infrastructure developed quickly with three Cape banks, three newspapers,
a telegraph office, and—most significantly—the ZAR's first official stock
exchange opening between May and December.[47]

By late 1885, more than a hundred different shares were quoted on
the Barberton's Transvaal Share and Claim Exchange, with the market
dealing in a total of more than four million shares.[48] The opening of
the Standard Bank's office in April 1886 further intensified the migration
of Kimberley's financial and human capital to the De Kaap Valley.[49] A
matter of particular significance for the international financial recognition
of the ZAR's early securities industry was that many of the Barberton
mining companies went on to produce significant amounts of gold, and
were consistently able to pay dividends on their shares.[50] More importantly for the industrial development of gold mining in the region, the
Barberton boom intensified the pace and (private and public) financing
of prospecting activities in the ZAR.[51] The share dealings in Barberton
were, however, marked by financial connections and problems very similar
to those in Kimberley. The depressing state of affairs in Barberton during
1886 and 1887 was summarised in the Standard Bank's Annual Report
(Fig. 2.1):

[46] See: Teisch, J., 2005. 'Home is not so very far away': Californian engineers in South
Africa, 1868–1915. *Australian Economic History Review*, 45(2), pp. 139–160.

[47] Henry, James. *The First Hundred Years of the Standard Bank*. 1963. pp. 60–61.

[48] Wheatcroft, G. *The Randlords*. p. 84.

[49] Henry, James. *The First Hundred Years of the Standard Bank*. 1963. pp. 60–61.

[50] Kubicek, Robert V. *Economic imperialism in theory and practice: the case of South
African gold mining finance 1886–1914*. 1979. pp. 57–58.

[51] WHP. *Committee on Discovery of Gold on the Witwatersrand*. Government of the
Union of South Africa. A102. pp. 25–42.

The current half year has witnessed the collapse of the reckless speculation in Barberton shares and properties, resulting in a severe check of
the general business there. Even the best companies appear to have been
mismanaged.[52]

James Benjamin Taylor, an early partner of Alfred Beit and one of the
few successful brokers in Barberton, kept Beit and Rhodes well informed
of the market situation on the Barberton Stock Exchange. In a series of
telegraphs to Beit in late 1886, Taylor spoke of the unstable speculative
share market and urged Beit to provide him with further capital for new
ventures on the Witwatersrand.[53] With his mind firmly set on the development of gold mining on the Rand, Taylor concluded that initiating new
gold ventures had become impossible not only in Barberton, but also
in London. He believed that the market for South African gold shares

Fig. 2.1 Barberton Stock Exchange in 1888 (*Source* Harris, Robert. *South
Africa: Illustrated by a Series of One Hundred and Four Permanent Photographs.*
Port Elizabeth: Robert Harris. 1888. p. 17

[52] SBA. GMO 3/1/21, 8 August 1887. p. 616.

[53] BWA. W.B. (J.P), 3. Incoming correspondences 1886–1889.

was 'too narrow,' stating that (after the decline of Kimberley in 1886/1887) very few of the big London financial houses such as the Rothschilds, Barings and Schröders were interested in financing gold mining in South Africa.[54] The critical assessment of the London market by Taylor was that 'there was not enough speculative capital available in London for anything big.'[55]

Rhodes, in particular, was very sceptical of the future of the Barberton Stock Exchange. On 12 December 1886, in a letter to his long-term financial partner Charles Rudd, who operated a number of mining syndicates in Barberton, Rhodes stressed the need to start investing in 'real mining plots' and 'real mining machinery,' as the collapse of the bogus dealings in Barberton was quickly approaching.[56] He also advised Rudd to make sure that he establish good contacts with the colonial banks, as the stock exchange in Barberton was not seen as a feasible gamble for the infant mining industry. According to Rhodes, a move westward to the new goldfields of the Witwatersrand was the only way forward.

GOLD AND THE LURE OF LONDON: OPPORTUNITIES AND LIMITATIONS

In 1886, the ZAR's most significant gold deposits were discovered on the range of hills known as the Witwatersrand plateau, changing the course of southern African history. The richest deposits of gold were located very close to the surface in the form of a 65 km-long reef near the Ferreira mining camp that quickly became known as Johannesburg.[57] The mining setttlement's origins began in 1853 when Pieter Jakob Marais, the first prospector officially appointed by the ZAR's Volksraad, panned small

---

[54] Rosenthal, E. On 'Change Through the Years: A History of Share Dealing in South Africa. 1968. pp. 140–143.

[55] Quoted in: Ibid. p. 142.

[56] BLA. MS 110/6, Cecil John Rhodes to Charles Rudd, 12 December 1886.

[57] Although a number of theories exist on the origins of the name Johannesburg, the only credible one came in the form of an official 1896 Pretoria inquiry into the early history of the City of Gold. According to the commission, the only documents dealing directly with the city's name, point to the name-bearers of Johann Friedrich Bernhard Rissik and Christiaan Johannes Joubert, the first two farm owners in 1886 of the settlement that grew into the city.

See: WHP. Committee on Discovery of Gold on the Witwatersrand. Government of the Union of South Africa. A102.

amounts of gold in the Jukskei River, a few miles north of the Witwa-tersrand's main reef.[58] Located 55 km south of the ZAR's capital of Pretoria, the new mining town of Johannesburg would have to be grad-ually integrated into a recovering regional economy, where capital, food, basic manufactured goods, energy resources and building material could be supplied. With no railway connection from the Rand to the coast at the time of the discoveries, the transportation of machinery for the produc-tion and the eventual delivery of gold to international markets was very limited and, in the case of most early mining initiatives, outright impos-sible. Although no place in South Africa responded to the news of the gold discoveries with greater enthusiasm than Kimberley, the first finan-cial tests of the ZAR's young gold industry would take place on the stock markets of London.[59]

The gold discoveries on the Witwatersrand came shortly after the industrialising world began adjusting to a trade and monetary system based on the gold standard. Gold was to provide greater price and exchange stability as a result of closer integration with the world finan-cial centres.[60] Throughout nineteenth-century Britain, and particularly the City of London, had been at the centre of the international demand for gold and silver, as well as a significant market force of the global gold supply.[61] Britain had already used the gold standard at various times during the eighteenth century, but officially adopted, implemented and advocated the monetary policy after the Napoleonic Wars in 1821. The British gold standard would still face much internal opposition well into the second half of the nineteenth century,[62] uniting the City-based *Gold Standard Defence Association* in strongly rallying against any resurgence of bimetallism in the 1890s, praising the gold standard as the main reason

---

[58] WHP. *Committee on Discovery of Gold on the Witwatersrand*. Government of the Union of South Africa. A102. pp. 12–13.

[59] Rosenthal, E. *Gold! Gold! Gold!* 1970. p. 124.

[60] Eichengreen, Barry and Marc Flandreau, eds. *The Gold Standard in Theory and History*. Abington: Taylor & Francis. 1997. p. 7.

[61] Flandreau, M. *The glitter of gold: France, bimetallism, and the emergence of the international gold standard, 1848–1873*. OUP Oxford. 2004. pp. 49–40.

[62] See: Howe, Anthony C. "Bimetallism, c. 1880–1898: A Controversy Re-Opened?" *The English Historical Review* 105, no. 415 (1990): 377–391.

for trade liberalisation and Britain's rise as a commercial power for over half a century.[63]

The gold standard's career as a global monetary guarantor was launched by the new united German Empire's step to adopt a gold currency over silver in 1871, quickly followed by Sweden in 1874, Holland in 1875, France and Spain in 1876, Russia in 1893, India in 1898 and the United States in 1900.[64] During this final quarter of the nineteenth century, it would be the newly mined gold from South Africa, Australia and Canada that, eased international liquidity constraints by facilitating an expansion of the gold base and money supplies without the dangers of inflation.[65] This flurry of gold and the rising demand for other base and precious metals, spurred European, and particularly British, investors to take greater interest in overseas mining investments.[66]

London's position at the centre of the international trade and payment system between 1870 and 1914 enabled the City's capital market to dominate international mining finance.[67] Although nominal capitalisation of the foreign mining sector on the London Stock Exchange grew steadily throughout the early 1880s, the phenomenon was largely based on the trading dynamics of an extensive London secondary stock market, rather than that of just the formalised stock exchange.[68] It was in the market for mining securities in particular that the LSE struggled to maintain its position as London's premier stock market in the face of growing competition from the unregulated curb market where banks and brokers traded in stocks readily accessible to the general investing public.[69] Despite its greater social accessibility and lower capital constraints, the 'curb' or 'over-the-counter' market, where the integrity of the transaction was guaranteed only by the reputation of the broker or bank offering the financial products, was a risky alternative to the mutual guarantee offered

---

[63] Cain, Peter and Anthony Hopkins. *British Imperialism 1688–2000*. 2002. p. 144.

[64] Ally, Russell. *Gold and Empire: The Bank of England and South Africa's Gold Producers*. 1994. pp. 4–7.

[65] Cain, Peter and Anthony Hopkins. *British Imperialism 1688–2000*. pp. 141–144.

[66] See: Harvey, Charles and John Press. "The City and International Mining, 1870–1914." *Business History* 32, no. 3 (1990): 98–119.

[67] Rönnbäck, K. and O. Broberg. *Capital and Colonialism: The Return on British Investments in Africa 1869–1969*. Springer. 2019. pp. 25–27.

[68] Michie, R. C. *The London Stock Exchange: A History*. 1999. pp. 16–35.

[69] Ibid. p. 92.

by the LSE. It was only towards the end of the 1890s that the LSE exercised a virtual monopoly on the trade of securities in London.[70]

At the beginning of the 1880s, an increasing number of large gold mining companies converted to the joint form and combined this with the issue of stocks and shares to the (largely) London-based investing public.[71] This was mainly a result of the growth in the number of different shares offered on the LSE, fuelled by the popularity and marketability of stocks on the Official List. Any company applying for admission of its shares to the Official List had to first be admitted to general trading on the LSE. At any time only around 10% of all quoted securities could command a ready market as long as the brokers had a realistic outlook over the trending stocks.[72] A look at the Official List shows that the entire mining and plantation sector made up only 2.5% of all quoted securities in 1853, and only 1.2% of official trade in 1913.[73] While the Official List only represented a small section of London's security trade, unfortunately for historians, it remains the best-documented and quantifiable sector of the LSE.[74]

Despite the fact that the LSE was always willing to accommodate new types and sectors of securities, the Official List was the best control mechanism the Quotation Committee of the Exchange had in place to determine, restrict or even prohibit trade in particular stocks on the floor.[75] The Economist stated that the Official List was developed according to the importance of security to the public, which was in turn driven by demand, and even more so, speculation.[76] Although the self-regulated practices of the LSE were put to the test on numerous occasions throughout the late nineteenth century, Exchange members were

[70] Neal, Larry and Lance Davis. "The Evolution of the Structure and Performance of the London Stock Exchange in the First Global Financial Market, 1812–1914." *European Review of Economic History* 10, no. 3 (2006): 280.

[71] Michie, R. C. *The London Stock Exchange: A History*. 1999. pp. 92–97.

[72] Ibid. p. 95.

[73] Ibid. p. 93.

[74] See: Rönnbäck, K. and O. Broberg. *Capital and Colonialism: The Return on British Investments in Africa 1869–1969*. Springer. 2019. pp. 77–79.

Hannah, Leslie. "The London Stock Exchange, 1869–1929: New Statistics for Old?" *The Economic History Review* 71, no. 4 (2018): 1349–1356.

[75] Michie, R. C. The London Stock Exchange: A History. 1999. p. 87.

[76] Quoted in Ibid. p. 95.

unwilling to compromise on the minimal requirements for a quotation on the Official List.[77] By refusing to grant a quotation the Stock Exchange was not denying that security a market, even on the floor itself.[78] What was however being denied was access to the world's most recognised stock exchange and the possible marketing premiums for shares that went with it. The Official List was in many ways the dividing factor for South African gold mines wanting to list at the LSE. By studying the records of the *Investors Monthly Manual* for the years 1880–1885, one can quickly conclude that very few mining companies were even able to make it onto the Official List.[79] Even if several British mining companies were able to trade on the LSE's premier market, Australian and South African stocks only made short appearances at irregular intervals.

South African-registered companies in particular found it extremely difficult to meet the LSE's listing requirement stipulating the two-thirds public allotment of issued capital and would regularly resort to dubious accounting practices by presenting two different sets of accounts with their listing applications.[80] This was further illustrated by the fact that most mining prospectors would obtain mining rights by allotting large proportions of the issued shares to the vendors of the mining plots. According to *The Economist's* analysis of London's mining sector, in such cases, "a quotation could never be obtained since according to the LSE rules, it is a *sine qua non* that no less than two-thirds of the capital must have been absolutely taken up by the (British) public."[81] This also goes to further prove that South African mining investors were so short of capital that they were not even in a position to purchase the mining plots that they would later 'market' as mining companies in London. Additionally,

---

[77] See: Van, Helten J. J. "Mining, Share Manias and Speculation: British Investment in Overseas Mining, 1880–1913." 1990. p. 166.
Michie, R. C. *The London Stock Exchange: A History*. 1999. p. 95.

[78] Michie, R. C. *The London Stock Exchange: A History*. 1999. p. 87.

[79] See: "Financial History of the Year." *Investors Monthly Manual*, December 1880–1885.

[80] Van, Helten J. J. "Mining, share manias and speculation: British Investment in overseas mining, 1880–1913." 1990. p. 166.
See also: Parker, Robert Henry. "Regulating British Corporate Financial Reporting in the Late Nineteenth Century." *Accounting, Business & Financial History* 1, no. 1 (1990): 51–71.

[81] "Mining Companies and Vendor's Shares." *The Economist*, 8 December 1888. p. 1541.

as the final point of the listing regulation stipulated, there is no evidence to show that any of the LSE-listed South African companies were officially quoted in Kimberley or Barberton before making their debut in London. With no start-up capital, no gold and very complicated mining land rights in the ZAR, South African companies could only, at best, 'try their luck' in London.[82]

A small number of South African mines were however able to register on the Official List of the LSE. The *Official Report Book* of the LSE, reporting on applications for quotations on the Official List or a special settling day, documents how several South African companies attempted and succeeded in registering on the Official List. Although Kimberley companies such as the Kimberley Waterworks Company and the Anglo African Diamond Mining Company were able to successfully apply for listing in 1881,[83] ZAR's new gold mining companies were put under far greater scrutiny.

The listing procedure was well illustrated in the company file of the Oceana Transvaal Land Company. Despite being incorporated in Britain and the ZAR in November 1886 and successfully applying for listing on the LSE for an initial allotment in February 1887, Henry Burdett, the secretary of the Share and Loan Department of the LSE, only allowed the application for listing to pass fully on 14 May 1889. Between November 1886 and May 1889, the company submitted three applications, using both British and South African prospectuses, official translations of incorporation at the Transvaal Chamber of Commerce, declarations and endorsements from various members of the board of directors and extensive collections of company financial reports.[84]

The case of Rhodes's Gold Fields was even more complicated and proved the extent to which LSE listing requirements were a risk for South African gold mines. Although Rhodes was able to allocate 100 000 shares in London in February 1887 and 25 000 shares in South Africa in August 1887 to the British public, the company did not feature on the Official List until November 1888.[85] The official application file showed a

---

[82] Rosenthal, *Gold! Gold! Gold!*, pp. 134–146; "Transvaal Mining Ventures on the Continent." *The Diggers' News*, 20 April 1889. p. 3.

[83] GLA. MS 29,797, S29797/001, *Report Book August 1881–November 1882*. p. 9 and p. 335.

[84] GLA. Company File 22B/343. *Oceana Transvaal Land Company*.

[85] GLA. Company File 14B/27. *Gold Fields of South Africa*.

number of legal documents justifying the company's name change from Gold Fields of Africa, a series of British prospectuses (and a letter by Charles Rudd explaining the reasons for the 'lost prospectuses from South Africa'), a long sequence of letters from Burdett stressing the need to send additional applications confirming share allocations in South Africa and a number of official LSE documents explaining why the company was not yet granted a place on the Official List. The reasons for prolonging the granting of the application, personally signed by Henry Burdett on 30 October 1888, can be summarised as follows: lack of certificate of incorporation, lack of share certificates of public allotments in London, lack of certificates from the company's London bankers, and no evidence of a statutory declaration from the Joint Stock Registry.[86] Although only some of these documents were promptly submitted, and Gold Fields was on the Official List the following month, the episode illustrated that even for a company with the best connections to capital houses and financial networks in London and South Africa, listing on the LSE was a complicated, lengthy and bureaucratic process, deliberately enforced to discourage suspicious commercial undertakings which could endanger the financial credibility of the LSE and the City of London as a whole.

Once on the Official List, such a privilege and opportunity would open up another set of trading hurdles and market constraints. The main problems with listing South African shares on the LSE and general trading in South African securities were later summarised in *the Statist*.[87] It was noted that the high amount of capital invested in the South African shares would need 'extensive' diggings of gold to give investors a yield that would encourage even the humblest of dividends to be paid out. This lack of economic and financial principles behind the investments made by the brokers illustrated that the share market was not driven by the capital needs and operational outcomes of the mines (even less so than in the case of diamond shares), but rather by the speculative dynamics of the London mining market and its influential figures. In addition, the large number of traders on the LSE made it very difficult to reach collusive agreements on

---

[86] GLA. Company Files 14B/27. *Gold Fields of South Africa*. Henry Burdett to of South Africa, 30 October 1888.

[87] "Transvaal Gold Companies." *The Statist*, 26 January 1889. pp. 103–105.

specific sectors of the share market.[88] Even though traders ensured that there was no shortage of capital flowing into the Exchange for various deals, financial product niches such as the South African mining shares were controlled by dealers who were only willing to drive the market with ready available capital.[89]

The reality of speculative trades on mining companies was that the properties were underfinanced, non-existent or, in the worst cases, both. *The Statist* quickly revealed that despite the geologically confirmed riches of gold and the generous supplies of coal and free-flowing water, only a selected few locally registered companies were able to make a slight profit. Those using British working capital and under British management were commercial failures.[90] A number of South African companies were discussed in the report, but the situation of most British-listed South African gold mining companies mirrored *The Statist's* description of the Balkis Company:

> The Balkis Company, after four years' work, and after spending a large amount of money, has yet practically to commence the business for which the company was originally formed- that of developing the gold-bearing properties it required.[91]

The Statist's message to the London (and global) investing public was clear: London-listed South African gold mining companies were still production failures and only a few South African-based, owned and managed companies were able to yield any profits from their small operations in the ZAR the Transvaal. With low production and a very poor financial reputation, the South African gold mining industry was still not ready to firmly establish itself in London's international mining market.

---

[88] Davis, Lance and Larry Neal. "Micro Rules and Macro Outcomes: The Impact of Micro Structure on the Efficiency of Security Exchanges, London, New York, and Paris, 1800–1914." *American Economic Review* 88, no. 2 (1998): 40–45.

[89] Michie, R. C. *The London Stock Exchange: A History.* 1999. pp. 95–106.

[90] "Transvaal Mining." *The Statist*, 3 September 1887. pp. 258–260.

[91] "Transvaal Mining." *The Statist*, 3 September 1887. p. 259.

THE RISE OF JOHANNESBURG'S CAPITAL MARKET

As the growing pool of international investors in the ZAR had predicted, Barberton lost its allure and financial significance by early 1887. The settler financial elite needed to move to Johannesburg in search of new investments and speculative transactions.[92] As later lamented by the manager of the Standard Banks branch in Barberton, the town had no basic infrastructure and no support from the ZAR's government to develop the mining industry:

> Contrary to general anticipation, the progress made on the De Kaap range (Barberton reef) has been slow, the Sheba and Union Gold Mining Companies being almost the only ones with a regular monthly output of gold. At present however the heavy duties imposed by the Transvaal Government upon all imported articles used by Miners, the absence of bridges, and difficulties of transport in a hilly country to mines in an almost inaccessible position, adversely affect the gold industry.[93]

The slow development of mining on the Rand did not encourage the rapid investments in infrastructure and mining technology Rhodes had hoped for. Although electricity was already available in 1888, there was no telephone or telegraph communication with the rest of South Africa and the supply of heavy machinery was hindered by the lack of a railway that ended in Kimberley (and only reached Johannesburg in 1892).[94] In 1886 the new industry produced only 10 032 ounces of gold,[95] and despite convincing geological reports stating the potential wealth of the goldfields, the speculative share market back in London was not interested in providing the dusty fields at the original Ferreira Camp with large sums of international financial capital.[96]

It was precisely this initial lack of commitment from European markets that set Johannesburg on a course of share market speculation from the

---

[92] Kubicek, Robert V. *Economic imperialism in theory and practice: the case of South African gold mining finance 1886–1914.* 1979. p. 57.

[93] SBA. GMO 3/1/23, 8 August 1888. p. 67.

[94] Henry, James. *The First Hundred Years of the Standard Bank.* 1963. pp. 93–94.

[95] Compared with 383 544 ounces in 1889. See: "Transvaal Gold Production." *The Economist*, 22 February 1890. p. 239.

[96] "Transvaal Mining." *The Statist*, 3 September 1887. pp. 258–260.

first days of its existence.[97] The first share transactions on the Rand took place in a rustic canvas tent with trade taking place on Sundays, as this was the only day when mining was not allowed due to a strictly enforced regulation prohibiting the entry of African workers to the gold reefs.[98] The Pretoria government used the measure as an early form of labour pass systems on the Rand, controlling the amount of African labour available for the mines and simultaneously imposing strict respect for the Calvinist principles of the South African Republic.[99] With the 'day of rest' reserved for finance, early trade was performed in such a hasty and indiscriminate manner that even the Cape Town office of the Standard Bank issued an official warning to prevent all bank managers from 'abetting the share mania by means of the Bank's funds.'[100]

Undeterred by the Rand's uncertain financial future, Rhodes made the first serious attempt to establish an organised stock exchange in Johannesburg when he published a prospectus of the Witwatersrand Club and Exchange Company in the first issue of the *Diggers' News*, the Rand's earliest newspaper, on 24 February 1887.[101] The capital of the proposed Exchange was £ 3 500 in debentures of £1. The prospectus stressed that the large sums of capital invested in the goldfields had made clear the need for a 'central spot of mutual information, disposal of stock, and for other gold mining business.'[102] Even with the seasoned support of Alfred Beit, the Kimberley and Barberton financier Hermann Eckstein, and the Barberton stock market expertise of James Taylor, the still very limited securities industry proved that the stock exchange project was over-ambitious and attracted absolutely no interest and support.[103]

The significance of gold mining for Johannesburg's economic future determined its spatial development and urban infrastructure system.

---

[97] See: "Speculation." *The Diggers' News*, 23 November 1889. p. 3.

[98] See: SACMA. *South African Chamber of Mines Annual Report for the Year Ending 1896.* 1897. p. 15.

[99] See: Du Toit, André. "No Chosen People: The Myth of the Calvinist Origins of Afrikaner Nationalism and Racial Ideology." *The American Historical Review* 88, no. 4 (1983): 920–952.

[100] SBA. GMO 3/1/20. *Special Report*, 2 August 1886. p. 151.

[101] Klein. H. *The Story of the Johannesburg Stock Exchange 1887–1947.* 1948. p. 11.

[102] Rosenthal. E. *Gold! Gold! Gold!* 1970. p. 179.

[103] Rosenthal. E. *On 'Change Through the Years; a History of Share Dealing in South Africa.* 1968. p. 141.

Similar to the gold rush in California and Australia,[104] the mining settlement on the Rand changed from a tent camp to a brick town in a very short amount of time. Even before any real mining output could be accounted for, the original tented camp had attracted a diverse host of diggers, miners, labourers and entrepreneurs from all over southern Africa and the world. By the middle of 1887, the original Ferreira Camp had almost been abandoned as a result of the multiple gold reefs beneath it, with most of the buildings being moved a few hundred meters further to the township of Johannesburg.[105] The early population was estimated to be between 8000 and 10 000 European settlers and Africans, with the extensive introduction of bricks and plaster creating a more permanent settlement out of the mining camp.[106]

Even with some early signs of optimism in the mining sector, the rugged landscape and makeshift housing—still evident in early 1887—showed few signs of economic development. Not surprisingly, and foreshadowing the town's speculative spirit, the first impetus of economic activity came from an organisation that was quintessentially all about risk and gambling. The Johannesburg Turf Club was established in June 1887 and quickly proved to be the desired destination for most mining and non-mining speculators. The Turffontein Racecourse soon hosted its first horse races, proving that games of chance were considered equally if not more appealing than the risky and rough trade in mining claims and land plots.[107]

Despite the financial dominance of Kimberley mining magnates such as Rhodes, Beit and Eckstein, the honour of successfully establishing the first stock exchange in Johannesburg went to a rather unknown and even less experienced gold prospector, Benjamin M. Woollan. Very little archival evidence exists on the flotation of the Exchange and Chambers

---

[104] See: "The California Delusion and The Crown and the Southern Cross." In: Fetherling, George, ed. *The Gold Crusades: A Social History of Gold Rushes, 1849–1929*. Toronto: University of Toronto Press. 1997. pp. 11–67.

[105] Rosenthal, E. *On 'Change Through the Years; a History of Share Dealing in South Africa*. 1968. p. 169.

[106] SBA. GMO 3/1/22, 6 February 1888. p. 334.

[107] Brodie, Nechama. *The Joburg book: A Guide to the City's History, People & Places*. Johannesburg: Pan Macmillan and Sharp Sharp Media. 2008. p. 178.

Company,[108] except that Woollan, a very ambitious young Londoner managed not only to acquire a building site on the corner of Commissioner Street and Simmonds Street, but—unlike Rhodes—was able to raise £ 5 000 in nominal capital. Even less is known about Benjamin Woollan himself, apart from a newspaper report revealing that he was declared insolvent in Kimberley on 20 July 1886.[109] Although the successful initiative rose out of the dust without the financial help of Kimberley's diamond elite, the inclusion of James Taylor on the original list of directors does trace financial expertise, South African stock exchange knowledge and European capital back to Rhodes, who was surprisingly, was never offered a seat on the board of directors (Fig. 2.2).

From the little evidence that the JSE has presented about the securities trade in canvas tents at Ferreira's Camp, 'in the latter half of 1887 the growing weight of share speculation on the Rand, and poor telegraphic and postal communication[110] with (exchanges in) Kimberley and Pietermaritzburg, made it imperative that a stock exchange be instituted in Johannesburg.'[111] The new organisation on the corner of Simmonds and Commissioner Street was officially opened on 8 November 1887, but until the builders were able to complete their work in late January 1888, the tent-styled informal trade continued with many transactions at bar counters, makeshift offices and in the open air.[112] Within a few months after the official opening, the designated area between the Exchange and Market Square was already known as *'Between the Chains,'* with street trading in shares and land taking place day and night, including Sundays.[113] As described by Rosenthal, 'on those iron barriers, at both ends of the little street sat exhausted brokers, hoarse and ready to collapse after the strain of twenty hours continuous business'[114] (Fig. 2.3).

[108] "Exchanage and Chambers, Co.Ltd." In: Goldman, Charles Sydney, ed. *The Financial, Statistical, and General History of the Gold & Other Companies of Witwatersrand, South Africa.* London: E. Wilson and Co. 1892. p. 38.

[109] *The Journal* (Graham's Town), 20 July 1886. p. 3.

[110] See: "Telegrams." *The Diggers' News,* 8 January 1890. p. 3.

[111] Klein, H. *The Story of the Johannesburg Stock Exchange 1887–1947.* 1948. p. 13.

[112] Rosenthal, E. *On 'Change Through the Years; a History of Share Dealing in South Africa.* 1968. pp. 143–144.

[113] Ibid. p. 183.

[114] Rosenthal, E. *Gold Bricks and Mortar: 60 Years of Johannesburg History.* Johannesburg: Printing House. 1946. p. 48.

Fig. 2.2 The first Johannesburg Stock Exchange building at end of 1887 (*Source* Gerhard-Mark Van der Waal. *From Mining Camp to Metropolis: The Buildings of Johannesburg, 1886–1940*. Chris van Rensburg Publishing: Johannesburg, 1987. [Permission to reproduce image was granted by Chris van Rensburg Publishing])

Due to time and labour-saving factors, the Exchange's original trading rules were based on those of the Transvaal Share and Claim Exchange in Barberton.[115] Although very little is known about the exact content of these initial rules, one strictly upheld rule that clearly differed from the fortnightly settlement procedure of the LSE was that of the daily settlement on all transactions. All stocks purchased or sold on the Exchange on one day had to be delivered by noon the following day and if the delivery would not take place before noon, the buyer had the option to declare the

[115] Klein. H. *The Story of the Johannesburg Stock Exchange 1887–1947*. 1948. pp. 13–16.

37.—SIMMONS STREET : BETWEEN THE CHAINS.—PHOTOGR PHED BY J. DAVIS.

Fig. 2.3 Outdoor Trading on the JSE 'Between the Chains' (*Source* Longland, Henry. *The Golden Transvaal, an illustrated review, descriptive, historical,* etc. London: Simpkin, Marshall, Hamilton, Kento & Co. 1896. p. 46)

purchase to be 'off.'[116] The system was specifically implemented to avoid the speculative deals that took place in Kimberley and Barberton, where the delivery date was decided by the two parties involved. This has led to multiple chains of different contracts for future delivery. Rules were, however, far more flexible for shares bought and sold in the Cape Colony or in London, where a perfectly legitimate delivery would be recognised for up to ten and thirty days respectively.[117]

Membership of the Exchange was open to anybody who could pay the necessary subscription fees. The initial pool of members included men from very different professions working alongside financial entrepreneurs

[116] Kennedy, E. E. *Waiting for the Boom.* London: Effingham Wilson and Co. 1890. pp. 23–24.

[117] Ibid. pp. 23–24.

who were the real drivers of the Exchange and its operational business.[118] The basic rules of membership were explained in the JSE prospectus on the opening day:

> Only members have the right of entry to the Exchange Building for the transaction of business. Office hours are from 9am to 4 pm daily, Sundays and holidays excepted. Members are represented on the committee by three of their own number, elected from themselves, who act in co-operation with the directors, and with them exercise control over the general conduct of the Exchange, and frame the rules concerning the same. Anyone is eligible for membership, who has been recommended by two members who have fulfilled their engagements. An Official Share List will be issued by the authority of the Exchange weekly. Very stringent rules have been framed and ascribed to, as to the manner in which the business of sharebroking shall be conducted and breaches of these rules are punishable by expulsion, defaulters being posted and publicly declared to be such by direction of two-thirds of the directors.[119]

On 11 January 1888 the founding members were introduced in a much-celebrated prospectus. They were H.T.B. Harrington, J Langermann, C.E Scott, W.A Wills, S. Nettleton, A.W.H Peacock, A.E. Ellis, E. Ellis, A. Bailey, M.S. Runchman, W.F. Morris, F.M. Woollan, J.P. Taylor, W.P. Taylor, L. Homan, D. Ziman, W.H.A. Pitschard, E. Jansch, F. Churchill, J. Gardener, T.A. Rance, Carl Hanau and H. Bettleheim.[120] Despite Taylor, Bettleheim and Hanau being his close business associates, Rhodes himself never became a member of the Exchange. By the end of March 1888 the Exchange had grown to 130 members.[121]

Becoming a member of the JSE was the goal of most financial investors hoping to get rich in the ZAR. The minimal demands and regulations presented many opportunities and caused a great influx of brokers and financial experts once the Rand caught the attention of the world in financial capitals such as London, Paris, Frankfurt and Berlin. The limited barriers to entry on the JSE created a new dynamic, allowing many British

---

[118] Bryant, Margot. *Taking Stock: Johannesburg Stock Exchange- the first 100 years.* 1987. p. 5.

[119] Quoted in: Rosenthal, Eric. *On 'Change Through the Years; a History of Share Dealing in South Africa.* 1968. p. 155.

[120] Klein, H. *The Story of the Johannesburg Stock Exchange 1887–1947.* 1948. pp. 16–18.

[121] Rosenthal, E. *Gold! Gold! Gold!* 1970. p. 181.

and continental Europeans to bypass the social constraints of metropolitan capitals and establish themselves in the rough and rustic financial world of the South African Republic.

CONCLUSION

As the fate of southern Africa would have it, the discoveries of gold on the Rand came at a critical time of financial globalisation with increasingly interconnected global commodity and capital markets. The early development of the gold mining industry ensured that the ZAR and later the whole southern African regional economy, experienced a fundamental economic transition. This quickly led to the birth of a new financial industry and the expansion of settler society beyond the British colonial frontier. Although the independent Boer Republic was not the first territory in southern Africa where stocks were traded, Barberton's and then the Rand's gold rush laid the economic foundations for the emergence of Johannesburg as the most important financial centre in southern Africa. Kimberley's diamond industry provided the initial institutional and organisational foundations of southern Africa's mining finance, but it would be Johannesburg's gold sector where colonial and international financial capital would be invested at a scale never before possible in the region.

This chapter has provided the historical and social context for how the crucial processes of capital formation were enabled and accelerated by the establishment of the JSE during South Africa's first 'Golden Decade.' Following the development of South African mining finance in Kimberley, Barberton, London, and finally Johannesburg, the chapter documented the social, financial and economic connections between the rise of the Cape Colony's diamond mining industry and Johannesburg's first stock exchange. In answering the question on the need for the establishment of the JSE, the chapter concludes with a combination of legislative, speculative and technological factors that shifted the interest and focus of South African gold mining shares from London back to the source of the gold mania, the main reef in Johannesburg, deep in the (still) independent ZAR.

Founded on 8 November 1887, the JSE redefined the operational capacity of South African mining finance, creating an alternative capital market to London and numerous southern African exchanges. The establishment of the JSE was no exceptional institutional project, but clearly one that was made unique in its legislative conduct and connections with regional, local and global financial institutions. With limited access to London's premier mining market, South African mines were exposed to an unpredictable and uncontrollable capital market, facing growing competition from alternative securities in an increasingly globalised mining market. As conducive as the LSE was to test the financial capacity of the young South African diamond and gold mining industry, it was the JSE where regulatory simplification and limited financial barriers to entry created a favourable financial climate for a young and capital-hungry mining industry.

Despite the multiple institutional connections between the economic, financial and demographic conditions leading up to the gold discoveries on the Rand, the case of powerful social groups and individuals has been stressed the most. The friends and enemies of Kimberley's diamond industry transferred their capital, social networks, and political ambitions to Johannesburg, raising liquidity for new speculative schemes and financial scams on non-British territory. It is striking, too, how speedily the presence and influence of major diamond magnates came to shape the infant Exchange: Rhodes, Beit, the Barnato brothers, the Ecksteins, Taylor and Woollan—names that are inextricable from the history of mining and finance in Kimberley—were all active within a mere two years of the discovery in 1886 of the main reef. Their financial foresight, greed and quest for political dominance in a frontier colonial society was reflected in most organisational undertakings of the early years of Johannesburg, with the JSE being the most significant financial and social intermediary of the 1880s.

CHAPTER 3

From Market to Exchange: The JSE's Early Rules, Regulations and Organisation

Speculations in shares may be, and often is, of a risky nature, but the functions of the Stock Exchange should be to curtail that evil by disseminating correct information, by official quotations and by a corporate body to control the conduct of its business.[1]
—Benjamin M. Wollan at the opening of the first JSE building on 16 January 1888.

The increase in gold production in and around Johannesburg generated a simultaneous explosion of growth in local and foreign financial intermediaries such as banks, insurance companies, brokers and, most significantly, the stock exchange. During the year 1887, the ZAR's state revenue almost tripled as a result of the economic and financial developments in Johannesburg.[2] With the formal establishment and incorporation of the JSE, Johannesburg possessed the capital market aimed at attracting local and foreign investors to the ZAR's young gold mining industry. While the LSE was conducive to testing the financial capacity of the young diamond and gold industries in South Africa, it was the JSE—less regulated, more easily entered, and more ad hoc than its

---

[1] Quoted in: Rosenthal, Eric. *On 'Change Through the Years; a History of Share Dealing in South Africa*. Cape Town: Flesch Financial Publications. 1968. pp. 143–144.

[2] Jeppe, F. 1889. *Jeppe's Transvaal Almanac and Directory for 1889*. Cape Town: The Argus Printing and Publishing Company. p. 51.

© The Author(s), under exclusive license to Springer Nature Switzerland AG 2024
M. Lukasiewicz, *Gold, Finance and Imperialism in South Africa, 1887–1902*, Cambridge Imperial and Post-Colonial Studies, https://doi.org/10.1007/978-3-031-51947-5_3

counterparts in Europe—that provided an initial spur to the flotation of companies and their capitalisation.

When informal stock markets transition into regulated stock exchanges, organisational decisions about the structure and content of operating rules must be made.[3] Before state governments began to increasingly regulate various aspects of stock exchange operations throughout the twentieth century, the development of rules and operations was left almost entirely to the proprietors and members of the exchanges. Although numerous financial crises in the eighteenth and nineteenth century led the British parliament to reconsider the practices of the self-regulating LSE, these political inquiries typically ended with minor pieces of new legislation to pacify the upper classes and preserve the existing organisation of the exchange.[4] With the notable exception of the Paris Bourse, which experienced significant legal and operational challenges from the French Republic and the mayor of Paris,[5] all the major stock exchanges of the nineteenth century were self-regulated and experienced limited government interference.

Given that the JSE was established at a time when major exchanges in London, New York and Paris already had distinct market structures and regulatory policies, the case of the JSE—a stock exchange in a buccaneering mining town in a settler republic—presents a unique example of institutional formation and adaptation during the first age of financial globalisation in an understandably colonial context.[6] Recently, financial

---

[3] Davis, Lance and Larry Neal. "Micro Rules and Macro Outcomes: The Impact of Micro Structure on the Efficiency of Security Exchanges, London, New York, and Paris, 1800–1914." *American Economic Review* 88, no. 2 (1998): 40.

[4] Davis, Lance, Larry Neal and Eugene N. White. "How It All Began: The Rise of Listing Requirements on the London, Berlin, Paris, and New York stock Exchanges." *The International Journal of Accounting* 38, no. 2 (2003): 117–143.

[5] Lehmann, Paul-Jacques. *Histoire de la Bourse de Paris*. Paris: Presses Universitaires de France. 1997. pp. 24–27.
See, also: Davis, Lance and Larry Neal. "Micro Rules and Macro Outcomes: The Impact of Micro Structure on the Efficiency of Security Exchanges, London, New York, and Paris, 1800–1914." *American Economic Review* 88, no. 2 (1998): 43.

[6] For qualification and quantification of "First Age of Financial Globalisation," see: Clemens, M. A. and Williamson, J. G. Wealth bias in the first global capital market boom, 1870–1913. *The Economic Journal* 114, no. 495 (2004): 304–337.
Ferguson, N. and Schularick, M. "The Empire Effect: The Determinants of Country Risk in the First Age of Globalization, 1880–1913." *The Journal of Economic History* 66, no. 2 (2006): 283–312.

literature on market microstructures has developed on the supposed link between stock exchanges' behaviour and their corporate organisation.[7] Microstructures reflect not only on the organisational structures of an institution, but also the social codex and norms that define the legislation of the market.[8] Despite the significance of market organisation in many historical studies of stock exchanges in Europe, North America and Australasia, microstructures have never been used to study corporate organisation in nineteenth-century colonial Africa. In contrast, the JSE's corporate evolution is here understood through the institutional context of settler colonialism and frontier capitalism.

This chapter documents the early development of rules and regulations on the JSE. The history of the development, adaptation and implementation of operating rules in Johannesburg is analysed in the context of an emerging exchange in a settler frontier economy. The core of the chapter examines the growth and development of the social organisation on the JSE, showing how the divisions in labour and decision-making were regulated in a booming mining town that increasingly came under the scrutiny of Pretoria's republican government. Additionally, and most importantly for the further political development of Johannesburg's capital market, the chapter follows the rise of the JSE's landlord, Barney Barnato's Johannesburg Estate Company, and its gradual dominance in shaping the regulatory and organisational structure of the JSE.

EARLY REGULATION

The JSE was initially an independently organised, managed and regulated financial intermediary, governed only by the rules and regulations approved by the JSE General Committee. The separation of ownership of the JSE building and the actual management of the Exchange created a complex web of stakeholders with very different economic and social objectives. The original owner and proprietor of the JSE, the *Johannesburg Exchange & Chambers Company* (JECC) was incorporated in

---

[7] O'Sullivan, Mary A. "Yankee Doodle Went to London: Anglo-American Breweries and the London Securities Market, 1888–92." *The Economic History Review* 68, no. 4 (2015): 1366.

[8] Davis, Lance and Larry Neal. "Micro Rules and Macro Outcomes: The Impact of Micro Structure on the Efficiency of Security Exchanges, London, New York, and Paris, 1800–1914." *American Economic Review* 88, no. 2 (1998): 40–45.

late 1887 by the London-born and Kimberley-trained mining speculator Benjamin Woollan but was only formally registered in the ZAR
on 28 February 1888.[9] Although the JECC was registered with the
ZAR Chamber of Commerce, the Pretoria government had no authority
to regulate trade in securities in Johannesburg and Barberton. It was
only in 1909 that the Transvaal Colony issued the first *Stock and Share
Dealings Regulation Act*.[10] In 1947, the Union of South Africa passed
its first Stock Exchanges Control Act to regulate the operation of the
stock exchange by implementing capital requirements for members and
setting out professional rules for brokers.[11] The JECC acted as the
owner, operator and regulator of the JSE until the formal take over by
Barney Barnato's Estate Company in April 1889, unleashing a new era of
institutional development.[12]

Unfortunately, only limited primary evidence existence on the earliest
rules and regulations used on the JSE's trading floor. As a time and
labour-saving method, the JSE immediately adopted the rules and regulations of the Transvaal Share and Claim and Exchange of Barberton.
It was only two years later, in December 1889, that the JSE hosted a
regional conference to coordinate the process of arranging standard rules
and regulations to govern all exchanges operating in South Africa.[13] It
would take three years from the official opening of the Exchange that the
JSE finally approved its own set of rules and regulations that would later
govern sharebroking practices throughout all exchanges in South Africa.[14]

[9] Jeppe, F. *Jeppe's Transvaal Almanac and Directory for 1889*. Cape Town: The Argus
Printing and Publishing Company. 1889. p. 105.

[10] Richards, C. S. Stock Exchange Facilities in the Union–The Open Call Exchange.
South African Journal of Economics 1, no. 4 (1933 December): 511–518.

[11] See: Richards, Cecil Sydney. "The Report of the Company Law Amendment Enquiry
Commission." *South African Journal of Economics* 17, no. 3 (1949): 229–251.

[12] See: "Johannesburg Exchange and Chambers Company." In: Goldman, Charles
Sydney, ed. *The Financial, Statistical, and General History of the Gold & Other Companies
of Witwatersrand, South Africa*. London: E. Wilson and Co. 1892. p. 38.

[13] JSEA. *Minutes of an Ordinary Meeting of the Committee*, 3 December 1889.

[14] Klein, H. *The Story of the Johannesburg Stock Exchange, 1887–1947*. 1948. p. 15.

The early evolution of JSE's rules represented the essential institutional component of corporate legitimisation.[15] What immediately gave the JSE a legislative advantage over the exchanges in Kimberley, Barberton, and—more significantly—London, was that the listing of companies for a quotation on the JSE's Official List was a very quick and relatively low-cost procedure. As opposed to London, there was no formal company screening, no close scrutiny of the company's financial history and most importantly, very lax requirements on the public subscription of issued capital. The JSE maintained a lenient policy to company listing and initial public offerings, being more concerned with growing the local securities market than verifying the legitimacy of financial products intended to capitalise on the mining industry. In the interest of creating business for the new intermediary, quantity preceded the quality and nominal value of companies being drawn to the market.

In the initial two years, listing on the JSE was only regulated by means of commercial registration certificates, a document that companies were legally obliged to obtain and supply to the Exchange when applying for a quotation.[16] This simple, largely non-bureaucratic and non-restricting nature of the early Exchange promoted a wave of initial registrations on the Official List with 68 companies by the end of November 1887. Just as at other established stock exchanges around the world at the time, the purpose of the JSE's Official List was to clearly separate regulated trade, legislation and the official market price from a potential curb market. The Official List further expanded to more than 300 companies by the end of January 1890.[17] Despite the fact that the Official List had already been adopted during the early tent trading days, additional corporate legislation was only finalised during the first boom of 1888/9. This resulted in the first formal set of rules and regulations for the quotation of companies, passed on 12 November 1889[18]:

---

[15] Strydom, N. T. *Stock exchange legitimacy: The case of the Johannesburg Stock Exchange, 1887–1945*. University of Johannesburg (South Africa). Unpublished dissertation. 2021. p. 99.

[16] JSEA. *Minutes of an Ordinary Meeting*, 29 October 1889.

[17] "Johannesburg Share Market." *The Diggers' News*, 8 January 1890. p. 3.

[18] JSEA. *Minutes of an Ordinary Meeting of the Committee*, 12 November 1889.

1. That subject to such rules and regulations, as may be from time to time passed, the stock or shares of any company or association may be admitted to the official list of this Exchange.
2. That every company applying for a quotation shall forward to the Secretary of this Exchange, a certified copy of any prospectus which may have been issued by such company, also a certified copy of the Trust Deed or Articles of Association, and a certificate of registration, as a Limited Liability Company, together with such other documents as the committee may require to establish the bona fide character of each company.
3. That such applications may be considered at any Ordinary or Special meeting of the Committee.
4. That mining companies applying to be quoted with a nominal capital not exceeding £100 000 shall have a paid up working capital of not less than 10% of the nominal capital. Mining companies having a nominal capital exceeding £100 000 shall have a minimum working capital of £10 000, provided that the Committee may in its discretion depart from this rule under special circumstances.
5. That a fee of three guineas (£ 3-3-0) per annum, shall be paid in advance by each company whose shares are quoted on this Exchange.
6. That no company's stock shall be quoted before the Committee shall have been satisfied that permanent scrip has been issued; satisfactory information to be given to the Committee in all cases as to the date of such issue.
7. That every company quoted shall give immediate notice to the Secretary of the Exchange, of any increase of capital, issue of new shares, declaration of dividends or other rights, liquidation or reconstruction of the company.
8. That the committee retains these rights, for reasons shown to its satisfaction of suspending for any period, or with drawing altogether from the official list, the name of any company quoted on this Exchange.

The General Committee's first complete set of quotation rules was significantly more lenient than those in London. Apart from verifying the value of the nominal capital, companies listed on the JSE had no obligation to disclose any financial documents to the Committee. What is however noteworthy is the special rule (#4) directed at the capital require-ments of mining companies. Although the rule did not prevent the large distribution of vendor shares, it did stipulate that at least 10% of the working capital had to be fully paid up. In this way, the JSE's legisla-tion allowed companies to avoid the far more stringent capital, legal and accounting requirements of the LSE. More importantly for the economic future of Johannesburg, the set of rules defined that the Exchange was to specialise in the trade of mining stocks, a financial sector that was still proportionally small on the Official List of the LSE by the late 1880s.[19]

Although the registration and operation rules were initially more accommodating than older exchanges in Europe and North America, they were closely monitored and strictly enforced by the JSE's General Committee. The Committee went to great lengths to ensure that registra-tion and trading occurred only under its control and jurisdiction.[20] There is no denying that share trading in Johannesburg began as an unofficial curb market, with various mining securities from the Cape Colony and Barberton changing hands before any JSE Official List was implemented. At first, the General Committee had no authority to ban the outdoor trade in unregistered shares, but it quickly became very clear that trade disputes would be settled according to the JSE's rules when it came to the trade in shares from the Official List. As the General Committee proved its secure market vision and commitment to the enforcement of rules, the JSE's Official List became an increasingly prized market component of Johannesburg's early financial architecture.

ORGANISATION: OPERATORS VS. OWNERS

Equivalent financial intermediaries, including stock exchanges, are never identical in form and function in any economy.[21] The JSE might have been located inside the ZAR, but was only minimally guided by regulatory

---

[19] See: Burt, Roger. "Segmented Capital Markets and Patterns of Investment in Late Victorian Britain: Evidence from the Non-ferrous Mining Industry." *Economic History Review* 51, no. 4 (1998): 709–733.

[20] Strydom, N. T. *Stock Exchange Legitimacy: The Case of the Johannesburg Stock Exchange, 1887–1945.* University of Johannesburg (South Africa). Unpublished disser-tation. 2021. p. 99.

[21] Michie, Ranald C. "The London and New York stock exchanges, 1850–1914." *The Journal of Economic History* 46, no. 1 (1986): 171.

and organisational influences from Pretoria. Given the early experiences of South African mining companies with mining finance in London, it comes as no surprise that the JSE's first organisational structures closely resembled those of the LSE. There was no explicit intention to transplant organisational and management structures from other local and foreign stock exchanges to Johannesburg's gold-driven financial environment. However, based on the financial developments in Kimberley and Barberton, there was an obvious bias towards the shared common institutional heritage in London. Furthermore, many Kimberley brokers had, at least in some part, learned their trade on the unofficial London security markets, bringing a diverse set of practices and regulatory expectations to Johannesburg.[22] From the day of its inauguration, the constant struggle for influence over governance between the owners, operators and the members created a hostile business environment on the trading floor.[23] The gradual decline of the Barberton Stock Exchange in 1887 meant that there was no local competition for the JSE inside the ZAR. With no close competition and no alternate financial intermediaries apart from the unregulated street trading, the first five years of the Exchange's operation showed how different stakeholders could make or break an institutional project. Although the basic structures of the JSE's corporate organisation resembled the LSE in many ways and principles, the early JSE operators did not intend to replicate London's stock trade system in an understandably very different financial and political setting. The initial and most obvious deviation from London's organisational structure came from the conflicting relationship between the JSE's operator and owner. At the LSE the separation of ownership of the marketplace from its operations meant that two committees, the Committee of Trustees and Proprietors (representing the owners) and the Committee for General Purposes (representing the users), were competing for influence over the organisation's governance and legal mechanisms.[24] The JSE was

---

[22] Kennedy, Edward E. *Waiting for the Boom*. London: Effingham Wilson and Co. 1890. pp. 1–14.

[23] Strydom, N. T. *Stock Exchange Legitimacy: The Case of the Johannesburg Stock Exchange, 1887–1945*. University of Johannesburg (South Africa). Unpublished dissertation. 2021. p. 90.

[24] Davis, Lance and Larry Neal. "Micro Rules and Macro Outcomes: The Impact of Micro Structure on the Efficiency of Security Exchanges, London, New York, and Paris, 1800–1914." *American Economic Review* (1998): 41.

not immediately established as a separate legal entity from its operators, leading to conflicting organisational and financial management strategies. Unlike in London, where the powers of the proprietors were already separated from the powers of the subscribers in the early 1830s,[25] the development of the JSE was guided by the rivalry for influence between the General Committee, representing the interests of the *Exchange and Chambers Company*, and the JSE's landlords, the Johannesburg Estate Company.

Before the takeover by Barney Barnato's Johannesburg Estate Company, the JSE's Committee for General Purposes was the main regulatory body with just about no interference from the original owner and operator, the *Exchange and Chambers Company*. It must however be emphasised that despite their different functions and separate legal identities, it was difficult to differentiate between the objectives of the Chambers Company and the JSE's General Committee. Both parties were virtually made up of the same individuals and, for the first two years of the JSE's existence, the same people represented the conflicting interests of the operators and members. Until the takeover by the Estate Company, the JSE's General Committee was made up entirely of the directorate of the original *Exchange and Chambers Company*, namely, Benjamin Woollan, Friedrich Eckstein, Carl Hanau, Andrew Jones, Richard Allan, James Hay, Henry Rogers and James Taylor.[26] The most significant division in power was that only the General Committee had the authority to regulate the JSE's operational activities and vote on all organisational decisions.

Not only did the broader organisational structure of the JSE resemble that of London, but more explicitly, significant portions of the governance structure of the Exchange were intentionally worded in a similar style and manner. Even if the JSE did not directly choose to resemble the governance structure of the LSE, modelling the initial stages of corporate development on the world's premier stock exchange was intended to create corporate legitimacy and public trust in an extremely unpredictable

---

[25] Neal, Larry and Lance Davis. "The Evolution of the Structure and Performance of the London Stock Exchange in the First Global Financial Market, 1812–1914." *European Review of Economic History* 10, no. 3 (2006): 291.

[26] "Johannesburg Exchange and Chambers Company." In: Goldman, Charles Sydney, ed. *The Financial, Statistical, and General History of the Gold & Other Companies of Witwatersrand, South Africa*. London: E. Wilson and Co. 1892. p. 38.

financial project. The two regulatory extracts from the two exchanges below demonstrate just how similar the definition and wording of the powers and functions of the general committees were:

LSE VERSION

The said Committee for General Purposes shall regulate the transaction of business on the Stock Exchange, and may make rules and regulations not inconsistent with the provisions of these presents respecting the mode of conducting the ballot for the election of the Committee and respecting the admission, expulsion and suspension of Members, and their Clerks, and the mode and condition in and subject to which the business on the Stock Exchange shall be transacted and the conduct of the persons transacting the same, and generally for the good order and government of the Members of the Stock Exchange; the power of amending, altering, or repealing such rules or regulations, and of making any new, amended, or additional rules and regulations for the purposes aforesaid.[27]

JSE VERSION

The Committee shall have the entire management and control of the internal affairs of the Exchange, including the conduct of business; the admission, expulsion, or suspension of members and their clerks; the hearing and adjudication on cases between members, or members and their clients, which may be submitted to them; the investigation and adjudication upon all charges, by whomsoever made, affecting the character or dealings of any member of the Exchange; the mode and conditions in, and subject to which the member of the Exchange shall be transacted, and the conduct of the persons transacting the same, the making of provisions for the good order and governance of the Exchange; the power of amending, altering, or repealing such rules or regulations, and of making any new, amended, or additional rules and regulations for the purposes aforesaid.[28]

Despite some initial organisational similarities, the JSE would eventually be forced to take on a fundamentally different organisational

---

[27] Levien, F. *Rules and Regulations for the Conduct of Business on the Stock Exchange.* 1888. p. 8.

[28] *Rules and regulations of the Johannesburg Stock Exchange, 1893.* Johannesburg: Argus Printing and Pub. Co., 1893. p. 1.

and regulatory course, largely due to Barney Barnato's dominance over the financial intermediary. After much hesitation and consultation with Kimberley business rivals, the first signs of a possible financial boom became clear when Barney Barnato transferred his business operations from Kimberley to Johannesburg. Having just fought and won a critical election that returned him to the Legislative Assembly of the Cape Parliament as the senior representative for Kimberley in 1888, Barnato made his way to what he called the 'financial Gibraltar of South Africa.'[29] The JSE's official Members' Roll books show that by the time Barnato made the move to Johannesburg in November, most of his Kimberley rivals, such as Hermann and Friedrich Eckstein, George Farrar, Julius Jeppe, Edward Lippert and Sigismund Neumann, had already become members of the Stock Exchange.[30] Seeing the rent-seeking potential of the new Exchange and more importantly, the ability to control the commercial activities of his business rivals, Barnato quickly set about taking physical control of it.

To make up for his late arrival on the Rand, Barnato invited his brother Henry and cousins Solomon (Solly) Barnato Joel and Woolf Barnato Joel to join him on the JSE.[31] Within a few months, the Barnatos and the Joels had established the Barnato Bank, Johannesburg Estate Company, Johannesburg Consolidated Investment Company and the Johannesburg Waterworks and Exploration Company.[32] Within this rapidly growing family business empire, the most important link to the Exchange was the Estate Company. In March 1889 Barnato established the Johannesburg Estate Company with the main objective of purchasing the JSE building and its adjacent commercial properties in the young town centre. After buying out most of the shares in the *Exchange and Chambers Company*, Barnato wasted no time in securing his own election to the JSE's General Committee and forced it to accept a new set of rules handed over by

---

[29] Cartwright, Alan Patrick. *The Corner House: The Early History of Johannesburg*. 1965. p. 86.

[30] See: JSEA. JSE Members Roll Books for year ending 1888 and 1889.

[31] "Joel family." In: Wills, Walter H., ed. *The Anglo-African Who's Who*. London: L. Upcott Gill. 1907. pp. 198–200.

[32] Cartwright, Alan Patrick. *The Corner House: The Early History of Johannesburg*. 1965. p. 8.

his Estate Company.[33] The arrival of Barnato had set the interests of the owners and members on a rapid course of divergence. Far more interested in membership fees and seeking rent from offices inside the JSE building, Barnato's dominance came in direct conflict with the General Committee's vision of growing the market for JSE-listed securities. The Committee felt strongly that Barnato's personal business interests had put the development of trade in securities in Johannesburg under considerable threat and pursued a strategic policy of appeasement in the hope that the Estate would work together with the JSE to ensure the financial stability of the local capital market.[34]

Although the JSE's contemporary documentation shows no exact date as to when brokers began to organise themselves, a brokers' association, the *Johannesburg Stock Exchange Association*, was established in early 1889 with more than 200 members.[35] The JSE Association's main objective was to counteract the growing influence of Barnato and limit the powers of the owners. Brokers were in direct conflict with the rent-seeking goals of the Estate Company and would eventually galvanise members to strive for greater control of the internal affairs of the Exchange. Despite having its own General Committee, the JSE was dependent on the fixed assets and working capital of the Estate Company, leaving it exposed to the regulatory dictatorship of Barney Barnato. Even if potential members were applying to join the JSE, it was the Estate Company that controlled the intake and expulsion of all financial professionals associated with the JSE.

The first five years were marked by an uncertain period of rapid institutional organisation, resulting in different forms of engagement with financial and political stakeholders. The early development of the Exchange can therefore be seen as an unsettled balance of organisational power between the JSE's regulatory and operational entities. The Exchange acted as a separate legal entity with the proprietors owning and maintaining the property that hosted it. Internal opposition from members, brokers and the General Committee would eventually isolate

---

[33] Rosenthal, Eric. *On 'Change Through the Years; a History of Share Dealing in South Africa*. 1968. p. 163.

[34] JSEA. *Minutes of an Ordinary Meeting of the Committee*. 24 December 1889.

[35] Rosenthal, Eric. *On 'Change Through the Years; a History of Share Dealing in South Africa*. 1968. p. 164.

the influence of the Estate Company, creating a stable, yet fragile organisational microstructure that closely resembled that of London. Although the power struggle was between the Estate and the General Committee, the real battles were for the loyalty of the growing pool of members.

Membership and Division of Labour

Although there was initially no minimum or maximum number of desired members, the divisions in the organisational structure of the JSE led to preconceived notions of how the expansion of the pool of members should be controlled. The profit-seeking motives of the Johannesburg Estate Company—which gained its income from membership fees—conflicted with the General Committee's strategy to control and regulate participation in the stock exchange. While JSE membership needed to be accessible to Johannesburg's gold prospectors, it also needed to be exclusive and of high financial credibility to ensure enough liquidity on the market. Most importantly, any desired strategy on the number and quality of participants in the expanding stock market, along with the rules governing trade, needed to promote the JSE as a premier financial organisation and discourage the development of an alternative exchange or a secondary market in securities in Johannesburg.[36]

Initially, membership of the JSE was open to anyone who could pay the necessary subscription fee, encouraging a very diverse social mix of financiers. Considering the requirements for joining were minimal and not intended to drive away any potential fee-paying members, there were several formalities associated with gaining membership. Here it is imperative to emphasise that, once again, most of these procedures resembled the rules for admission to the LSE, with the intended difference of being less demanding of prospective candidates. Unlike in London where three recommendations were needed, every applicant at the JSE had to be recommended by only two members of the Exchange who had themselves been members for at least twelve months.[37] These two members would also commit to guarantee an amount of no more than £200 each as liability security for the new applicant.[38] In London, each of the

---

[36] See: Michie, Ranald. *The Global Securities Market: A History.* 2007. p. 103.

[37] Rule 37. *Rules and Regulations of the Johannesburg Stock Exchange.* 1893. p. 9.

[38] Rule 43. *Rules and Regulations of the Johannesburg Stock Exchange.* 1893. p. 9.

three guarantors had to put down £500 for a period of four years.[39] The directors of the Johannesburg Estate Company could also become regular members of the Exchange, subject to the approval of the General Committee, which was, of course, strategically elected among themselves.[40] Even candidates under the legal age of twenty-one were able to apply for admission provided they were recommended by a member who was willing to make themselves liable for all the transactions the young candidate would undertake.[41] With these minimal requirements in the early days, it comes as no surprise that the social makeup of the JSE did not resemble the specialisation of financial professionals plying their trade on the exchanges of London, New York and Paris:

> The members were men who had been store-keepers, canteen-keepers, lawyers, policemen, farmers, ostrich feather dealers, clerks, bookmakers, one or two defaulting brokers from London, and there were some who were said to have been dealers in old clothes, and a good many of them looked as if that was their natural calling. There were men from Kimberley too, some of whom were known to have taken the degree of Illicit Diamond Buyer, which in South Africa is a past master's degree in the art of roguery.[42]

The rules for admission were particularly lenient on the nationality of potential candidates, giving the JSE a cosmopolitan character, albeit with a clear racial and settler bias. Using Kimberley as a model for enhancing international partnerships, the JSE actively promoted international access to its products through the global financial networks of its founding members. Unlike in London, where no foreigners could become members unless they had been a naturalised British citizen for at least two years, the JSE initially had no regulation on nationality, religion and gender.[43] With non-Afrikaners effectively disenfranchised and in no legal position to become citizens of the ZAR, only a very small number of the JSE's

[39] Rule 22. Levien, F. *Rules and Regulations for the Conduct of Business on the Stock Exchange*. 1888. p. 14.

[40] BLA. *Minutes of the Board of the Johannesburg Estate Company*, 4 April 1889.

[41] Rule 37. *Rules and Regulations of the Johannesburg Stock Exchange*. 1893. p. 9.

[42] Kennedy, E. E. *Waiting for the Boom*. 1890. pp. 10–11.

[43] Non-British citizens were only admitted to the LSE from 1971. Michie, Ranald. *The London Stock Exchange: A History*. 1999. p. 483.

initial members were ZAR citizens. The general body included members with various national and professional backgrounds who, along with the experienced European-trained traders, gave the JSE a very flamboyant character. As observed by the young London broker, Edward Kennedy, who arrived in Johannesburg in June 1889 and joined the Exchange in September 1889:

> To a man fresh from the London Exchange, where the individual is chaffed for a whole day if he wears a very loud necktie, a gaudy pair of trousers, or something very special in waistcoats, and where it would simply be seeing the destruction of the offensive article to walk in with any hat on your head but the time honoured and universally respected chimney-pot, the costumes of the Johannesburg Stock Exchange were a rude shock. In the matter of hats they wore all kind of head-gear except the chimney-pot. The weather was cold in the early morning, so there were many ulsters, some of remarkable design and colour; there were men in riding-breeches and top-boots, who carried a hunting-crop, and looked as unlike stockbrokers as anything we could imagine.[44]

It is also imperative to critically consider how the social identities of race and gender in Johannesburg intersected to create a financially inclusive yet socially exclusive economic and political space. Although the JSE's rules and regulations had no explicit racial and gender bias on membership, Johannesburg's financial sector in general, and the stock exchange in particular, was almost exclusively dominated by white men of European ancestry. Although the General Committee reported of a 'certain lady admitted to the Exchange,' on a temporary membership in November 1889,[45] the JSE's early social identity was forged through male initiation rituals and regular displays of masculine bravado such as bouts of boxing and cricket on the trading floor.[46] These early membership structures enhanced Johannesburg's male-dominated settler colonial model and the

---

[44] Kennedy, E. E. *Waiting for the Boom.* 1890. pp. 9–10.

[45] JSEA, *Minutes of an Ordinary Meeting of the Committee,* 26 November 1889.

[46] Bryant, Margot. *Taking Stock: Johannesburg Stock Exchange- The First 100 Years.* 1987. p. 22.

accelerated racialisation of the mining economy, with Africans effectively excluded from all operations of the stock exchange.[47]

The notable membership procedural difference between the LSE and the JSE was that the candidate's financial history and credit worthiness were never questioned or scrutinised in Johannesburg. The financial credibility and integrity of the candidate was only assessed on the recommendation of the two members who were required to 'have personal knowledge of the past and present circumstances of the applicant whom they recommended for admission.'[48] This was, consequently, a major source of attraction for many London brokers who were barred from the LSE after bankruptcy during the copper speculation of the mid-1880s.[49] The 'no questions asked' policy would however go through much testing during the first JSE boom of 1888/9 and would eventually lead to a great deal of cooperation with the LSE. By the mid-1890s, the JSE and LSE would send monthly lists of defaulters and members in arrears, intended to prevent, or at least deter, the migration of brokers with unfulfilled financial obligations.[50]

Despite the uncertain future of Johannesburg as a mining and financial centre, the JSE experienced rapid growth in membership numbers. At the beginning of January 1888, less than two months after the official opening, the Exchange already had more than 100 paid-up members.[51] The most significant and rapid rise in membership came with the arrival of Barney Barnato as director of the Johannesburg Estate Company. Some 700 new members were introduced to the Exchange during the year of 1889 (See Fig. 3.1). Barnato was instrumental in opening the doors of the Exchange to a wide cross-section of Johannesburg's general public, encouraging miners and prospectors with no previous financial experience to join the JSE.

---

[47] See: Harrison, P. and Zack, T. "The Power of Mining: The Fall of Gold and Rise of Johannesburg." *Journal of Contemporary African Studies* 30, no. 4 (2012): 551–570.

[48] Rule 39. *Rules and Regulations of the Johannesburg Stock Exchange, 1893.* 1893. p. 9.

JSEA. *Minutes of an Ordinary Meeting of the Committee*, 30 December 1889.

[49] Kennedy, E. E. *Waiting for the Boom.* 1890. p. 10.

[50] See: JSEA. *Minutes of an Ordinary Meeting of the Committee*, 1 June 1897.

[51] Rosenthal, Eric. *On 'Change Through the Years; a History of Share Dealing in South Africa.* 1968. pp. 146–147.

JSE membership

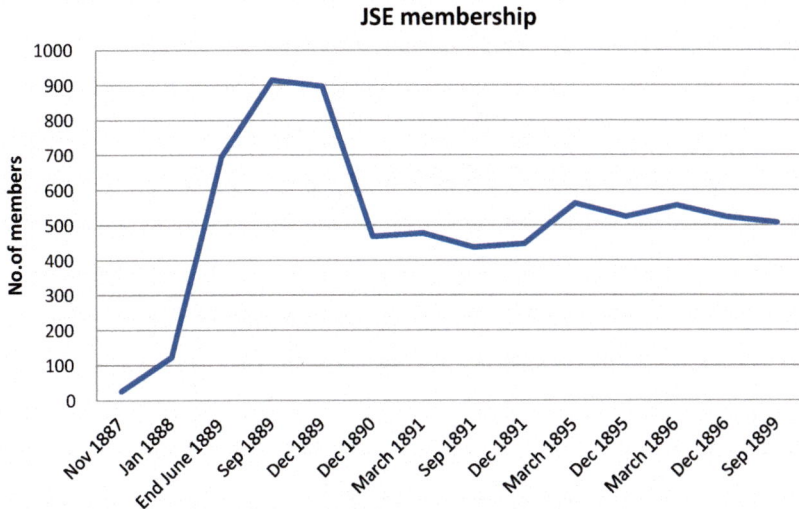

Fig. 3.1 JSE Membership. 1887–1899 (*Source* Own calculations from JSE Members Roll Books 1889–1899. Figures for the period November 1887–June 1889 from Klein, Harry. *The story of the Johannesburg Stock Exchange: 1887–1947.* The Committee of the Johannesburg Stock Exchange. 1948. p. 33; Rosenthal, Eric. *On 'Change Through the Years; a History of Share Dealing in South Africa.* 1968)

The Estate's Board of Directors,[52] represented by Barnato's cousin Woolf Joel, Harry Caldecott, James Leonard, Henry Rogers and James Taylor, assisted Barnato in consolidating his power over the JSE with only limited internal opposition. With power came confidence, and soon enough the Exchange became too small for Barnato's financial ambitions in Johannesburg. Even at this early stage, Barnato was convinced that the original Stock Exchange hall was inadequate for the several hundred members and their clerks who were operating at the time.[53] Barnato immediately insisted that the fees were to be doubled to six guineas (£

[52] All members of the Board were members of the Exchange before the Johannesburg Estate Company was formed.

[53] Klein, Harry. *The Story of the Johannesburg Stock Exchange: 1887–1947.* 1948. p. 24.

Table 3.1 JSE
Membership Fees,
1887–1893

Date	Member's Quarterly	Partner/Clerk Quarterly	Visitor's Monthly
December 1887	£ 0. 10. 6	x	x
March 1889	£ 1. 1. 0	£ 1. 1. 0	£ 1. 1. 0
April 1889	£ 3. 3. 0	£ 1. 1. 0	£ 3. 3. 0
January 1890	£ 6. 6. 0	£ 3. 3. 0	£ 5. 5. 0
May 1893	£ 6. 6. 0	£ 3. 3. 0	£ 6. 6. 0

Source Klein, Henry. *The story of the Johannesburg Stock Exchange: 1887–1947.* 1948. p. 33. JSE Members Roll Books 1889–1899; *Rules and regulations of the Johannesburg Stock Exchange, 1893.* 1893

6. 6. 0) under the pretext that the increase was due to extra funds needed for the expansion of the Exchange building (See Table 3.1).[54]

The separation of ownership from the operation of the stock exchange was a fundamental factor in influencing the institutional evolution of the Exchange. The significant increase in the number of memberships was a typical management strategy to compensate for poor revenue during financial slumps. Furthermore, by increasing the price of membership, the Exchange ensured that new members would need adequate financial resources, forcing them to reconsider their liquidity before applying for membership. Most of the costs incurred in operating the JSE had to be directly financed using membership fees and were supplemented by other sources of income such as quotation fees, legal fees, and irregular contributions by the Estate Company.

The division of labour on the JSE's trading floor was already formally discussed at the opening of the first JSE building on 16 January 1888. The specialisation of stockbrokers on the Exchange was aimed at encouraging a professionalisation of the industry in an expanding financial community.[55] During the opening speech, Benjamin Woollan described

[54] Rosenthal, Eric. *On 'Change Through the Years; a History of Share Dealing in South Africa.* 1968. p. 163.

[55] Michie, Ranald. *The London Stock Exchange: A History.* 1999. p. 40.

the different professions of members—dealers, jobbers,[56] and brokers—urging brokers to respect 'the utility of an honest dealer.'[57] Although all members could engage in the duties associated with the buying and selling of stocks, the privileges of brokers were clearly defined in their financial service to the non-member investing public.[58] Brokers were to be responsible for 'all transactions, whether for cash or on time, (and) on account of non-members.'[59] Differentiating between brokers and dealers was particularly important when brokers took on orders from multiple clients. Private clients had to be very careful when choosing their financial services since brokers never purchased and sold on their own accounts. Provided they revealed the name of their customers, brokers had no responsibility or liability for losses resulting from poor transactions.[60] This legal clause gave brokers a significant amount of influence over all members, allowing them to abuse their power when it came to testifying against defaulting clients, who would be suspended immediately.[61] However, Johannesburg's jobbers were the real drivers of the stock trade that made the market. The reason for the professional separation of brokers and dealers was that brokers were not authorised to purchase or sell for their own account (i.e. to job) unless this was done and declared by another registered broker.[62] Jobbers operated in the capacity of their principal, buying and selling on their own trading accounts and dealing only with fellow jobbers or brokers. As opposed to the dealers, jobbers took personal ownership of the shares they were trading, quite often only for the duration of the trading day. Officially, jobbers had no clients from Johannesburg's investing public and it was only brokers who traded on behalf of non-JSE members in return for a regulated fee. Jobbers made

[56] See: Bowen, Huw V. "The Pests of Human Society': Stockbrokers, Jobbers and Speculators in Mid-Eighteenth-Century Britain." *History* 78, no. 252 (1993): 38–53.

[57] *On 'Change Through the Years; a History of Share Dealing in South Africa.* 1968. p. 149.

[58] "The Brokers and the Exchange." *Standard and Diggers News*, 18 April 1889. p. 3.

[59] Rule 113. *Rules and Regulations of the Johannesburg Stock Exchange, 1893.* 1893. p. 27.

[60] Kennedy, E. E. *Waiting for the Boom.* 1890. pp. 24–25.

[61] JSEA. *Minutes of an Ordinary Meeting of the Committee*, 3 December 1889.

[62] See: Brokers and Brokerage. *Rules and Regulations of the Johannesburg Stock Exchange, 1893.* 1893. pp. 31–32.

their income from the profits they made by adjusting their buying and selling prices to those of the Official List.

In summarising the traders' division of labour, brokers were dealers who were not allowed to job, meaning they could not trade on their own account and could only trade for non-member customers. To avoid the ambiguity of these intermediate functions, a list of the members of the Exchange distinguishing brokers from dealers was posted on the main notice board with changes taking place almost daily.[63] The specialisation of financial professionals and their regulation inside the JSE served to divide the trading floor into groups of buyers who served clients with different needs. Large clients such as the colonial and local banks, medium clients such as brokerage companies and smaller individual speculators were thus able to introduce their shares to the market through different professionals depending on the types and quantities of stock they were holding.

Unlike at the LSE, where there was still no fixed regulation on brokers' commission by the end of the 1880's,[64] the JSE set the transaction fees for brokerage on all sales and purchases inside the Exchange. The brokerage charge on all transactions closed was 1% or £ 1 on sales below £ 100.[65] The fees were strictly enforced, and any broker found to have charged less than the set rates was to be fined £ 25 for the first offence, £ 50 for a second, and excluded from membership for the third.[66] As defended in the official records of the General Committee, this rule was not intended to harm any brokers, but was strategically crafted to discourage small financiers with low-cost stock purchases from investing on the JSE.

[63] *Rules and Regulations of the Johannesburg Stock Exchange, 1893.* 1893. p. 19.

[64] Davis, Lance and Larry Neal. "Micro Rules and Macro Outcomes: The Impact of Micro Structure on the Efficiency of Security Exchanges, London, New York, and Paris, 1800–1914." *American Economic Review* 88, no. 2 (1998). p. 41.

[65] *Rules and Regulations of the Johannesburg Stock Exchange, 1893.* 1893. p. 31.

[66] See: Rule 143. *Rules and Regulations of the Johannesburg Stock Exchange, 1893.* 1893. p. 31.

THE TRADING SYSTEM OF HIGH 'CHANGE

The Exchange's members traded using an open outcry system, which matched buyers and sellers in deals through verbal and non-verbal communication.[67] Johannesburg's auction-based system defined the JSE's operations and served as a daily spectacle even for those not directly associated with the Exchange. As described by Anna Comtesse de Bremont in her 1899 novel, when 'High 'Change was on, and men of every age, clime, and complexion were shouting in every variation of voice and tone, according to the capacity of each individual's lungs and throat.'[68] The trading system of High 'Change was introduced to the JSE in March 1888 and was based on the system of calling out the stocks by the JSE's secretary in alphabetical order beginning at 10.00 a.m.[69] Kennedy described the process from a broker's point of view:

> To a Johannesburg broker, High 'Change seems such an absolute necessity, that he finds it hard to understand Stock Exchange business conducted without it. At the official opening of the Exchange in the morning at ten o'clock, the Secretary, an amiable gentlemen, but possessed of a voice which unfortunately failed him frequently, and went into a squeak or a groan, to the amusement of the members, mounted the rostrum and commenced to call over the stocks alphabetically.[70]

During High 'Change, members called out their share orders which would then be recorded by officials on a central chalkboard. Completed 'deals' would then be documented on paper cards as broker's notes, which could in turn be re-traded after High 'Change.[71] The early adaptation of these broker's notes significantly increased the number of daily transactions and provided liquidity before a clearing house was officially

[67] Strydom, N. T. *Stock exchange legitimacy: The case of the Johannesburg Stock Exchange, 1887–1945.* University of Johannesburg (South Africa). Unpublished dissertation. p. 107.

[68] Comtesse de Bremont, Anna. *The Gentlemen Digger.* London: Greening and Co. 1899. 2021. p. 97.

[69] Rosenthal, Eric. *On 'Change Through the Years; a History of Share Dealing in South Africa.* 1968. p. 155.

[70] Kennedy. E. E. *Waiting for the Boom.* London. 1890. p. 13.

[71] Strydom, N. T. *Stock Exchange Legitimacy: The Case of the Johannesburg Stock Exchange, 1887–1945.* University of Johannesburg (South Africa). Unpublished dissertation. 2021. p. 108.

established in Johannesburg. The transactions (or the lack of them) for each stock called out at High 'Change were recorded and were the only official business done during the trading day.[72] With the rapid expansion of stocks on offer during the 1888/9 boom, the daily documentation of transactions was restricted to only those stocks that were purchased or sold, thereby avoiding publishing long price lists of stocks with no daily market.[73] As soon as High 'Change was over (even during the peak of the boom the procedure would take no longer than two hours) brokers would leave the trading floor and continue to bid for or sell stocks in other parts of Johannesburg.[74] All the prices quoted in newspapers in South Africa and abroad were the transactions registered during High 'Change and it was only the trade that took place during High 'Change was regulated by the JSE.

The auction-based system was anything but perfect and offered ample opportunities for illicit trading. The perceived deliberateness of High 'Change led some brokers to collude and manipulate the volume of transactions for their personal gains. As observed by Kennedy on his first day of trade on the JSE, the teams of brokers worked hand in hand to influence the price in whichever direction it suited them:

> The dealings in stock were just closing, there had been transactions at 36/6. "I'll buy at 36/-," said my friend. "I'll sell at 36/6,"says another broker. "I'll sell at 36/6, too," says my friend, and the knowledge that there were two sellers on the market at the price would have the effect of weakening the shares, and give the buyers a better opportunity of getting them at the lower price. It also led to a great many bogus bargains, with the object of affecting the price one way or the other.[75]

The system created so many trading disputes for the General Committee that in February 1890 it even suggested that it be scrapped together. Many brokers considered High 'Change to be a dull ceremony with no practical value for promoting the trade in shares, forcing them to listen to the calling out of hundreds of different stocks that could be

---

[72] JSEA. *Minutes of an Ordinary Meeting of the Committee*, 22 April 1890.

[73] JSEA. *Minutes of an Ordinary Meeting of the Committee*, 29 August 1890.

[74] Kennedy. E. E. *Waiting for the Boom*. 1890. p. 14.

[75] Ibid. pp. 14–15.

left unsold for weeks and even months during quiet periods of trade.[76] A special investigative committee was eventually formed to consider the question of discontinuing High 'Change.[77] The report presented to the General Committee and members in February 1890 proposed a suspension of the auction system in the near future.[78] The Chairman of the Exchange, James Hay, attempted to encourage the members to support the immediate suspension of High 'Change, but after a very heated series of public debates, the Brokers' Committee suggested a formal vote to decide on the future of High 'Change. After a week of negotiations between the Management Committee and the Brokers, the ballot yielded a result of '271 (votes) for High 'Change and 97 against.'[79] As controversial as High 'Change might have been, the brokers and members were able to use the internal democratic system of the Exchange to their advantage. Most members of the General Committee were forced to concede that, even with its lengthy proceedings, High 'Change was beneficial to the growth of Johannesburg's securities market. Despite occasional further protests and votes against High 'Change, the trading system remained an integral aspect of the JSE's early operations.[80]

PRETORIA: COMPETING INSTITUTIONS OR POLITICAL BLUFFS?

The growth of Johannesburg's financial sector did not go unnoticed in Pretoria. Although President Kruger's attitude to economic development in the Republic was often labelled as 'anti-capitalist' and his contempt of Johannesburg's mining houses is well documented, there is no evidence to suggest he was against the opening of the JSE.[81] The little evidence available shows that not only did Kruger's government have no intention of interfering with the JSE,[82] it eventually responded to the JSE's

---

[76] JSE. *Minutes of an Ordinary Meeting*, 25 February 1890.

[77] JSE. *Minutes of an Ordinary Meeting*, 11 February 1890.

[78] Ibid.

[79] JSEA. *Minutes of an Ordinary Meeting*, 18 February 1890.

[80] JSEA. *Minutes of an Ordinary Meeting*, 18 February 1894.

[81] Marks, Shula and S. Trapido. "Lord Milner and the South African State." *History Workshop Journal* 8, no. 1 (1979). pp. 50–80.

[82] SBA. GMO 3/2/1/1, 10 February 1890. p. 34.

near-monopoly on regulated security trade in the ZAR by establishing Pretoria's own *South African Share and Claim Exchange* in February 1889.[83]

As early as June 1886, newspapers in the Cape Colony were reporting on the unorganised trade of mining stocks in Pretoria.[84] Although the trade in shares in the ZAR's capital was far smaller than in Barberton, it did have the official backing of the South African government and the personal endorsement of President Paul Kruger. Pretoria-based mining companies with names such as the *Paarl-Pretoria Gold Mining & Exploration Company* and the *Zuid Afrikaansche Exploratie en Land Maatschappij* were also early Afrikaner attempts to enter the Republic's British-dominated mining sector and growing capital market. Sometime in early 1888, a political push was made to organise the Pretoria share market into a formal stock exchange. However, it would not be until February 1889 (the peak of Johannesburg's first gold mining boom) that an effective institution was established.[85]

In February 1889, President Kruger officially opened the South African Exchange at a stately ceremony attended by the highest ranked politicians and judges of the Republic. In his opening speech, Kruger praised Pretoria's new 'spirit of speculation' and encouraged the brokers to make 'Pretoria the centre of share speculation and other business connected with the gold mining industry.'[86] The Pretoria-based *Transvaal Advertiser* published the opening speech of the Chairman of the new South African Share and Claim Exchange, Joseph William Mogg:

This Exchange has been established to facilitate in this city transactions in the stocks of those mining and commercial companies which are going to develop the resources of this Republic; and not only to facilitate, but to put these transactions under regulation and control. The necessity of such an exchange has been long-felt, and the lack of it has been the means of diverting from Pretoria, a large amount of capital and energy. It is believed by the promoters of this Exchange, that after it has been in operation

[83] Rosenthal, Eric. *Other Men's Millions*. Cape Town: Howard Timmins. 1965. p. 106.

[84] Rosenthal, Eric. *On 'Change Through the Years; a History of Share Dealing in South Africa*. 1968. p. 130.

[85] Ibid. p. 131.

[86] Quoted in Rosenthal, Eric. *On 'Change Through the Years; a History of Share Dealing in South Africa*. 1968. pp. 130–133.

for a short period, capitalists and financiers who are investing their money in Barberton, the Rand, Klerksdorp, Malmani, Waterberg, Zoutpansberg, Lydenburg, Heidelberg, Pretoria and other properties, will find that they can come here and obtain a central and reliable market for the stocks of the before-mentioned districts and the whole of this Republic. They will then take up their residence here and make Pretoria, as it naturally should be, the financial centre of this country.[87]

Despite the official support of Kruger's government, the great lack of documentation on the existence of the exchange in Pretoria shows just how unimportant the development was for the financial infrastructure of the ZAR. The shortage of the Exchange's operational evidence is, however, overshadowed by the social connection of two founders of the South African Share and Claim Exchange, D. B. Rush and J. R. Dyer. The Member's Book of the JSE clearly states that both financiers were members of the JSE at the time of the great boom of 1889.[88] As confirmed by Rosenthal, at the time of the Pretoria Exchange's ultimate closure in March 1891, 'like their colleagues in other parts of South Africa they are all members of the Johannesburg Stock Exchange.'[89]

CONCLUSION

The establishment of the JSE as a formal stock exchange in November 1887 prompted the official organisation and regulation of the financial intermediary and its commercial activities in an unpredictable mining economy. Confronted by many decisions that needed to be made on the Exchange's future in an uncertain economic and political climate, the owners and management needed to turn regulatory challenges into business opportunities. Using the London Stock Exchange as a comparative institutional model for some aspects of the JSE's formative development, this chapter analysed the regulatory and organisational evolution of the JSE, listing its legal advantages and regulatory omissions, specially adjusted to the gambling spirit of Johannesburg's financial and mining industries.

---

[87] Ibid. p. 131.

[88] See: JSEA. *Members Roll Book for 1889.*

[89] Rosenthal, Eric. *On 'Change Through the Years; a History of Share Dealing in South Africa.* 1968. p. 133.

Like most financial and economic intermediaries in Johannesburg, the Exchange developed independently of strict political control from the ZAR government, allowing the JSE to adapt its regulations to the needs of the mining economy it was serving, with minimal concern for opposition and competition from Pretoria. Despite borrowing many rules and regulations from other exchanges in Kimberley, Barberton, and London, the JSE quickly adapted and adjusted its policies to meet the demands of Johannesburg's emerging capital market. With different stakeholders such as owners, directors, members and clients advocating competing visions of institutional organisation, the first three years of the JSE's existence tested its ability to balance the needs of operational regulation and promoting access to capital market.

The formal organisation of the JSE positioned the financial intermediary as a capital market specialising in the trade of mining securities. Although financial products from other sectors of South Africa's economy were not formally excluded, a clear preference was given to the introduction of shares in gold mining and exploration companies. For all the enthusiasm and urgency displayed by many investors in expanding the volume and value of securities on the Official List, the early development of the Exchange was constrained by the power struggle between the General Committee and the JSE's landlords, the Johannesburg Estate Company.

The organisational aspects of the JSE's evolution documented how the arrival of Barney Barnato and the establishment of his Johannesburg Consolidated Estate altered the Exchange's initial development. Barnato's dominance in shaping the regulatory and organisational structures of the Exchange was a key feature of the JSE's development during the first financial boom of 1888/9. By increasing the number of members and the membership fees during the height of the first boom, Barnato was able to turn the JSE into a strategic rent-seeking organisation within his personal portfolio of Johannesburg businesses. The organisational microstructures at the JSE were not entirely unique to the global financial industry of the late nineteenth century but were embedded in the broader social environment of a young mining city and infant finance industry. The balance of power and interest between the General Committee, the Johannesburg Consolidated Estate Company and the JSE's growing pool of members produced many conflicting views on how the capital market was to operate. With the institutional objectives of growing the capital market and reinforcing the legitimacy of its members, the General Committee came into direct conflict with the Johannesburg Estate Company's development strategy of not excluding any potential paying participants.

The qualitative evidence presented in this chapter confirms that the General Committee of the JSE developed its new rules and regulations based on explicit references to the LSE's legislation of the same period. Although the JSE initially used the Barberton Stock Exchange's rules and regulations, the legislation developed during and after the 1888/9 boom showed a clear resemblance to the LSE. More importantly, the division between ownership and operations, a characteristic of the late Victorian corporate sector, facilitated the emergence of regulatory sub-committees tasked with investigating disputes and controversies over the rights and obligations of members.

CHAPTER 4

Finance, Industry and Information: The JSE and the Chamber of Mines

The instrument for complete control of the native and white labour market will be the Chamber of Mines.[1]
—John Atkinson Hobson

The early financial momentum in the development of gold mining promoted much more than just the establishment of intermediaries aimed at mobilising local and foreign sources of capital. The expansion of Johannesburg's capital market depended on the productivity of the gold mining sector in an uncertain political environment. Although the JSE was specialised in the trade of mining securities, the Exchange initially had no official representation in Johannesburg's gold mining industry and even less authority in political stakes in Pretoria. Even if the JSE had quickly positioned itself at the centre of the growing financial industry and gained the active support of most Johannesburg-based capitalists, its official mandate did not include the promotion of industrial interests in the ZAR's mining sector. If the Exchange was to facilitate and coordinate the capital accumulation process of Johannesburg's mining industry, a closer organisational link was needed between finance, industry, and imperial politics.

[1] Hobson, John Atkinson. *The War in South Africa: Its Causes and Effects.* 1900. p. 236.

© The Author(s), under exclusive license to Springer Nature Switzerland AG 2024
M. Lukasiewicz, *Gold, Finance and Imperialism in South Africa, 1887–1902*, Cambridge Imperial and Post-Colonial Studies, https://doi.org/10.1007/978-3-031-51947-5_4

Mining and colonial politics in southern Africa were always inextricable, mutually reinforcing one another.[2] Kimberley's diamond industry demonstrated that formal industrial organisation was needed to centralise the interests of mine owners vis-à-vis the Cape's colonial legislation.[3] Johannesburg's mine owners, the Randlords (as they would come to be known), were well aware that they were dealing with an unpredictable and yet malleable government in a Boer settler republic that was divided about the socioeconomic impact of the expanding gold industry.[4] Although initially largely of social rather than industrial value, Johannesburg's mining community was resolute that a centralised organisation was needed to represent the interests of the gold mines and protect these from the inconsistent and inefficient mining legislation being issued in Pretoria under President Kruger.[5] Johannesburg's first Chamber of Mines was founded during a meeting at the Central Hotel on 7 December 1887, marking the beginning of not only a strategic political partnership between mine owners, but also, more importantly for the mines' factors of production, an alliance between the gold industry and the capital market that was to finance its development.[6] Established just a month apart in late 1887, the JSE and the Chamber of Mines became responsible for reorganising the flows of financial capital and labour to the gold mines of the Rand.

The forging of ties between the mines and the capital market was not only an attempt at securing collective financial and political interests but had another far more crucial function in managing collective industrial relations between the Rand's employers and mine workers. South African historian Cornelis De Kiewiet assessed that modern South Africa was not built on gold and diamonds alone, but on the availability and regulated

[2] Van-Helten, J. J. Mining and Imperialism. *Journal of Southern African Studies* 6, no. 2 (1980): 230–235.

[3] Newbury, Colin Walter. *The Diamond Ring: Business, Politics, and Precious Stones in South Africa, 1867–1947.* 1989. pp. 10–28.

[4] See: Trapido, Stanley. "Landlord and Tenant in a Colonial Economy: The Transvaal 1880–1910." *Journal of Southern African Studies* 5, no. 1 (1978): 26–58.

[5] See: Jeeves, A. The Control of Migratory Labour on the South African Gold Mines in the Era of Kruger and Milner. *Journal of Southern African Studies* 2, no. 1 (1975): 3–29.

[6] Lang, John. *Bullion Johannesburg: Men, Mines and the Challenge of Conflict.* 1986. p. 25.

mobility of African labour that was used to exploit the mineral resources.[7] The mining sector's recruitment system and the associated racialisation of labour through the introduction of the industrial colour bar became the industry's most notorious feature.[8] The first stage of surface mining in the mid-1880s had assigned small groups of African labourers, living on the outskirts of the new reefs, to minimum-paying, unskilled employment in digging and washing out of gold-bearing gravel.[9] Although the demand for African wage labour for African labourremained relatively low in these initial stages of outcrop mining, the fluctuations in Johannesburg's capital market and international mining finance eventually forced the Rand's mines to consider a long-term strategy for the institutionalisation of a coercive labour regime based on racial discrimination. Due to the fixed price of gold on the international market, when profits were squeezed, mining companies intensified their efforts to replace white settler and colonial workers with African labour. With the extensive application of local, colonial, and transimperial labour recruitment networks, mining companies were able to collectively control African labour costs for a prolonged period.[10] Despite different operational objectives, the two most influential economic organisations on the Rand, the JSE and the Chamber of Mines, would soon engage in a common effort to control the physical and social mobility of African labour.

This chapter widens the analytical scope of Johannesburg's capital market to include organisational impact of the mining industry. The chapter examines the two organisations' interdependence by demonstrating their mutual contribution and commitment to the development of the ZAR's young gold mining industry. The chapter proceeds to connect the rise of the two Johannesburg-based organisations to British imperialism in the Cape Colony and situates the formation of the early

[7] De Kiewiet, Cornelis. *A History of South Africa: Social and Economic.* 1941. p. 3.

[8] Jeeves, A. Migrant Labour in South Africa's Mining Economy: The Struggle for the Gold Mines' Labour Supply, 1890–1920. McGill-Queen's Press-MQUP. Vancouver. 1985. p. 5.
See, also: Levy, N. *The Foundations of the South African Cheap Labour System.* Vol. 12. Taylor & Francis. 2022.

[9] Richardson, Peter and Van Helten, Jean Jacques. "Labour in the South African Gold Mining Industry: 1886–1914." In: Marks, Shula and Rathbone, Richard, eds. *Industrialisation and Social Change in South Africa.* 1982. pp. 77–78.

[10] Harrison, P. and Zack, T. The Power of Mining: The Fall of Gold and Rise of Johannesburg. *Journal of Contemporary African Studies* 30, no. 4 (2012): 554.

social network connections in the brewing Anglo-Afrikaner conflict of the 1890s. Furthermore, the chapter argues that it was the attempt to create a cartel on the production and distribution of financial intelligence that prompted influential members of the JSE to restructure the Chamber to suit the needs of the financial industry in the wake of the capital crisis of 1889.

The First Chamber of Mines and the JSE

The origins of commercial mining in Johannesburg are shrouded in uncertainty and conflicting evidence.[11] The first fifty years of gold mining in the ZAR produced so many different accounts of the discoveries of the gold reefs that the South African Union Government 'fact-finding commission' was established in 1938 to enquire into the origins of gold extraction on and near the Witwatersrand.[12] Although focusing mainly on the individual contributions of 'small capitalists from Kimberley and Pietermaritzburg,' the commission's final report emphasised the many unsuccessful campaigns of financiers and miners attempting to form a central organisation for the coordination of gold exploitation and government representation in 1886 and 1887.[13] At the beginning of the gold rush to the Rand in 1886, the township of Johannesburg was governed by the ZAR's mining commissioner, Captain Carl von Brandis who proclaimed the opening of the goldfields as public diggings in accordance with President Kruger's orders on 20 September 1886.[14] With a population of some 1000 people by the end of that first year of outcrop mining, the Pretoria government authorised a diggers' committee, modelled on those active in Barberton and Pilgrim's Rest, as the first form of local governance. The nine members of the Diggers' Committee replaced the mining commissioner of the original mining camp in November 1886

[11] Harrison, P. and Zack, T. The Power of Mining: The Fall of Gold and Rise of Johannesburg. *Journal of Contemporary African Studies* 30, no. 4 (2012): 551–570.

[12] WHP. *Committee on Discovery of Gold on the Witwatersrand. Government of the Union of South Africa.* A102. p. 1.
    See also: Petterson, Donald R. "The Witwatersrand a Unique Gold Mining Community." *Economic Geography* 27, no. 3 (1951): 209–221.

[13] WHP. *Committee on Discovery of Gold on the Witwatersrand. Government of the Union of South Africa.* A102. pp. 102–104.

[14] Rosenthal, Eric. *Gold! Gold! Gold!* 1970. p. 145.

and became the official authority responsible for all municipal affairs. Although the Diggers' Committee exercised all authority over the gold-fields on behalf of the ZAR government, it was a political institution and not an organisation representing the economic and legal interests of the mining community. The first formal steps in the organisation of the mining industry were closely linked to Johannesburg's financial industry. In addition to the financial infrastructure in the form of local and colonial banks, the most significant organisation for the mining sector to have emerged during the final months of 1887 was the *first* Chamber of Mines.[15] By the beginning of 1888, the Chamber consisted of 140 member mines, all committed to the development of gold mining in Johannesburg.[16] The Chamber was established as a voluntary business association committed to closer cooperation between members of the mining community and encouraging the exchange of resources and information in a growing industrial community.[17]

It must here be emphasised that the Chamber of Mines was established much earlier than 1889, when some studies suggest it was founded, and initially not for the purposes of exercising greater control over the gold industry's factors of production.[18] Johannesburg's limited and unreliable communication technology proved to be a significant setback for the international aspirations of many mining companies opening for business on the Rand. With the stock market in operation, however, there was absolutely no organisation that could provide the Exchange with industrial data and statistics on gold mining production. Initially, the great amount of publicity that was devoted to the discoveries of gold in 1886/7 with the intention of bringing financial capital to the Witwatersrand came from the media houses of Kimberley.[19] It was this lack of crucial information on the gold output of the mines and its potential commodification that incentivised the financial community to take the first step in creating

---

[15] See: *Organisation and Administration of the Witwatersrand Gold Mining Industry.* In: Jeppe, Carl Wilhelm Biccard, ed. *Gold Mining in South Africa.* 1948. pp. 77–83.

[16] Ibid.

[17] McCulloch, J. *South Africa's Gold Mines & the Politics of Silicosis.* Vol. 30. Boydell & Brewer Ltd. 2012. p. 11.

[18] Du Toit, Darcy. *Capital and Labour in South Africa: Class Struggle in the 1970s.* 1981. p. 74.

[19] WHP. *Committee on Discovery of Gold on the Witwatersrand.* Government of the Union of South Africa. A102. p. 104.

a central agency for industrial data capturing and analysis. As argued for and documented by Lang, the Chamber's origins were as a data-collecting and consultative body that could publish 'authoritative information' on the goldfields which would be accepted as such in colonial South Africa and the financial capitals of the world.[20]

Industrial information for the financial sector was the Chamber's original mandate, something that was clearly reflected in the professional occupations of the individuals who would serve it. The first Chamber of Mines in Johannesburg held its founding meeting at the town's Central Hotel, just a few days after the opening of the JSE, on 7 December 1887. The original Executive Committee was elected on 21 December and consisted of Carl Jeppe, Hermann Eckstein, Joseph Benjamin Robinson, John Stroyan, John Griffin Maynard, John Dell, Edward Hancock, Harry Wright, and Augustus Charles Baillie.[21] The management of the Chamber reflected the urgency to form a strategic alliance between the mining and financial industry. The Chamber's Executive Committee was made up of the most influential representatives of the young financial industry, who were already, or would in the course of the next few months become members of the JSE. Apart from Joseph B Robinson, all the members of the Executive Committee became members of the JSE before the end of March 1888.[22] The Chamber was, however, not intended to be a social club for Johannesburg's aspiring industrial capitalists, but an industrial organisation with the mandate of collecting and distributing mining intelligence for a politically sensitive economic sector.[23]

Generations of economic and social historians of South Africa have argued that the Chamber of Mines was originally formed to eliminate the competition of labour and regulate the labour market in the interest of the mine owners.[24] Although the firm stance on labour coercion became the main mandate of the Chamber in the early 1890s, in the late 1880s the organisation was still primarily committed to the distribution of industrial

---

[20] Lang, John. *Bullion Johannesburg: Men, Mines, and the Challenge of Conflict*. 1986. p. 27.

[21] Ibid. p. 30.

[22] JSEA. *Members' Roll 1888–1889*.

[23] Lang, John. *Bullion Johannesburg: Men, Mines, and the Challenge of Conflict*. 1986. p. 28.

[24] Giliomee, Hermann Buhr, and Bernard Mbenga. *New History of South Africa*. 2007. p. 201.

data and, most importantly, defending the international commercial reputation of the ZAR's mining industry from the financial irregularities that emerged at the beginning of 1887 and were widely publicised throughout Europe.[25] The Chamber was strongly opposed to the many bogus share flotation and false prospectuses misleading potential investors in Johannesburg and London.[26] During the early months of 1888, the Chamber gained global recognition and wrote to the London Stock Exchange, the Colonial Institute, *The Times,* and many other newspapers in London, warning international financiers to carefully investigate the South African companies they were investing in.[27] Contrary to literature suggesting that the Chamber was only established in 1889,[28] publications dating from as early as 26 December 1887 show the London *Times* was already corresponding with the Chamber on issues such as South African import duties and mining output.[29] The Chamber's international network of stakeholders in mining and finance has often been overlooked in favour of more narrow interpretations of the organisation's later specialisation with industrial labour relations and the social engineering of African workers' lives.

The Chamber's early association with the JSE was never meant to be a secret and the two organisations worked conjointly on many common commercial, and eventually, political objectives. One of the most prominent early collaborations took place on 4 July 1888 during a public meeting organised to address the growing commercial problems associated with President Kruger's concessions for the manufacture of explosives, a key component of the mining process . From the earliest days of mining on the Witwatersrand, the ZAR government allowed

See also: Jeeves, Alan. "The Control of Migratory Labour on the South African Gold Mines in the Era of Kruger and Milner." *Journal of Southern African Studies* 2, no. 1 (1975): 3–29.

Harries, Patrick. "Capital, State, and Labour on the 19th Century Witwatersrand: A Reassessment." *South African Historical Journal* 18, no. 1 (1986): 25–45.

[25] "South African Gold Fields." *The Economist,* 17 December 1887. p. 1596.

[26] Lang, John. *Bullion Johannesburg: Men, Mines, and the Challenge of Conflict.* 1986. p. 31.

[27] Ibid. p. 28.

[28] Du Toit, Darcy. *Capital and Labour in South Africa: Class Struggle in the 1970s.* 1981. p. 74.

[29] "South Africa." *The Times,* 26 December 1887. p. 3.

mine owners to import quotas of explosives (mostly dynamite) under a heavily regulated permit system.[30] A major change took place towards the end of 1887 when Alfred and Otto Beit's cousin, Edward Lippert, obtained exclusive monopoly rights to manufacture and distribute dynamite in the ZAR. Lippert, who at the beginning of 1888 was both a founding member of the Chamber of Mines and the JSE, was called upon by both organisations to officially respond to the strong public opposition to his government concessions. During the official public meeting, conveniently held at the Exchange on 4 July 1888, Lippert was able to convince the Chamber and JSE members that despite its higher price (£7 9s 9d), his dynamite was of far greater quality than the imports (at £5 a case). Representing the Chamber, Joseph Robinson issued an official government petition with a price ceiling of £ 7 10d per case of dynamite, stating that the growth of the ZAR's mining industry depended on the stable price and secure supply of industrial explosives.[31] Despite the successful appeasement of all the parties concerned, this controversy was indicative of how the institutional entanglement of mining and finance was being positioned to challenge the political authority of Kruger's government in Pretoria.[32]

The Chamber's early political activities and international lobbying revealed concerns about the organisation's impact on bringing about economic reforms to the Rand. Even if no primary documentation from the Chamber of Mines is available for the first two years of its existence, contemporary sources nonetheless refer to the lack of financial support for the young organisation.[33] The Chamber's limited capacity and authority to confront the Pretoria government and regain commercial autonomy for Johannesburg's mining industry eventually led to a significant loss of confidence among its members and financial backers. Towards the end of 1888, only one single member company had paid the subscription fee of

---

[30] Marais, Johannes S. *The Fall of Kruger's Republic*. Oxford: Clarendon Press. 1961. p. 28.

[31] Lang, John. *Bullion Johannesburg: Men, Mines, and the Challenge of Conflict*. 1986. pp. 34–35.

[32] See: Jeeves, Alan H. "The Rand capitalists and the coming of the South African war 1896–1899." *South African Journal of Economic History* 11, no. 2 (1996): 55–81.

[33] See: SACMA. *South African Chamber of Mines Annual Report for the Year Ending 1889*. 1890.

one guinea for the next year.[34] At the beginning of the following year, the Chamber was only able to rely on its most loyal beneficiaries, the colonial banks who were dependant on the Chamber's industrial statistics for debtor management. To keep the Chamber afloat, the Standard Bank, Natal Bank, the Bank of Africa, and the Cape of Good Hope Bank each guaranteed a monthly sum of £10 to keep the organisation in operation and safeguard the interests of the financial sector.[35]

The international outreach of the Chamber must also be contrasted with the lack of official recognition in the ZAR. Despite the Rand's first Diggers' Committee having close personal ties to President Kruger's government in Pretoria, the Chamber of Mines had no official recognition and political status with the Ministry of Mines. In April 1889, the ZAR government even stated that not only did the Chamber have no judicial power to represent any aspect of mining inside the ZAR, it had very little support from members of Johannesburg's mining industry, rendering any communication with the organisation obsolete.[36] The government did, however, concede that the Chamber's unofficial status could be elevated to official representation in the future, but only with the explicit support of President Kruger and the Ministry of Mines.[37]

The Chamber's most staunch supporters were based outside the Republic. Just months after its official establishment, the Chamber of Mines was able to represent the Johannesburg gold industry at a special meeting of the Royal Colonial Institute in London on 11 April 1888. The Institute had already supported political initiatives in Kimberley and saw Johannesburg as a perfect opportunity to promote British imperial politics in the Boer Republic.[38] Most importantly, the Chamber of Mines received the Institute's official backing to represent Johannesburg's gold industry.[39] The chairman of the Colonial Institute, Lord Thomas Brassey, even suggested that the early signs of commercial prosperity in the ZAR

[34] Lang, John. *Bullion Johannesburg: Men, Mines, and the Challenge of Conflict.* 1986. p. 35.

[35] Ibid.

[36] "Concerning Mining." *Standard and Diggers News*, 9 April 1889. p. 3.

[37] Ibid.

[38] See: Reese, Trevor R. *The History of the Royal Commonwealth Society 1868–1968.* 1968.

[39] "Royal Colonial Institute." *The Times*, 12 April 1888. p. 13.

and their dependence on British capital investments would probably lead to an economic, and later political union with the Cape Colony and Natal.[40]

Despite its organisational mission of providing the mining and finance sector with industrial intelligence, the Chamber lacked the authority and resources to pressure mine owners into action on common strategies of sharing production data and political resources for developing Johannesburg's mining industry. Most of the Rand's mining companies were still able to exploit the relatively low institutional barriers to entry in the South African gold industry and lacked the collective will to better control the factors of production.[41] As much as the Chamber tried to protect the autonomy of the mining industry and the needs of its members, it was virtually powerless in its mandate to resolve many legal issues with the government in Pretoria on the application of the ZAR's Gold Law.[42] Mining claims in 1886 were standardised at 155 feet by 413 feet, granting the owner the right to mine on or beneath the surface of the claim, but explicitly prohibited following a reef underground outside the limits of the surface boundary.[43] While the pioneering mines on the main reef operated as open-air trenches or shallow underground mines up to 100 feet in depth, as soon as mining companies went deeper into the pyritic zone and marginal production costs increased considerably,[44] the Gold Laws added a higher degree of bureaucracy, making it very difficult to recognise and uphold the boundaries of the claims.[45]

When the Chamber sent a memorandum to the Pretoria Government in early 1888 pleading not to grant any new mining concessions without consulting the Chamber, the State Secretary rebuffed the request and urged the Chamber to avoid meddling in affairs that were a matter for the

---

[40] Ibid.

[41] Frankel, S. H. *Capital investment in Africa*. 1938. pp. 80–81.

[42] See: Barber, Sydney Hilton. *Transvaal Gold Law. Translation into English of Law No. 15 of 1898*. Cape Town: T. Maskew Miller. 1904.

[43] Kubicek, Robert. *Economic Imperialism in Theory and Practice: The Case of South African Gold-Mining Finance 1886–1914*. 1979. p. 40.

[44] Katz, E. N. "Outcrop and Deep Level Mining in South Africa Before the Anglo-Boer War: Re-Examining the Blainey Thesis." *Economic History Review* (1995): pp. 304–328 and pp. 308–310.

[45] SACMA. *South African Chamber of Mines Annual Report for the Year Ending 1889*. 1890. p. 15.

republican state.[46] A similar episode was then repeated in May 1889 when the Chamber tried to prevent changes to the Gold Law. The Volksraad in Pretoria once again dismissed the direct involvement of the Chamber in any official negotiations with the state on the grounds that the Witwatersrand was represented in the government and the interests of the goldfields were to be handled by the official delegation.[47] The Minister of Mines, Christiaan Joubert, was particularly critical of the Chamber, stating that its leaders were unfit to hold office, and showed no intention of cooperating with the Ministry of Mines in any way that would benefit the economic and social development of the ZAR.[48]

Despite Carl Jeppe, Joseph Robinson and several other members of the Chamber's Executive Committee having strong commercial and political connections to President Kruger, as an industry representative organisation, the first Chamber of Mines was virtually powerless against the government's policies for the Witwatersrand. By June 1889 the Chamber struggled to maintain any position of political influence in Pretoria. The Ministry of Mines refused to recognise the Chamber in any representative capacity of Johannesburg's mining industry and stood firm in its efforts to uphold the political status quo of the Diggers' Committee.[49] The Ministry of Mines was additionally convinced that the Chamber was not the appropriate partner for any discussion on reforming the Gold Law and had lost all industrial recognition in Johannesburg, forcing many mines to consult directly with the government on all official issues pertaining to their industrial development in the ZAR.[50] Although some attempts were made to revive the 'old' Chamber of Mines, it became clear that a far more radical reconstruction was needed.[51] With potential

---

[46] Lang, John. *Bullion Johannesburg: Men, Mines, and the Challenge of Conflict.* 1986. p. 36.

[47] Ibid.

[48] "Truth and its Statements." *Standard and Diggers News*, 18 May 1889. pp. 2–3.

[49] "Chamber of Mines." *Standard and Diggers News*, 4 June 1889. p. 3.

[50] "Chamber of Mines." *Standard and Diggers News*, 15 August 1889. p. 2.

[51] Lang, John. *Bullion Johannesburg: Men, Mines, and the Challenge of Conflict.* 1986. p. 37.

new organisations such as *the Mining Protection Association*, the Chamber's Executive Committee decided to dissolve the organisation at the beginning of October 1889.[52]

THE REBIRTH OF THE CHAMBER

The failure of the Chamber to gain legitimacy and exert authority over the young mining sector served as an important lesson for future industrial organisation on the Rand. The Chamber only had a minor impact on local politics and needed a complete realignment of its engagement with the mining industry and the Pretoria government. A new initiative would need to take a different approach to the goldfield's geological constraints and adapt to the growing industrialisation and internationalisation of the Rand's economy. The irony of the situation was that gold mining was indeed the economic sector that could potentially lead the whole ZAR into industrialisation, but was already collapsing from poor financial management, share market speculation, and inefficient government regulation.[53] The 1889 capital slump, disastrous as it was for Johannesburg's economy, provided the mining industry with a new organisational prospect by eliminating some fifty or sixty companies whose only assets were share certificates.[54] While some share syndicates still believed in quick profits towards the middle of 1889, the leading mining and investment houses began to focus on long-term developments of the reefs. As summarised by Fitzpatrick, Johannesburg's investors soon found it necessary to establish a stronger and more comprehensive intelligence capacity to protect their political interests and collect industrial information for the mining industry as a whole.[55] This section therefore argues that it

---

[52] "Chamber of Mines." *Standard and Diggers News*, 9 May 1889. p. 3.
"Chamber of Mines." *Standard and Diggers News*, 15 August 1889. p. 2.

[53] Webb, Arthur. "Blainey and Early Witwatersrand Profitability Some Thoughts on Financial Management and Capital Constraints Facing the Gold Mining Industry 1886–1894." *South African Journal of Economic History* 12, no. 1–2 (1997): 139.

[54] Cartwright, Alan Patrick. *The Corner House: The Early History of Johannesburg*. 1965. p. 103.

[55] Fitzpatrick, Percy. *The Transvaal from Within: A Private Record of Public Affairs*. 1899. p. 61.

was the JSE and its most influential members who prompted the re-establishment of the Chamber in the interest of forming an information cartel to rehabilitate the share market.

Following the failure of all attempts by the Wernher & Beit mining partnership to revive the old Chamber in an organisational structure that could meet the new industrial demands had failed, the new *Witwatersrand Chamber of Mines* was formed on 4 October 1889 at the height of Johannesburg's first share market slump.[56] According to the first available annual report, the newly established Chamber's initial duty was to settle the 'old' Chamber's debts and stabilise the London's share market with an extensive exhibition of South African gold at the 1889 Paris *Exposition Universelle* and London's Mining and Metallurgical Exhibition.[57] The most obvious organisational relationship between the Chamber and the JSE was in its physical location. The first meeting of the representative members of the 'new' *Witwatersrand Chamber of Mines* was held on 5 October 1889 inside the boardroom of the JSE building. At the time of the publication of its first annual report in 1891, the Chamber was managed from just a few offices inside Barnato's Building that housed the JSE.[58] It was only in April 1891 that the Chamber moved out of the Exchange and into the Bettelheim Building, one block away on the corner of Simmonds and Fox Streets, which it then used for the next four years.[59] What is, however, important to note here is that, for the first two years of its existence, the new Chamber of Mines operated from underneath the same roof as the JSE.

The significance of the physical location is, however, only secondary to the argument. The two organisations were not only run from the same building but, more importantly, they were virtually managed by the same people. As president of the Chamber of Mines, Hermann Eckstein, needed only to descend one flight of mahogany-wood stairs to attend to his duties as a member of the JSE's General Committee. Apart from the president, there was a dominant presence of JSE members on the Chamber's *Council of Representative Members*. Of the initial 21 members of

[56] Ibid.

[57] SACMA. *South African Chamber of Mines Annual Report 1890*. 1891. p. 11.

[58] Ibid. p. 11.

[59] SACMA. *South African Chamber of Mines Annual Report for the Year Ending 1890*. 1891. p. 7.

the Council, all but 5 were JSE members (see Table 4.1). More importantly, these were not just any ordinary voting members who could enter the trading floor of the Exchange, but influential decision-makers at the centre of the mining and financial industries. At a further meeting on 10 October 1889, Eckstein was officially elected as the Chamber's president, with Hollins and Hanau as vice-presidents. The rest of the standing committee was made up of James B. Taylor, Carl Goch, William F. Lance, Francis J. Dormer, George Richards, William H Rogers, and Frank C Liddle.[60] With the exception of Hollins, Richards, Hosken, Richards, and Phillips, the Chamber's whole standing committee was able to join Eckstein on the trading floor of the Exchange.

Table 4.1 Chamber of Mines Council Members and their JSE affiliation

Name	JSE member	Date joined	General Committee
R. R. Hollins	NO		
W. Y. Campbell	Yes	June 1889	Yes
C. Hanau	Yes	December 1887	Yes
C. Goch	Yes	December 1887	No
E. Lippert	Yes	June 1889	No
H. A. Rogers	Yes	August 1888	No
J. B. Taylor	Yes	December 1887	No
W. H. Rogers	Yes	December 1888	No
H. Eckstein	Yes	December 1887	Yes
F. C. Liddle	Yes	June 1889 (Expelled January 1890)	No
T. M. C. Nourse	Yes	June 1889	Yes
J. Hay	Yes	April 1889	Yes (Director)
W. Hosken	No		
W. F. Lance	Yes	June 1889	No
G. Richards	No		
G. Farrar	Yes	June 1889	Yes
F. Spencer	No		
H. L. Currey	Yes	June 1889	No
L. Phillips	No		
F. J. Dormer	Yes	June 1889	No
W. Ross	Yes	February 1889	No

Source JSEA. JSE Members Roll Book for 1889

[60] Ibid. p. 42.

The main objectives of the 'new' Chamber were aimed at overcoming the failures of the old organisation and, more specifically, at establishing an official working relationship with the government in Pretoria. The new objectives were formally announced in *The Star* on 3 September 1889[61]:

1. To promote and protect the mining interest and industries of the South African Republic, and in particular the mining interests and industries of the Witwatersrand Gold Fields.
2. To consider all questions connected with the mining industry, and to promote public discussion thereon.
3. To promote legislative or other measures affecting such mining industry.
4. To collect and circulate statistics relating to such mining industry.
5. To communicate with and exchange information upon mining matters with Chambers of Mines or Government Departments of Mines in the South African Republic and other countries.
6. To procure information as to mines, mining companies, and all matters relating thereto.
7. To establish, form, and maintain a library, and museum of models, specimens, designs, drawings, and other articles of interest in connection with the mining industry.
8. To act as arbitrators in the settlement of any disputes arising out of mining.
9. To sell, manage, improve, lease, mortgage, dispose of, turn to account, or otherwise deal with any part of the property of the Chamber.
10. To invest the money of the Chamber not immediately required upon such security or securities, and on such terms or otherwise, in such manner as may from time to time be determined.
11. To borrow any money required by the Chamber
12. To obtain, whenever determined upon, an Act of the Volksraad, for the incorporation of the Chamber, and any other Act that may be deemed conducive to any of these objects.

The new mandate specified the tasks of the restructured organisation. This focus was given to clearly outlining the problems of the Rand's mining

---

[61] "The Chamber of Mines." *The Star*, 3 September 1889. p. 3.

industry and how the Chamber intended to respond to them. The collection of industrial information, its circulation, and its archival management were, however, at the core of the initial mandate. For the significance of this chapter's argument, it is also important to emphasise that, at this point in time, there was still no explicit reference to policies directed at the supply, control, or price of labour in the mining industry.

With the Chamber located inside Barnato's JSE building at the time of the 1889 financial slump, the two organisations were ideally positioned to alleviate some of the financial challenges and begin work on a common strategy to strengthen the cooperation between mining and finance.[62] A joint JSE sub-committee was appointed to oversee the partnership between the two organisations in March 1890 and was instructed to explore different procedures for improving the flow of information between the Chamber's member mines and the JSE's General Committee.[63] It was also immediately settled that the Chairman of the Chamber would become an *ex-officio member* of all JSE sub-committees, giving the Chamber direct access (but not voting rights) to all JSE committees.[64]

The first step of the renewed organisational partnership was to review the property rights of all JSE-listed mining companies. The Exchange requested the Chamber to conclude an investigation into the 'security of tenure of the gold mines' owning land plots on the Rand.[65] The JSE instructed the Chamber to contact each of its member mines and formally request the proof of land titles to be sent to the Exchange. The sub-committee's report led to a significant overhaul of the criteria for listing on the Official List with all companies now required to submit proof of land titles when applying for JSE quotations.[66] Although the Chamber's actions in creating an extra layer of legal control for JSE-listed mines did much to rectify a working relationship between the two institutions, the main reason behind fostering a deeper engagement between finance and industry was still focused on the collection and exchange of vital

---

[62] See: "The Chamber of Mines." *Standard and Diggers News*, 14 February 1890. p. 3.

[63] JSEA. *Minutes of an Ordinary Meeting of the Committee*, 25 March 1890.

[64] Ibid.

[65] Ibid.

[66] JSEA. *Minutes of an Ordinary Meeting of the Committee*, 1 April 1890.

mining intelligence. From the perspective of the JSE and Johannesburg's financial community, industrial statistics were the Chamber's core function and were to be commodified for the benefit of the capital market. By the end of 1892, several hundred copies of monthly output figures were being sent out by the Chamber to the JSE and the Kimberley Stock Exchange every month.[67] Mining output statistics were a key analytical tool for the JSE's General Committee, its customers, local banks, and foreign investors questioning the legitimacy of the ZAR's goldfields.[68] As admitted by the Chamber at its first annual general meeting, new statistical efforts and methods were employed to calculate the milling returns of all member mines, making all the data available for publication by the international press.[69] Between 1888 and 1893, the Chamber provided *The Economist*, *The Financial Times*, and the London *Times* with gold production reports, all clearly aimed at stimulating London's international market for ZAR mining securities.[70]

The Chamber's statistical work and mining intelligence were also recognised in France. The French financial expert and pioneer of data collection on South African mines, Henry Dupont, published the first edition of the *Revue Sud-Africaine* on 21 May 1893, emphasising his publication's close ties to the Chamber.[71] Furthermore, Henry Dupont went beyond the data collection and stressed the growing political aspirations of the Chamber in defending the mining industry's interests

---

[67] SACMA. *South African Chamber of Mines Annual Report for the Year Ending 1892.* 1893. p. 33.

[68] See: Mining Intelligence. JSEA. *Minutes of an Ordinary Meeting of the Committee,* 15 August 1890.

[69] SACMA. *South African Chamber of Mines Annual Report for the Year Ending 1890.* 1891. p. 12.

[70] See: "The Gamble in South African Mining Shares." *The Economist*, 8 December 1888. p. 1537.
"The Witwatersrand Gold Fields." *The Economist*, 22 December 1888. p. 22.
"South African Gold Production." *The Economist*, 2 November 1889. p. 1392.
"South African Gold Shares." *The Economist*, 14 December 1889. p. 2416.
"Transvaal Gold Production." *The Economist*, 22 February 1890. p. 2426.
"News from the Rand." *The Financial Times*, 19 February. 1890. p. 2.
"Royal Colonial Institute." *The Times*, 12 April 1888. p. 13.
"South Africa." *The Times*, 18 January 1889. p. 13.

[71] *Revue Sud-Africaine. Paris: Henry Dupont*, 21 May 1893.

in Pretoria.[72] As Dupont emphasised, the 'new' Chamber's quest for political legitimacy and industrial cohesion was backed by the honorary function of President Paul Kruger. Although the exact procedure of his appointment remains unclear, President Kruger approved the Chamber's invitation to make him the honorary president of Johannesburg's main mining organisation towards the end of October 1889.[73] The President's only request was that in addition to his position, the Ministry of Mines was also given honorary status.[74] Kruger's position on the role and function of the new Chamber is nevertheless very difficult to assess, but it was at the Chamber's invitation that he travelled to Johannesburg in January 1890 on an official visit to inspect the city. Despite the Chamber's meeting with Kruger focusing on the possible extension of railway lines to Johannesburg, the Chamber used the opportunity to extensively advertise that Kruger was willing to support the Chamber in its mission to improve the local and international reputation of the gold industry.[75]

The most comprehensive assessment of the 'new' Chamber's activities and impact on the mining industry was published in the first official internal report, which was delayed by a year due to a fire at the premises of the *Argus Publishing Company*, in which the complete manuscript was destroyed.[76] By 28 January 1891 the Chamber had 86 paying members, representing 51 mining companies.[77] In an analysis by the Chamber's president, Hermann Eckstein, the main work of the Chamber for the post-1889 financial crisis was to actively encourage the rapid expansion of railway connections to the Rand, convince the government to allow the import of dynamite, secure the mining results of all mines associated with

---

[72] (My own translation from French.) Dupont, Henry. *Les mines d'or de l'Afrique du Sud*. Paris: Lemaire & Dupont, 1893. p. 26.

[73] SACMA. *South African Chamber of Mines Annual Report for the Year Ending 1890*. 1891. p. 7.

[74] Lang, John. *Bullion Johannesburg: Men, Mines and the Challenge of Conflict*. 1986. p. 79.

[75] SACMA. *South African Chamber of Mines Annual Report for the year ending 1890*. 1891. p. 11.
See also: "Public Meetings." *Standard and Diggers News*, 14 February 1890. p. 3.

[76] SACMA. *South African Chamber of Mines Annual Report for the Year Ending 1890*. 1891. p. 11.
See also: "A Disastrous Fire. Star Works Destroyed." *The Star*, 27 May 1890. p. 3.

[77] SACMA. *South African Chamber of Mines Annual Report for the Year Ending 1890*. 1891. p. 13.

the Chamber and expand the membership to more non-mining companies.[78] The report also provided a brief explanation of the mining labour
situation, but refrained from adopting an authoritative agenda.

In the initial stages of the Rand's gold production in the 1880s,
the question of mining labour was left to free competition, leaving
demand and supply to dictate the market.[79] Johannesburg's labour
history provided unique insights into the racialisation of industrial relations in South Africa's labour-repressive economic development path of
the nineteenth century.[80] Given that the growing demand for labour in
the early years of Johannesburg's mining development presented African
and European settler labour with a relatively strong wage bargaining position, the racial bias of economic development in southern Africa set in
very quickly. Many thousands of African seasonal labourers left in late
1889 and refused to come back to work in Johannesburg the following
year.[81] Despite the fact that African workers were paid far less than European settlers before and after the period of depression between 1889 and
1892, before any collective wage ceilings and 'industrial colour bars' were
institutionalised by the mining industry, mine owners were soon struggling to pay even these suppressed wages. The pressure from mining
employers resulted in the Chamber of Mines issuing a collective plea
to all members to change their payment systems from monthly to daily,
making the employment and retrenchment of African labour more flexible.[82] The Chamber argued that with 15 000 African workers on the
goldfields, a 'great sum' of £45 000 had to be spent at an average monthly
wage of £ 3 per worker. Apart from the suggested change in payment
structures, there is no evidence to prove that any collective attempts by
the Chamber were made to reduce the wages of European and African
workers before May 1890. It was only in mid-1890 that the issue of wage
ceilings was first raised by the Chamber's most influential member, the

[78] Ibid. pp. 11–13.

[79] Lang, John. *Bullion Johannesburg: Men, Mines and the Challenge of Conflict*. 1986.
p. 79.

[80] Trapido, S. "South Africa in a Comparative Study of Industrialization." *The Journal
of Development Studies* 7, no. 3 (1971): 314.

[81] "The Native Labour Question." *Standard and Diggers News*, 23 January 1890. p. 2.

[82] SACMA. *South African Chamber of Mines Annual Report for the Year Ending 1890*.
1891. pp. 12, 61 and 64.

Wernher, Beit & Co. group of companies.[83] United within the Chamber, the actions suggested towards the end of 1890 would set the organisation on a new course of labour mobility control and wage suppression in the mining industry. As summarised by the *Standard and Diggers' News*, greater control over the cost and movement of labour would soon need to become the Chamber's '*raison d'etre*.'[84]

FINANCIAL INTELLIGENCE, IMPERIALISM AND THE PRESS

The organisational entanglements between gold mining and finance must also be viewed through the consolidation of Johannesburg's press and printing industry. The role and function of press as a tool for capital mobilisation was a dominant feature of finance's information infrastructure.[85] The global expansion of financial intelligence and financial press throughout the late nineteenth century facilitated the diffusion of financial information to a broad social demographic of investors and financial intermediaries.[86] With the publishing and greater circulation of price lists, a wider cross-section of the population engaged in commercial activities could exploit financial information which was previously restricted to a small merchant elite.[87] The mining sector in particular suffered from major information asymmetries between company managers and investors, creating many opportunities for market manipulation and insider trading.[88] The simultaneous development of mining and finance in Johannesburg would attract the ZAR's press to capture and control the most accessible channels of financial information.

---

[83] Lionel Phillips (Johannesburg) to Messrs. Wernher, Beit & Co. (London), 23 May 1890. HE 149. In: Fraser, Maryna and Alan Jeeves., eds. *All that Glittered: Selected Correspondence of Lionel Phillips, 1890–1924.* 1977. p. 37.

[84] "The Native Labour Question." *Standard and Diggers News*, 23 January 1890. p. 2.

[85] Marks, S. G. *The Information Nexus: Global Capitalism from the Renaissance to the Present.* Cambridge University Press. 2016. p. 83.

[86] Baldasty, G. J. *The Commercialization of News in the Nineteenth Century.* University of Wisconsin Press. 1992. pp. 3–6.

[87] Ibid.

[88] Rönnbäck, K. and O. Broberg. The Crumble in the Jungle: The London Financial Press and the Boom-and-Bust Cycles of the Ashanti Goldfields Corporation, 1895–1914. *Enterprise & Society* 22, no. 4 (2021): 972–973.

For a young frontier mining town, Johannesburg already had an active press interest by the end of 1887. Although little information exists about print and circulation figures, *The Mining Argus*, *The Standard and Transvaal Mining Chronicle*, *Standard and Diggers News*, the *Advertiser*, *The Eastern Star*, and the Pretoria-published Dutch- and English-language *Republikein*, were readily available to the growing public.[89] The rise of English-language press in the ZAR in general, and the newspaper landscape in Johannesburg in particular, was closely related to the development of the goldfields and the growing demand for financial intelligence.[90] English-language newspapers and journals devoted considerable attention to the ZAR's economic progress t and became the main source of financial information from which prospecting miners developed their sense and vision of frontier capitalism on the Rand.

Financial intelligence on the early stock trade on the Barberton Stock Exchange encouraged the migration of English-language newspapers and colonial financial journalists to the Boer Republic.[91] Thomas and George Sheffield, two brothers from the Cape Colony who had previously followed the diamond booms as journalists in Grahamstown and Kimberley, established *The Eastern Star* in Barberton in 1886.[92] Lionel Phillips, the later president of the Chamber of Mines, also began his career on Barberton's goldfields as a financial correspondent for the Cape's *The Independent*.[93] In November 1887, the Sheffield brothers joined the rush of mining prospectors and financiers to Johannesburg, where they quickly

[89] Jeppe, F. *Jeppe's Transvaal Almanac and Directory for 1889*. Cape Town: The Argus Printing and Publishing Company. 1889. p. 125.

See, also *Press* in: Musiker, Naomi and Reuben Musiker. *A Concise Historical Dictionary of Greater Johannesburg*. 2000. p. 216.

Rosenthal, Eric. *Gold ! Gold ! Gold !* 1970. p. 171.

[90] See: Robinson, Cynthia A. *The Power Behind the Press. English Newspapers in the Transvaal, 1870–1899.*

Unpublished Dissertation. University of British Columbia. 1989.

[91] The Star. *Like it Was: The Star 100 Years in Johannesburg*. The Star: Johannesburg. 1987. pp. 1–2.

[92] Plug, C. Early scientific and professional societies in the Transvaal: Barberton 1887–1889. *South African Journal of Cultural History* 4, no. 3 (1990): 190–199.

[93] Turrell, Robert Vicat. *Capital and Labour on the Kimberley Diamond Fields, 1871–1890*. 1987. p. 117.

became members of the first Chamber of Mines.[94] *The Eastern Star* re-established itself in Johannesburg as the unofficial press organ of the Rand's mining industry. The newspaper worked closely with the original Chamber and used its readership in the mining camp to consolidate the political voice of the mining community.[95] It must, however, be empha-sised that despite printing the JSE's daily price lists since early 1888, the newspaper initially had a limited focus on Johannesburg's financial sector, devoting more coverage and entire sections to advertising mining equipment, which provided the great majority of its revenue base.[96] Notwithstanding the newspaper's support for the collection of financial intelligence, it would take a stronger colonial connection to propel *The Eastern Star* closer to Johannesburg's financial community.

The earliest plans to lay the political foundation of a closer union between financial capital and the local press were conceived in the Cape Colony by Cecil John Rhodes and the Cape journalist Francis Dormer. The strategic partnership between the two committed imperialists was originally forged in 1881 when, after taking his seat in the Cape Parlia-ment, Rhodes acquired influence in the *Cape Argus* by assisting its editor, Francis Dormer, in becoming the main owner of the Cape Colony's most-read newspaper.[97] In the same year, Dormer purchased the *Cape Argus* for £6 000, and with Rhodes' political influence and financial backing, turned the paper into a political platform for the doctrine of 'impe-rial progressivism.'[98] With extensive personal experience and knowledge of the Kimberley's share trade, Dormer was one of the main colonial loyal-ists to have used journalism as an apparatus of imperial accountability and speculation in South African financial circles.[99]

[94] Lang, John. *Bullion Johannesburg: Men, Mines, and the Challenge of Conflict*. 1986. p. 29.

[95] Gale, William D. *The Rhodesian Press*. Salisbury: Rhodesian Printing and Publishing Company. 1962. pp. 2–3.

[96] The Star. *Like it Was: The Star 100 Years in Johannesburg*. The Star: Johannesburg. 1987. p. 2.

[97] Tamarkin, Mordechai. *Cecil Rhodes and the Cape Afrikaners: The Imperial Colossus and the Colonial Parish Pump*. London: Frank Cass and Co. 1996. p. 134.

[98] Kwasitsu, Lishi. "Promoting Commercial Activities in Cape Town Newspapers, 1876–1901." *Social Dinamics* 30, no. 1 (2004): 171–172.

[99] See: Dormer, Francis. In: Wills, Walter H., and R. J. Barrett. *The Anglo-African Who's Who and Biographical Sketch-book*. 1907. p. 106.

Encouraged by the *Argus'* success in the Cape and the growing readership throughout South Africa, Rhodes urged Dormer to join Johannesburg's gold rush and establish a British loyalist newspaper in the ZAR.[100] Dormer benefited from his Cape financial connections to become both a member of both the JSE and the Chamber of Mines in January 1888.[101] With a recommendation from Rhodes and further endorsements from various Kimberley capitalists, Dormer was invited to join the Chamber's Board of Directors and became the organisation's first secretary.[102] Dormer was open about the imperial visions he shared with Rhodes and, once firmly established in his new role in Johannesburg, he turned to London for further financial and political support. It was in London, where Dormer, representing the Chamber of Mines at a meeting with the Royal Colonial Institute in April 1888,[103] was able to convince Donald Currie, founder of the Castle Steamship Line, to provide him with £ 5000 in debentures.[104] Ships such as the *Carisbrooke Castle* (from 1889) and later the *Armadale Castle* (from 1903) were directly insured by N. M. Rothschild and Sons, and responsible for the majority of shipments of the ZAR's gold out of Cape Town up until 1910.[105] With Currie's Castle Steamship Line being the largest transporter of South African gold to the City of London,[106] the imperial triangle between printed media, mining

---

[100] Robinson, C. A. *The Power Behind the Press: English Newspapers in the Transvaal, 1870–1899* (Doctoral dissertation, University of British Columbia). 1989. p. 61.

[101] JSEA. *Members' Roll 1888–1889.*
Lang, John. *Bullion Johannesburg: Men, Mines, and the Challenge of Conflict.* 1986. p. 42.

[102] SACMA. *South African Chamber of Mines Annual Report for the Year Ending 1890.* 1891.

[103] "Royal Colonial Institute." *The Times,* 12 April 1888. p. 13.

[104] Robinson, Cynthia A. *The Power Behind the Press. English Newspapers in The Transvaal, 1870–1899.*
Unpublished Dissertation. 1989. p. 61.

[105] Van Helten, Jean Jacques. "Empire and High Finance: South Africa and the International Gold Standard 1890–1914." *Journal of African History* 23, no. 4 (1982): 543.

[106] See: Porter, Andrew. "Britain, the Cape Colony, and Natal, 1870–1914: Capital, Shipping, and the Imperial Connexion." *The Economic History Review* 34, no. 4 (1981): 554–577.

finance, and gold exports was exposed.[107] Profiting from this new injection of financial and social capital, Dormer was in an excellent position to establish the most influential and pro-British newspaper in Johannesburg. Considering that Johannesburg already had numerous newspapers in print and circulation, Dormer's financial backers decided to purchase an existing paper rather than to start a completely new publication.[108] Dormer was well informed about the political alliance between the old Chamber of Mines and *The Eastern Star*, prompting him to move ahead with a plan to take full control of the newspaper.[109] More importantly, *The Eastern Star* was significant with regard to the Chamber's intended impact—as of beginning of 1888, it was Johannesburg's best-selling paper and the most critical of the Pretoria government.[110] The small circle of Johannesburg's capitalists and journalists who managed to weather the financial storm of early 1889 felt they were constantly being attacked by the government-subsidised *Standard and Diggers News*.[111] After a short period of negotiations with Thomas and George Sheffield, *The Eastern Star*'s owners, publishers, and editors, Dormer's takeover of the *Argus Printing and Publishing Company* was completed with a buyout deal struck on 1 May 1889, a process which resulted in the creation of the 'new' *Star* newspaper.[112] With the direct intervention of Hermann Eckstein, the Argus was listed on the JSE. It also needs to be emphasised that ever since Eckstein had acquired an interest in the *Argus Printing and Publishing Company* in 1889, the Corner House group of mining firms had taken a great interest in the appointment of the editor of *The*

[107] See: Van Helten, Jean Jacques. "Empire and High Finance: South Africa and the International Gold Standard 1890–1914." *Journal of African History* 23, no. 4 (1982): 529–548.

[108] Robinson, Cynthia A. Robinson, Cynthia A. *The Power Behind the Press. English Newspapers in the Transvaal, 1870–1899.* 1989. p. 63.

[109] Lang, John. *Bullion Johannesburg: Men, Mines, and the Challenge of Conflict.* 1986. p. 26.

[110] Robinson, Cynthia A. *The Power Behind the Press. English Newspapers in the Transvaal, 1870–1899.* 1989. p. 63.

[111] Ibid. p. 4.

[112] See: *Argus Printing and Publishing Company.* In: Goldman, Charles Sydney. *The Financial, Statistical, and General History of the Gold & Other Companies of Witwatersrand, South Africa.* 1892. p. 13.

Star.[113] Additionally, and even before Dormer managed to take over *The Eastern Star*, he was able to secure the financial support of Joseph Robinson, the owner of the most productive and capitalised mine on the Rand.[114] By securing the patronage of influential Randlords such as Rhodes, Eckstein, and Robinson, Dormer forged Johannesburg's new union between the press, financial capital, and an increasingly anti-Kruger mining sector. The reorganised newspaper started with £70 000 in fixed capital, with Dormer instated as chairman and a board of directors made up of Edmund Powell (Editor of the *Cape Argus*), James Smith, William George Vos, Alexander Schmidt, and Thomas Sheffield.[115] The newspaper quickly set out its anti-government agenda and retained Thomas Sheffield as editor. Sheffield intensified the rhetoric against Kruger's administration by using the first issue's editorial to announce its political position:

> Loyalty to the institutions of a country does not mean subservience to those in power for the time being...but doing that which is best calculated to preserve its constitution intact, at the same time endeavouring to bring about such reforms as will give all who submit to its laws a voice in their government...To bring about such reforms shall be one of the aims of *The Star*.[116]

More significantly for the developments in the crisis-stricken financial sector, Francis Dormer aspired for *The Star* to create a closer financial and operational relationship with the JSE. Dormer and Barnato had maintained a good business relationship since their days in Cape Town and Kimberley.[117] Undeterred by the fact that Dormer continued to work for Rhodes, Barnato mobilised the JSE to take advantage of Johannesburg's growing demand for financial reporting and secure a strategic information

---

[113] Kubicek, Robert V. *Economic Imperialism in Theory and Practice: The Case of South African Gold Mining Finance 1886–1914.* 1979. p. 82.

[114] Robinson, Cynthia A. *The Power Behind the Press. English Newspapers in the Transvaal, 1870–1899.* 1989. p. 63.

[115] *Argus Printing and Publishing Company.* In: Goldman, Charles Sydney, ed. *The Financial, Statistical, and General History of the Gold & Other Companies of Witwatersrand, South Africa.* 1892. p. 13.

[116] Quoted in: Rosenthal, Eric. *Gold ! Gold ! Gold !* 1970. p. 172.

[117] Robinson, Cynthia A. *The Power Behind the Press. English Newspapers in the Transvaal, 1870–1899.* 1989. pp. 65–66.

distribution platform with *The Star*. By the end of 1891 Barney Barnato's team of JSE directors became major shareholders in the Argus Company. Fritz Eckstein, Alphone Lilienfeld, Solly Joel, Woolf Joel, Gustav Sonn, Fritz Mosenthal, and Victor Woolf were all influential members of the JSE and were continuously encouraged by Barnato to increase their stakes in the Argus Publishing Company.[118]

The Star became the JSE's official printer and distributor of the Official List. During the market's recovery towards the end of 1889, *The Star* published the JSE's Official List up to three times a day.[119] Along with the price lists, the Argus Printing and Publishing Company was responsible for the binding and publishing of all JSE Minute Books until the beginning of 1902.[120] Although the Argus Company operated from its own building on the corner of President and Sauer Street, *The Star* occupied the largest office in the new JSE building from 1890 onwards.[121] With the majority of the JSE's directorate having a financial stake in *The Star*, Dormer had no problems eliminating any newspapers that stood in the way of the partnership between the Argus and the JSE. By the end of 1891, Dormer was able to run four of the six competing newspapers out of business.[122] More significantly for the industrial link to the Chamber of Mines, in addition to the services for the JSE, the Argus Company also became the official publisher of the new Chamber's reports and journals.[123] With the active support of the Argus Company and *The Star*, the Chamber, the Exchange, and the local press were firmly united and well positioned to guide the development of deep-level mining into the hands of local and increasingly international financial capital.

[118] JSEA. *JSE Members Roll Book for 1891.*

Argus Printing and Publishing Company. In: Goldman, Charles Sydney. *The Financial, Statistical, and General History of the Gold & Other Companies of Witwatersrand, South Africa*. 1892. p. 13.

[119] See: "The Stock Exchange." *The Star*, 22 September 1889. p. 6.

[120] See: Inside Cover of JSEA. *General Committee Minute Meetings*. 29 October 1889–27 October 1891.

[121] BL. *Minutes of the Board of the Johannesburg Estate Company*, 12 May 1890.

[122] Robinson, Cynthia A. *The Power Behind the Press. English Newspapers in The Transvaal, 1870–1899*. 1989. p. 66.

[123] See: *Argus Printing and Publishing Company*. In: Goldman, Charles Sydney, ed. *The Financial, Statistical, and General History of the Gold & Other Companies of Witwatersrand, South Africa*. 1892. p. 13.

CONCLUSION

The establishment of the Johannesburg Stock Exchange encouraged the formation of strategic institutional partnerships and closer cooperation between the finance industry and the gold mines they were promoting. Despite operating the capital market for mining finance, the JSE had no official mandate and only limited capacity to influence the development of the ZAR's mining industry. Founded just weeks apart at the end of 1887, the establishment of the Witwatersrand Chamber of Mines and its close institutional link to the JSE was a crucial step in the mines' early industrial organisation and the long-term development of the goldfields. Additionally, and more importantly for the growing demand in financial intelligence, with the stock market in operation and multiple mining companies applying for admission onto the JSE's Official List, there was still little industrial information and mining data available to the financial community. The new cooperation between finance and mining would need to secure a unified channel of information collection and dissemination for a growing local and international investing public.

In taking the analysis back to the JSE's organisational infancy, this chapter investigated the common origins of the JSE and the Chamber of Mines, mapping the convergence of Johannesburg's industry, finance and politics. Most importantly for the institutional development of the JSE, the chapter explored the personal connections between Johannesburg's finance and mining industry through interlocking committee appointments, the exchange of information and joint political actions carried out by both organisations. Established just weeks after the JSE, the Chamber was seen as the first independent representation of Johannesburg's mining industry. The main argument posited here was that despite past studies emphasising the organisation's capacity and ability to influence Johannesburg's racialised industrial relations, the Chamber's original mission was to collect and control the distribution of statistics on the mines' industrial output. The close ties of the two organisations with the Cape Colony, and London reinforced the imperial connection and the strategic value of mining intelligence for the international financial sector. Although the chapter outlined the ambitions and ultimate failures of the early Chamber of Mines, it was the growing links to the financial and press industries that defined the organisation's operational capacity and service to Johannesburg's commercial society. The liquidation of the old Chamber and the restructuring of the new Witwatersrand Chamber of Mines on 5 October

1889 are viewed as a long-term commitment to the political and financial demands of the mining industry that struggling with the ramifications of Johannesburg's first financial crisis. The widening of the re-established Chamber's operational mandate beyond industrial statistics confirms that the focus on the supply and control of African labour came after May 1890, more than two years after the Chamber was initially established, as an industrial response to the capital crisis of early 1889.

Additionally, this chapter documented the evolution of the strategic information nexus between Johannesburg's mining, finance, and press industries. The emergence and the distribution of the *Standard and Diggers News* and *The Star* was a crucial step in securing publication channels for financial information in a boomtown dominated by rumours and speculative reports. The Argus Publishing Company and its close affiliation with the Chamber of Mines and the JSE constituted the consolidation of media ownership in Johannesburg's financial press. Financial intelligence and its narrow distribution channel through the local press are seen as the strategic capitalist link between Johannesburg, the Cape Colony, London, and increasingly Paris.

CHAPTER 5

Between Johannesburg, London and Paris: Deep-Level Mining and International Finance

The consolidation of the partnership between finance, industry, and the press came at a time of great transformation for Johannesburg's economy. The financial crisis of late 1889/90, created by the simultaneous problems associated with the banking system and the treatment of pyritic ore, left the ZAR's gold mining sector in the state of uncertainty and vulnerability. The first boom defined the speculative nature of Johannesburg's mining finance and as soon as it became evident that many of the early mining companies were financially mismanaged and technically unprepared for new extraction methods that would be needed to exploit the pyric reef at greater depths, the capital market crashed with the JSE suffering its worst losses since it was founded in 1887. The immediate implication and concern for Johannesburg's young financial industry was that with increasing unpredictability over future production capacity and rising costs of gold exploitation, most Rand shares were now overvalued, and some of ZAR's earliest company flotations turned out to be worthless.[1] At the end of 1891, some 73 mining companies were still in operation, but

---

[1] Cartwright, A. P. *The Corner House: The Early History of Johannesburg.* London: McDonald. 1965. p. 103.

© The Author(s), under exclusive license to Springer Nature Switzerland AG 2024
M. Lukasiewicz, *Gold, Finance and Imperialism in South Africa, 1887–1902*, Cambridge Imperial and Post-Colonial Studies, https://doi.org/10.1007/978-3-031-51947-5_5

at least 89 had been shut down between 1889 and 1891.[2] Moreover, the financial failures of 1889 left the Rand with a poor commercial reputation in London and took most Johannesburg brokers out of business.[3]

Operating from its new building in Commissioner Street, the JSE faced the most difficult business environment in its formative years. Local sources of capital from Johannesburg, Kimberley, and Barberton had started the Rand's gold mining industry during the 1886–1888 period, but as the first crisis proved, the large-scale development of mining required greater and more varied sources to finance the operations.[4] Mining finance on the goldfields was either restricted to companies with strong connections to diamond mining in the Cape Colony or inadequate to incur the large fixed costs that were needed for the expansion of the relatively (and absolutely) more capital-intensive deep-level industry, and that urgently needed to be supplemented by financial and human capital from Europe,[5] and, hopefully, North America.[6] Just as in the early days of Johannesburg, Kimberley's diamond industry would serve as a valuable planning and management tool for mining finance on the Rand.[7] The high risk of new mining undertakings would need to be spread among a few influential and highly capitalised enterprises. The 'rationalisation' of this corporate structure came by merging a number of profitable mines together into specific industrial groups and, in the process, bringing a large number of smaller subsidiary mines (up to 16) under single control.[8] The JSE and the Chamber of Mines were ideally positioned to coordinate this commercial transition into the group system through their shared financial, technological, and increasingly political objectives.

---

[2] Katz, Elaine N. "Outcrop and Deep Level Mining in South Africa Before the Anglo-Boer War: Re-examining the Blainey Thesis." *The Economic History Review* 48, no. 2 (1995): 309.

[3] "Financial History of the Year." *Investors Monthly Manual*, 31 December 1890. p. 574.

[4] Kubicek, Robert V. *Economic Imperialism in Theory and Practice: The Case of South African Gold Mining Finance 1886–1914*. 1979. p. 61.

[5] Innes, Duncan. *Anglo: Anglo American and the Rise of Modern South Africa*. 1984. p. 54.

[6] "About Kafir Finance." *New York Times*, 31 May 1896. p. 22.

[7] See: JSEA. *Minutes of an Ordinary Meeting of the Committee*, 15 March 1893.

[8] Innes, Duncan. *Anglo American and the Rise of Modern South Africa*, 1984. p. 54.

The economic, social, and political transformation from outcrop to deep-level operations on the Rand constitutes a central aspect of economic historiography on the motives for the South African War (1899–1902).[9] This chapter traces and situates the development of deep-level mining in the debates on the pivotal role of financial capitalism in Johannesburg's political evolution through the institutional lens of the JSE. The function of this chapter within the greater historical analysis of the JSE's institutional development is to bridge the Exchange's transition from the failures of the first boom to the development of deep-level mining. More importantly for its industrial transition, the chapter investigates Johannesburg's rise of monopoly capitalism and the new social class of 'capitalists,' 'millionaires,' 'magnates,' more commonly known as 'Randlords,'[10] who developed the group system and firmly entrenched themselves in the JSE's organisational and operational structures. The mining groups were not only concerned with the direct management of deep-level mines, but used their local and increasingly international networks to influence share market operations. By combining and coordinating their financial efforts in the form of the group system, the Randlords amalgamated their capital investments to consolidate and expand their dominance of Johannesburg's mines and the international financial system that served them. Although much has been written about the Randlords' international financial networks,[11] very little is

---

[9] Katz, E. N. "Outcrop and Deep Level Mining in South Africa Before the Anglo-Boer War: Re-examining the Blainey Thesis." *Economic History Review* (1995): 304–328.

Richardson, Peter, and Jean-Jacques Van Helten. "The Development of the South African Gold-Mining Industry, 1895–1918." *Economic History Review* (1984): 319–340.

Blainey, G. "Lost Causes of the Jameson Raid." *The Economic History Review* 18, no. (2) (1965): 350–366.

Mendelsohn, R. Blainey and the Jameson Raid: The Debate Renewed. *Journal of Southern African Studies* 6, no. (2) (1980): 157–170.

Kubicek, R. V. "The Randlords in 1895: A Reassessment." *Journal of British Studies* 11, no. (2) (1972): 84–103.

[10] "Campaign of Slander." *The Rhodesia Herald*, 1 November 1906. p. 4.

[11] This is just a small intorduction to a vast body of litarature on a relatively narrow subject. See: Wheatcroft, Geoffrey. *The Randlords*. 1987.

Denoon, Donald. "Capital and Capitalists in the Transvaal in the 1890s and 1900s." *The Historical Journal* 23, no. 1 (1980): 111–132.

Kubicek, Robert V. "The Randlords in 1895: A Reassessment." *The Journal of British Studies* 11, no. 2 (1972): 84–103.

Emden, Paul Herman. *Randlords*. 1935.

known about their direct connections to Johannesburg's capital market. Crucially, this chapter maps the development of their strategic relationships with the JSE, the Chamber of Mines, and the holding companies that the Randlords were servicing. The final section of the chapter investigates the internationalisation of the market for South African mining securities, illustrating how the interest in deep-level stocks spread from Johannesburg to London and continental Europe.

CRISIS AND REORGANISATION

The JSE's first phase of institutional development was marked by increasing exposure to international financial, human, and social capital. When looking at Johannesburg's economic climate in the early 1890s, the relatively small but increasingly international financial industry must be examined within the global context and severity of the Barings Crisis.[12] Along with the causally related Australian banking crisis and the American currency panic of 1893,[13] the global financial climate of the early 1890s threatened the recovery of share trade in Johannesburg.[14] The international crisis was fuelled by Argentina's bond which led to the near collapse of the Barings Bank and the Bank of England's bailout interventions to rescue London's banking sector in November 1890.[15] The immediate capital market reaction in London was a reduction in the amount of securities listed on the LSE and a decrease in their nominal capitalisation by almost half.[16] More significantly for ZAR's mining finance, London investor sentiments towards colonial and foreign stocks took a significant blow after the collapse of several colonial trust schemes that catered to

[12] See: Mitchener, Kris James and Marc D. Weidenmier. "The Baring Crisis and the Great Latin American Meltdown of the 1890s." *Journal of Economic History* 68, no. 2 (2008): 462–500.

[13] See: Carlson, Mark. "Causes of Bank Suspensions in the Panic of 1893." *Explorations in Economic History* 42, no. 1 (2005): 56–80.

[14] "Financial History for the year 1891." *Investors Monthly Manual*, 31 December 1891. p. 616.
"The Financial Outlook." *The Rhodesia Herald*, 19 October 1891. p. 2.

[15] Turner, J. D. *Banking in Crisis: The Rise and Fall of British Banking Stability, 1800 to the Present*. Cambridge University Press. 2014. pp. 152–156.

[16] "The Growth in the Field of Investment." *The Economist*, 5 March 1892. pp. 316–317.

the risk apetites of the late 1880s.[17] The effects of the subsequent credit tightening were felt as far away as Australia, where the sources of financial distress lay in private sector banking rather than government borrowing,[18] leaving many to expect similar problems in the Cape Colony, Natal, and the ZAR. Although some of these initial fears gradually dissipated, Johannesburg's share trade was not liquid enough to withstand the global consequences of the Barings Crisis.[19] According to the 1895 investigation of South African mining finance by Hatch and Chalmers, the crisis led to a significant stagnation of foreign capital investments—at a time when local credit was hardly available.[20] As later confirmed by Kubicek, the financial slump in Johannesburg was indeed intensified by the Barings Crisis due to the acknowledged over-commitments of the Baring Brothers to ZAR mining finance.[21]

The global financial crisis exposed the fact that the JSE's legal mechanisms in place were not strong enough to ensure capital market stability and mitigate share transaction risks. The local stock market was riddled with illicit trading, indicating to the local and foreign investing public that not much had changed since the trough of the slump in 1889. The Johannesburg Estate Company was particularly concerned about numerous complaints from municipal authorities criticising the unresolved trading practices of betting 'Between the Chains.'[22] According to the General Committee, it often remained unclear when brokers were selling out

[17] See: Chambers, David and Rui Esteves. "The First Global Emerging Markets Investor: Foreign & Colonial Investment Trust 1880–1913." *Explorations in Economic History* 52 (2014): 1–21.

[18] Hickson, Charles R., and John D. Turner. "Free Banking Gone Awry: The Australian Banking Crisis of 1893." *Financial History Review* 9, no. 2 (2002): 150.

James, Harold. '"International Capital Movements and the Global Order." In: Neal, Larry, and Jeffrey G. Williamson, eds. *The Cambridge History of Capitalism: Volume 2, The Spread of Capitalism: From 1848 to the Present.* Cambridge University Press. 2014. p. 273.

[19] SBA. GMO 3/2/11, 9 August 1893. p. 616.

[20] Hatch, Frederick and John Alexander Chalmers. *The Gold Mines of the Rand.* 1895. p. 3.

[21] Kubicek, Robert V. *Economic Imperialism in Theory and Practice: The Case of South African Gold Mining Finance 1886–1914.* 1979. pp. 26 and 31.

[22] JSEA. *Minutes of an Ordinary Meeting of the Committee,* 4 July 1893.

or buying in on account of other members, leading to regular break-downs of trade during daily settlements.[23] Despite the mining industry working closely together to facilitate a technological transition to the demands of industrial capitalism, the JSE had done very little to change its trading practices and was openly criticised by the Chamber of Mines in an industry report for 1892:

> The arrangements for the settlement of bargains and differences remain today as crude as when share transactions were first introduced in South Africa. The dangers, difficulties and temptations to which dealers and spec-ulators are exposed are constantly on the increase and, unless immediate steps be taken to introduce improvements into the present system of trans-acting business, a recurrence of the financial scandals of some months ago may be regarded as imminent.[24]

In addition to the JSE's dwindling reputation in share trade, the finan-cial intermediary's future was threatened by declining membership. As late as May 1892, many members were still struggling to pay their subscriptions fees and those in arrears were wiped off the members' list by the dozen each week.[25] Members' lists were regularly updated and posted in the Exchange Hall to warn and publicly humiliate potential offenders. Although the major drop in numbers came between December 1889 and December 1890, when membership decreased from 896 to 467, the regular expulsions were not immediately balanced out by new applications and the arrival of experienced stockbrokers from Kimberley. The establishment of De Beers Consolidated and the amalgamation of Kimberley's diamond mines reduced the number of quoted companies on the Kimberley Stock Exchange to an unprofitable level.[26] In 1888 there were still 60 brokers and 12 dealers working on the Exchange, but by 1893 these figures had dropped to 29 brokers and no dealers.[27] Although

---

[23] JSEA. *Minutes of an Ordinary Meeting of the Committee*, 1 September 1892.

[24] *South African Mining Journal*, 30 July 1892. Quoted in: Rosenthal, Eric. *On 'change Through the Years: A History of Share Dealing in South Africa*. 1968. p. 171.

[25] JSEA. *Minutes of an Ordinary Meeting of the Committee*. 29 March 1892.

[26] Rosenthal, Eric. *On 'change Through the Years: A History of Share Dealing in South Africa*. 1968. p. 73.
Newbury, C. Technology, capital, and consolidation: the performance of De Beers Mining Company Limited, 1880–1889. *Business History Review* 61, no. 1 (1987): 1–42.

[27] Ibid. p. 74.

many unemployed brokers and other financial professionals moved to Cape Town and planned their return to Europe, a significant number of the Kimberley Stock Exchange's members left for Johannesburg. Of the KSE's 56 members at the end of 1890, 22 joined the JSE during the 1891 financial year.[28] This number might have been relatively small, but clearly proved that, just as with the migration from Barberton, most financial professionals believed Johannesburg was the only place in South Africa with the financial infrastructure that could accommodate their trading skills. Confronted by this new mobility of financial professionals, it would still take another two years before the JSE's General Committee installed a special new rule requiring further guarantees for new applicants to encourage the growth of a more 'legitimate' pool of members.[29]

The majority of the JSE's internal disciplinary system and legal resources during the recovery period between 1889 and 1893 were however assigned to settling trade disputes. Legal charges for dispute settlement generated significant revenue for the Exchange, rivalled only by the members' subscription fees.[30] Despite this secure source of income, the legal hearings were not intended to be exploited for profit, but acted as a significant publicity tool to illustrate the JSE's renewed commitment to reforming Johannesburg's financial industry. As a gesture of goodwill, and an expression of confidence in Johannesburg's socioeconomic transformation, the General Committee decided that at least half of the income raised from the legal hearings would be donated to Johannesburg's public hospital and the public library.[31]

Low liquidity in the capital market remained the key constraint in the JSE's recovery efforts.[32] Despite the opening of Pretoria's new *Nationale Bank der Zuid-Afrikaansche Republiek* in April 1891, and the Dutch-owned *Nederlandsche Zuid-Afrikaansche Hypotheek Bank* in August 1888 forcing most ZAR-based banks to lower their interest rates to below 5%, Johannesburg's banks remained reluctant to support a greater flow of

---

[28] Own calculations from JSE Members Roll Books 1889–1890.

[29] Ibid.

[30] JSEA. *Minutes of an Ordinary Meeting of the Committee*, 9 February 1892.

[31] Ibid.

[32] SBA. *Inspection Report of Johannesburg Branch as at 15 October 1892*. The Standard Bank of South Africa Limited, 17 February 1893. p. 72.

liquidity to the JSE.[33] Looking towards more established capital markets in Europe and North America for guidance, the JSE's General Committee attempted to reform the local securities market by introducing new trade and settlement methods that were more compatible with the growing availability of ZAR stocks in international markets. One important move towards reducing liquidity risks and facilitating faster transactions was seen in the establishment of a clearing house.[34] More urgently for the envisioned international expansion of the market for deep-level securities, the introduction of a clearing system was also intended to reduce the JSE's lengthy delivery times on stocks held in other parts of southern Africa and Europe.[35] According to the General Committee, the establishment of a clearing house in Johannesburg would lead to improving the volume and value of stock trade in periods of liquidity constraints.[36] By the early 1870s most financial centres in Western Europe had clearing houses devoted to national and international trade.[37] In London, the LSE's official clearing house was set up in 1880, replacing an earlier private initiative intended to leave members to pay for the balance, rather than complete every transaction.[38] In New York, an official clearing house was established by the New York Stock Exchange in the early months of 1892, but a similar organisation had already been in operation since the late 1860s with the objective of speeding up the transactions of purchases and sales between a growing pool of brokers.[39] The clearing process in Johannesburg was intended to replicate the institutional aspects of the trading systems already implemented in London and New York.[40] The proposition gained significant support throughout the latter half of 1892, only to be challenged for final approval by Friedrich Eckstein, the single

---

[33] SBA. GMO 3/2/1/1, 17 February 1892. p. 43.

[34] JSEA. *Minutes of an Ordinary Meeting of the Committee*, 29 December 1891.

[35] JSEA. Disorderly Conduct in the Exchange. *Minutes of an Ordinary Meeting of the Committee*, 11 October 1892.

[36] JSEA. *Minutes of an Ordinary Meeting of the Committee*, 26 April 1892.

[37] Kindleberger, Charles P. *A financial history of Western Europe*. 2015. pp. 78–79.

[38] Michie, Ranald C. *The London Stock Exchange: A History*. 1999. p. 78.

[39] Noyes, Alexander D. "Stock Exchange Clearing Houses." *Political Science Quarterly* 8, no. 2 (1893): 252–267.

[40] JSEA. *Minutes of an Ordinary Meeting of the Committee*, 29 December 1891.

JSE veto-holding member on the *Quotation Sub-Committee*.[41] Much to the disappointment of the *Quotation Sub-Committee* and the Brokers' Association, after a passed amendment issued by Eckstein, the General Committee voted against a plan to establish an official clearing house for the Exchange.[42] Despite further recommendations and internal assessments, the General Committee dismissed the whole proposal, stating that the JSE still possessed the limited technical operational capacity to implement such a system.[43] Although the establishment of Johannesburg's first clearing house was an administrative failure, the General Committee proved that significant steps were being debated and executed in an attempt to reform the JSE's trading system from within.

The objective of accelerating clearing procedures between buyers and sellers was soon extended to increasing the variety of securities listed on the JSE. Up until the beginning of 1893 only mining stocks were permitted to appear on the Official List.[44] This was seen as Johannesburg's comparative advantage and share trade was based on the growing institutional links between the mining industry and finance. An operational feature of these converging commercial interests was that all companies on the Official List were required to provide monthly statistics on their industrial output.[45] The diversification of financial products on offer at the JSE was also seen as an integral part of reforming the organisation and the growing international market it was serving.[46] The *Quotation Sub-Committee* was again tasked with investigating the possibility of introducing new types of securities to the Exchange, such as trust companies, banks, public utilities providers, and even sovereign debt.[47] The diversification of JSE stocks beyond the mining sector was seen as a new commitment to facilitating wider industrial participation in Johannesburg's capital market but, more importantly, was an opportunity to open the JSE to more risk-averse investors who were discouraged by the high volatility of the international mining market. It was on 9 May 1893

---

[41] JSEA. *Minutes of an Ordinary Meeting of the Committee*, 28 March 1893.

[42] Ibid. 25 April 1893.

[43] Ibid. 1 August 1893.

[44] Ibid. 17 May 1892.

[45] Ibid. 15 May 1894.

[46] Ibid. 5 January 1892.

[47] Ibid.

that the quotation of non-mining stocks was officially permitted with the National Bank of the ZAR being the first non-gold stock on the Official List.[48] The second notable quotation was the colonially underwritten British South Africa Company in September 1893.[49]

A far more urgent operational challenge for the JSE's General Committee was the continued access to the premises that were leased from the Johannesburg Estate Company. The JSE was plagued by a series of new disagreements with the landlords since moving into the new Exchange building in September 1890. Although the General Committee was able to navigate reoccurring disputes over the rights of the Estate Directors to automatically join the JSE as members, the continued right of the Estate to use the Exchange for non-commercial activities,[50] constant restrictions on the Dealers and Brokers Association[51] and the rescheduling of personal trading debts by the Barnato brothers,[52] meant that the JSE had very little say on how much it paid to rent the Exchange Hall, the adjacent offices and the bar. Barnato's Estate Company used the financial crisis to increase its power over the Exchange. A series of negotiations on new contractual agreements with the Estate Company that commenced in late 1893 threatened the sole existence of the JSE as a financial organisation.[53] The Brokers' Association felt that the Estate's persistent attempts to regulate the Exchange's constitution were a threat to the unity of all JSE committees and even went as far as investigating the possibility of renting alternative premises to establish a new home for the Exchange.[54]

The internal organisational crisis escalated further when the Estate demanded a 25% increase in the JSE's rent from £ 2 000 to £ 2 500 per year, citing the need to renovate and expand the new Exchange building as a reason for the contractual adjustment.[55] The new rental contract, starting in June 1893, created a major division between the General

[48] Ibid. 2 May 1893.
[49] Ibid. 5 September 1893.
[50] Ibid. 22 April 1890.
[51] Ibid. 13 March 1893.
[52] Ibid. 18 July 1893.
[53] Ibid. 15 December 1893.
[54] Ibid. 20 February 1894.
[55] Ibid. 4 July 1893.

Committee, the Brokers' Association, and the Estate Company. Although the Brokers' Association seized the opportunity to a gain a permanent seat on the General Committee and more direct power to influence the JSE's constitution, the disputes nearly led to the liquidation of the JSE as a corporate body.[56] The breakdown in negotiations with the Estate after the JSE's counter offer of £ 2 250 was rejected led to the walkout of most JSE members and the official resignation of the General Committee, leaving the Exchange without any official representation.[57] The constitution had no emergency provisions for such a scenario, forcing the JSE to employ a team of Johannesburg's top lawyers to guide the Exchange through the leadership crisis with its own landlord.[58]

The Estate eventually allowed the JSE to continue to use the Exchange Hall until the new committee was officially appointed. Although Henry Salomon was re-elected as chairman, the new committee lacked bargaining power against Barnato and was forced to succumb to the Estates contractual demands, signing the new lease with the inflated price of £ 2 500. The crisis reaffirmed the dominance of the Estate and the Barnato brothers during a period of industrial and commercial reorganisation in Johannesburg. The JSE was still dependent on the Estate and lacked the banking sector's support to establish itself at a new location. More significantly for the JSE's operational recovery, with limited administrative room for significant regulatory improvements and constant internal tension provided by the Estate Company, the initiative to reignite Johannesburg's capital market would need to be closely coordinated with the new deep-level mining houses.

The Making of the Group System

The post-1889 financial environment and the growing mining industry commitment to deep-level operations encouraged the creation of a new corporate system. Although outcrop mines remained in operation and continued to produce the great majority of the Rand's gold until 1895, from 1890 they represented a declining share of output and dividend

---

[56] Ibid. 13 March 1894.

[57] Ibid. 19 June 1894.

[58] Ibid.

payments as deep-level mines increased their production capacity.[59] The most common business strategy was for smaller outcrop mines to be integrated into the portfolios of large holding companies, allowing for a transfer of investment risk to the most profitable mining companies within the group. This new form of corporate organisation required the large mining groups and mining houses to raise substantial sums of financial capital that was needed to distribute the combined risk between the new deep-level and old outcrop operations and, in the short run, sustain business activities through the maturation period necessary to bring a the newmine into operation.[60] Using the groups to pool technological and administrative resources helped the companies to achieve rapid economies of scale and greater technological breakthroughs.[61] Most importantly for company organisation, the high amount of fixed capital needed reduced the participation of individual speculators and land claim syndicates operating on the JSE.[62]

The first notable mining financier and unintended initiator of the group system was Cape Colony-born Joseph Benjamin Robinson. After serving as mayor of Kimberley in 1880 and the representative of Griqualand West in the Cape Parliament for four years, Robinson was encouraged by Rhodes' German business partner, Otto Beit, to begin a mining partnership on the Rand in late 1887.[63] Although he did not immediately join the JSE as a member, Robinson was actively involved in the JSE's first share listings, working from his office inside Beit's building, conveniently located across the street from the original JSE hall on Commissioner

[59] Blainey, G. "Lost Causes of the Jameson Raid." *The Economic History Review* 18, no. 2 (1965): 351.

[60] Feinstein, Charles Hilliard. *An Economic History of South Africa: Conquest, Discrimination, and Development.* 2005. p. 103.
Katz, Elaine N. "Outcrop and Deep Level Mining in South Africa Before the Anglo-Boer War: Re-examining the Blainey Thesis." *The Economic History Review* 48, no. 2 (1995): 304–308.

[61] Ibid.

[62] Richardson, Peter and Jean Jacques van Helten. "The Development of the South African Gold-Mining Industry, 1895–1918." *The Economic History Review* 37, no. 3 (1984): 335.

[63] Cartwright, Alan Patrick. *The Corner House: The Early History of Johannesburg.* 1965. p. 2.

Street.[64] Robinson signalled confidence in early Johannesburg investments and exploited personal Kimberley experience to avoid possible feuds with old financial rivals. Suspicious of all the new mining associations, including the Digger's Committee and the Chamber of Mines, Robinson focused on establishing closer business and political links to Kruger's administration in Pretoria. With his intimate knowledge of the Afrikaner settler society and the Dutch language, Robinson was tasked with identifying the best mining land for the Kimberley firm of French diamond dealer Jules Porges & Co. Using his Pretoria government contacts and a £ 25 000 loan from Beit, Robinson purchased a number of properties on the farms of Turffontein and Langlaagte which proved to have some of the best accessible outcrop diggings on the Rand.[65] Although extremely distrustful, after much pressure from Beit and his Johannesburg representatives, Hermann Eckstein and James Taylor, he sold off his Robinson Land Syndicate for £ 250 000 in 1889.[66]

Robinson's sale paved the way to the establishment of the famed Corner House and initiated the corporate amalgamation of the group system. Largely organised and financed by Otto Beit's brother operating out of London, Alfred Beit, Hermann Eckstein was given full support to begin buying out undercapitalised (or already liquidated) casualties of the first financial crisis. Eckstein spent the early months of 1889 settling his affairs in Kimberley, but by the end of August 1889 was able to report to Beit and Porges the purchase of six stands on Commissioner Street; these became the site of the firm's Johannesburg office.[67] By locating the headquarters on Commissioner Street, the Eckstein partnership would be placed directly on the corner between the Main Reef's goldfields and the JSE, coincidentally perfectly suited to the English translation of his Germanic surname, corner stone.[68] The firm of H. Eckstein & Co. was established as a partnership under the control of Jules Porges & Co. which

---

[64] Ibid. pp. 2–3.

[65] Kubicek, Robert V. *Economic Imperialism in Theory and Practice: The Case of South African Gold Mining Finance 1886–1914.* 1979. pp. 126–127.

[66] Wheatcroft, Geoffrey. *The Randlords.* 1987. p. 113.

[67] BWA. Fraser, Maryna. *Inventory of the Archives of H. Eckstein & Co. 1887–1910.* Barlow Rand Limited. 1975. p. 1.

[68] Cartwright, Alan Patrick. *The Corner House: the early history of Johannesburg.* 1965. p. 71.

was reconstituted as Wernher, Beit & Co. when Porges retired from business in South Africa in 1889 and moved back to Paris.[69] With Alfred Beit managing most of the partnership's mines from London, the group took advantage of Johannesburg's need for finance and the process of company amalgamation by drawing on their valuable City of London connections and the Rothschilds' close association with the bullion market.[70]

The Corner House (Fig. 5.1) was well positioned to weather Johannesburg's financial storm and enjoyed the first-mover advantage in the JSE's deep-level initiatives. All of the directors of the mining group became members of the JSE and occupied some of the most strategic positions within the Chamber of Mines.[71] Beit and Porges also invited James Taylor, South Africa's most experienced stock broker, to join Hermann Eckstein at the new offices directly opposite the Exchange building.[72] With Julius Wernher, James Taylor, and Hermann Eckstein all on the JSE's General Committee by the end of 1889, the Corner House used its expanding capital and engineering networks in southern African and Europe to invest in more mining ground and began applying its corporate strategy to overcome Johannesburg's subdued financial reputation.[73] Not only was further European capital drawn in through the firm's London, Paris, and Berlin representatives, but Alfred Beit was able to encourage Rhodes to return to Johannesburg's mining industry in 1892 as a means of further strengthening the political links with British colonial and metropolitan capital[74] (Fig. 5.1).

---

[69] Ibid. p. 3.

[70] Cain, Peter J. and Anthony G. Hopkins. *British Imperialism: 1688–2000.* 2002. pp. 323–324.
See also: Turrell, Robert Vicat, and Jean-Jacques Van Helten. "The Rothschilds, the Exploration Company and Mining Finance." *Business History* 28, no. 2 (1986): 181–205.

[71] Lang, John. *Bullion Johannesburg: Men, Mines, and the Challenge of Conflict.* 1986. pp. 41–44.

[72] Fraser, Maryna. *Inventory of the Archives of H. Eckstein & Co. 1887–1910.* 1975. p. 1.

[73] Kubicek, Robert. *Mining: Patterns of Dependence and Development 1870–1930.* In: Konczacki, Zbigniew, Parpart, Jane and Shaw Timothy, eds. *Studies in the Economic History of South Africa: Volume II: South Africa, Lesotho and Swaziland.* 1991. p. 69.

[74] Webb, Arthur. "Blainey and Early Witwatersrand Profitability Some Thoughts on Financial Management and Capital Constraints Facing the Gold Mining Industry 1886–1894." *South African Journal of Economic History* 12, no. 1–2 (1997): 141.

Fig. 5.1 The First Corner House in Johannesburg in 1890 (*Source* Barlow *Rand* Archives Photographic Collection) (Photo in public domain-Wikimedia Commons)

Between 1890 and 1892, Wernher, Beit, and Co. Restructured its mining portfolios to distribute profits generated by outcrop mines to operating subsidies for the new deep-level projects.[75] The Corner House floated the Bantjes Gold Mining Company and theLanglaagte Estate in mid-1889, and the Randfontein Estates Gold Mining Limited at the peak of Johannesburg's depression in April 1890.[76] Following the Corner House's lead, new holding groups such as Rhodes' Gold Fields and even the Barnato Brothers' smaller Barnato Group used the corporate restructuring period between 1889 and 1892 to extend their interests on the JSE.[77] Through the group system's control over separate mining companies, and the close organisational collaboration within the JSE, local

[75] Van Onselen, Charles. *Studies in the Social and Economic History of the Witwatersrand 1886–1914. New Babylon.* 1982. p. 11.

[76] See: Goldman, Charles Sydney. *The Financial, Statistical, and General History of the Gold & Other Companies of Witwatersrand, South Africa.* 1892. pp. 16, 66 and 106.
See also: JSEA. *Minutes of an Ordinary Meeting of the Committee,* 5 August 1890.

[77] See: The Search for Clients and Capital. In: Kubicek, Robert V., ed. *Economic Imperialism in Theory and Practice: The Case of South African Gold Mining Finance 1886–1914.* 1979. pp. 61–68.

investor confidence and resurgent foreign interest promoted a new wave of company flotations and listings by the end of 1892 (Fig. 5.2).

The first major commercial undertaking of the deep-level mining transition was achieved with the floating of Rand Mines Ltd.[78] The establishment of the company was a carefully orchestrated process intended to diversify capital portfolios across Johannesburg and Europe. Furthermore, the strategy of first floating the company in London and then Johannesburg was Corner House's pre-emptive move to support the management's eventual relocation to Britain. It was Hermann Eckstein who drafted the final trust deed stating that the directors of the new company would be Julius Wernher, Hermann Eckstein, Lionel Phillips, Harry Mosenthal, Sigismund Neumann, and Charles Rudd.[79] Additionally, Eckstein, Wernher, and Neumann would chair the London

Companies listed on JSE Official List

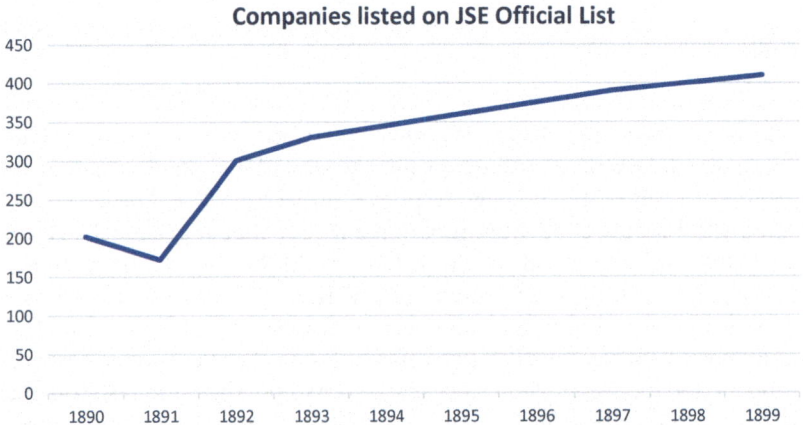

Fig. 5.2 Companies listed on JSE official list, 1890–1899 (*Source* Adapted from Fig. 4.5 Average number of JSE-listed shares, 1890–1902 in Strydom, N. T. *Stock exchange legitimacy: The case of the Johannesburg Stock Exchange, 1887–1945.* University of Johannesburg [South Africa]. 2021. p. 10 and "The Stock Exchange." *The Star.* 1887–1899)

[78] See: Rand Mines Ltd. In: Cartwright, Alan Patrick, ed. *The Corner House: The Early History of Johannesburg.* 1965. pp. 118–133.

[79] Cartwright, Alan Patrick. *The Corner House: The Early History of Johannesburg.* 1965. p. 138.

committee, which was intended to become the Corner House's headquarters as early as 1892. With all the directors of Rand Mines established members of the JSE and Lionel Phillips as the new chairman of the Chamber of Mines, the new deep-level initiative enjoyed the support of the most influential mining financiers in Johannesburg.

The development of Rand Mines demonstrated how deep-level companies intended to use the JSE as a strategic capital market that was located just a few kilometres from the actual gold mines. Until the floating of Rand Mines, the Corner House had not been directly concerned with mining operations and each mine was established as a separate joint-stock company with its own directors and managers.[80] Contrary to the group's previous promotions, which focused mainly on the potential gains of the share trade, Rand Mines was started as an ambitious mining site with two shafts over 800 feet deep being drilled before the end of the first full year of operations in 1893.[81] Rand Mines was the most valuable of the deep-level mining projects of the early 1890s and consistently paid high dividends, with a dividend of 100% on the profits declared in 1898.[82]

Beyond Johannesburg and its financial intermediaries, Rand Mines' London office was strategically positioned to foster the link between deep-level mining and European capital.[83] Alfred Beit had been converted to the idea of Johannesburg's deep-level mining promoted by the Corner House's American engineers,[84] Joseph Curtis, Henry Perkins, Hennen Jennings, and Hamilton Smith.[85] Although the Rand Mines Ltd. was first registered in the ZAR on 22 February 1893, with a nominal capital of £400 000 in £1 shares,[86] Corner House's management insisted that

[80] Wheatcroft, Geoffrey. *The Randlords*. 1987. pp. 132–133.

[81] Hatch, Frederick and John Alexander Chalmers. *The Gold Mines of the Rand*. 1895. p. 98.

[82] "Kaffir Mining Results." *The Financial Times*, 11 January 1899. p. 6.

[83] Turrell, Robert Vicat, and Jean-Jacques Van Helten. "The Rothschilds, the Exploration Company and Mining Finance." *Business History* 28, no. 2 (1986): 188.

[84] See: Katz, Elaine. "The role of American mining technology and American mining engineers in the Witwatersrand gold mining industry 1890–1910.' *South African Journal of Economic History* 20. 2 (2005). pp. 48–82.

[85] Meredith, Martin. *Diamonds, Gold, and War: The British, the Boers, and the Making of South Africa*. 2008. p. 302.

[86] Fraser, Maryna. "International Archives in South Africa." *Business and Economic History* (1987): 165.

the first public allotment was to be distributed on the LSE. More significantly for strengthening the European capital connection, in addition to the original vendor shares, Rand Mines issued another 100 000 shares to strategic partners in London and Paris.[87] Rudolf Kahn, an influential mining market promoter in Paris, received 3000 shares and Ernst Cassel, a German-born London banker with close ties to the Rothschilds, received 6 000. A further 8 400 shares went to members of the Kimberley Diamond Syndicate of H. Hinrichsen, R. Hinrichsen, Harry Mosenthal, and Sir. Horace Farquar. Nathaniel Rothschild was personally presented with 27 000.[88] An engineering syndicate, represented by E.G. de Crano, Hamilton Smith, H. C. Perkins, and Hennen Jennings was given a total of 15 000 shares. The largest allotment to investors outside the Corner House was 30 000 shares. These were given to Rhodes' Gold Fields. This strategy illustrated how the Corner House was determined to gain international allies in what was still an unpredictable financial undertaking, as the trading climate on the JSE would prove.[89]

According to Frankel's investigation into the history of capital accumulation and financial capitalism in colonial Africa, the Rand's most important corporate feature was the way the mining industry had dealt with the problems of financial control and technical organisation.[90] The Corner House's initial competitive advantage over its Johannesburg rivals lay in its unrivalled access to financial and geological information. The Corner House had its own 'Intelligence Department' before any other corporate entity in Johannesburg thought this would be necessary.[91] Eckstein's leading position in the Chamber of Mines gave him unprecedented access to mining intelligence, keeping him well ahead of all engineering and legal

---

[87] Kubicek, Robert V. *Economic Imperialism in Theory and Practice: The Case of South African Gold Mining Finance 1886–1914.* 1979. pp. 64–65.
    See also: Rand Mines Ltd. In: Cartwright, Alan Patrick. *The Corner House: The Early History of Johannesburg.* 1965. pp. 118–33.

[88] See: Cooper, John. *The Unexpected Story of Nathaniel Rothschild.* London: Bloomsbury Publishing. 2015. pp. 160–162.

[89] Wheatcroft, Geoffrey. *The Randlords.* 1987. p. 134.

[90] Frankel, Sally Herbert. *Capital Investment in Africa: Its Course and Its Effects.* 1938. p. 81.

[91] Cartwright, Alan Patrick. *The Corner House: The Early History of Johannesburg.* 1965. p. 101.

developments, even allowing him to withhold strategic industrial information and directly influence the Chamber's publication practices. With the ZAR Telegraph Office and *The Star* newspaper in close proximity on Commissioner Street, the Corner House was strategically positioned to collect and distribute critical mining intelligence to its financial partners in Johannesburg and Europe.

The Corner House's close affiliation with the Rothschild banking family promoted a technocratic approach to the international financing and management of deep-level mines.[92] The London branch of the Rothschilds had an extensive global information network at disposal,[93] including Johannesburg's Carl and Emmanuel Rothschild, two local agents on the floor of the JSE.[94] The Rothschilds demanded expert analysis on all mining projects before considering any financial undertakings, preferring their own sources of information to the reports of the Chamber of Mines and Johannesburg's newspapers.[95] A whole host of international, but mostly American, engineers was sent by the Rothschilds to work with the Corner House in Johannesburg, leaving a significant American technological influence on the city's mining practices and industrial objectives.[96] The Rothschild's greatest engineering partnership for the Corner House was with the two Californians,[97] Hamilton Smith and Edmund de Crano, who also joined the JSE as members immediately after

---

[92] See: Turrell, Robert Vicat and Jean Jacques Van Helten. "The Rothschilds, the Exploration Company and Mining Finance." *Business History* 28, no. 2 (1986). pp. 181–205.

[93] See: Liedtke, Rainer. "Modern Communication: The Information Network of N.M. Rothschild and Sons in Nineteenth-Century Europe." In: Feldman, Gerald D. and Peter Hertner, eds. *Finance and Modernization.* London: Ashgate. 2008. pp. 155–161.

[94] JSEA. *Members Roll Books 1889–1891.*

[95] Teisch, Jessica B. *Engineering Nature: Water, Development, and the Global Spread of American Environmental Expertise.* 2011. pp. 99–102.

[96] Cartwright, Alan Patrick. *The Corner House: The Early History of Johannesburg.* 1965. pp. 97–98.
See also: Katz, Elaine. "The Role of American Mining Technology and American Mining Engineers in the Witwatersrand Gold Mining Industry 1890–1910." *South African Journal of Economic History* 20, no. 2 (2005): 48–82.

[97] See: Teisch, Jessica. "'Home is Not So Very Far Away': Californian Engineers in South Africa, 1868–1915." *Australian Economic History Review* 45, no. 2 (2005): 139–160.

their arrival in Johannesburg in 1889. In addition to their technical expertise and more importantly for the Chamber's increasing preoccupation
with labour politics, American engineers exerted a powerful ideological
influence over the racialised transformation of the Rand's industrial relations, viewing the racial segregation of labour in southern Africa through
their own experiences in Arizona, California, and Colorado.[98]

CONVERGENCE OF INTERESTS:
THE RANDLORDS AT THE JSE

The active participation and partnerships of foreign financiers in the
commercial expansion of Johannesburg's goldfields has long been a topic
of investigation and debate for economic historians of South Africa.
Although much has been written about the Randlords' connections to
British imperialism in southern Africa,[99] very little is known about their
interaction with the JSE, a central financial intermediary of their engagement with the ZAR's mining economy. The London press viewed the
Randlords as two dozen powerful and rich financiers who had come to
South Africa and mastered their financial trade in Kimberley in the 1870s
and 1880s before moving to the Rand after 1886.[100] Although the Randlords infiltrated London's financial society of the late Victorian period,
due to Johannesburg's absence of a large community of British loyal-
ists, and the fact that the ZAR's mining frontier was largely removed
from Britain's commercial and social conventions, they were not considered 'gentlemanly capitalists' who directly influenced imperial politics but
rather frontier magnates who remained dependant on favourable imperial
and republican treatment.[101] Indeed, it was only after the South African

---

[98] Tuffnell, Stephen. "Engineering Inter-imperialism: American Miners and the Transformation of Global Mining, 1871–1910." *Journal of Global History* 10, no. 1 (2015):
55.

[99] See, for example: Wheatcroft, Geoffrey. *The Randlords*. 1987.

Denoon, Donald. "Capital and Capitalists in the Transvaal in the 1890s and 1900s."
The Historical Journal 23, no. 1 (1980): 111–132.

Kubicek, Robert V. "The Randlords in 1895: A Reassessment." *The Journal of British
Studies* 11, no. 2 (1972): 84–103.

Emden, Paul Herman. *Randlords*. 1935.

[100] Wheatcroft, Geoffrey. *The Randlords*. 1987. p. 7.

[101] Cain, Peter J. and Anthony G. Hopkins. *British Imperialism: 1688–2000*. 2002.
p. 322.

War, when many of Johannesburg's Randlords moved the majority of their financial operations to London, that they gained greater acceptance and imperial approval in the higher circles of Edwardian society with the help of extensive philanthropic campaigns.[102]

As highlighted by Kubicek, despite many economic studies on the financial portfolios of the more prominent mining groups, larger questions surrounding the corporate organisation strategies of the Randlords, how they developed claim holdings, and how they accumulated and distributed capital, have yet to be answered in full.[103] Despite the methodological challenges in quantifying and qualifying the Randlords' international capital accumulation,[104] the JSE's internal records provide original insights and crucial evidence that connects the group system's corporate organisation to Johannesburg's capital market and its international networks. The industrial transition to deep-level operations operationalised the group system's relationship with the JSE, where ten main mining houses exercised financial control over several subsidiary mines, managing the extensive share portfolios by the same boards of directors.[105] Using this system of mixed portfolios to diversify between gold producing and dividend paying companies, the Rand's financial houses supplied their contracted mines with all the financial, technical, managerial, and administrative services needed for company

---

[102] See: Stevenson, Michael. *Old Masters and Aspirations: The Randlords, Art and South Africa*. Unpublished Dissertation. University of Cape Town. 1997.

[103] Kubicek, Robert V. *Economic Imperialism in Theory and Practice: The Case of South African Gold Mining Finance 1886–1914*. 1979. pp. 17–18.

The most successful academic response to Kubicek's call for investigations into the capital accumulation of the Randlords has been that of Jean-Jacques van Helten.

Van Helten, Jean Jacques. "Mining and Imperialism." *Journal of Southern African Studies* 6, no. 2 (1980): 230–235.

Van-Helten, Jean Jacques. *British and European Economic Investment in the Transvaal: With Specific Reference to the Witwatersrand Gold Fields and Disctricts, 1886–1910*. Unpublished dissertation at the University of London. Institute of Commonwealth Studies. 1981.

[104] See: Rönnbäck, Klas, and Oskar Broberg. *Capital and Colonialism: The Return on British Investments in Africa 1869–1969*. Springer. 2019. pp. 70–74.

[105] Giliomee, Hermann Buhr and Bernard Mbenga. *New History of South Africa*. 2007. pp. 200–201.

flotations in Johannesburg,London and Paris.[106] With regard to their modus operandi, many of the group system's subsidiary mining companies were never intended to be gold producing, but rather their financial objective was to raise capital through stock offerings and, in most cases, to sell the majority of a mine's shares once stock prices had risen.[107] It therefore becomes imperative to identify that whatever the profit-maximising strategy, it was the stock exchange and not the gold reef that formed the Randlords' main focus and organisation of financial operations in Johannesburg in the early 1890s.

The ten largest capitalised mining groups of the early 1890s all owed their origin as much to the first financial crisis associated with the decline of Johannesburg's mining market in 1889 as to the increasing capital requirements of deep-level mining.[108] The Corner House, Rhodes' Gold Fields, the Barnato Group, Robinson Mines, and Farrar Investments were all closely linked to the JSE's organisational evolution and management structures from its earliest days. The groups' directors were at the forefront of shaping the JSE's early rules and regulations, using the JSE to foster their industrial and political needs with the active support of the Chamber of Mines (See Table 5.1). The other significant five mining groups that made up the 'Big Ten,' were George Albu of General Mining, A. Goerz and Company, S. Neumann and Company, the Lewis and Marks partnership, and the Abe Baily investment portfolio.[109] By the mid-1890s, not only did the 'Big Ten' dominate Johannesburg's market for mining securities, but more importantly, their directorship constituted the leadership of the JSE's General Committee and various sub-committees.

The impact of the deep-level transformation within corporate organisation in Johannesburg's young capitalist society was pronounced in that it united company directors and major shareholders underneath the same

[106] Katzenellenbogen, Simon E. "The Miner's Frontier, Transport and General Economic Development." In: Duignan, Peter, and Lewis H. Gann, eds. *Colonialism in Africa 1870–1960*. 1975. p. 363.

[107] Graham, Wayne. *The Randlord's Bubble 1894–6: South African Goldmines and Stock Market Manipulation*. Discussion Papers in Economic and Social History. Paper 10. University of Oxford. 1996. p. 7.

[108] Richardson, Peter and Jean-Jacques Van Helten. "The Gold Mining Industry in the Transvaal 1886–99." 1980. p. 28.

[109] Kubicek, R. *Economic Imperialism in Theory and Practice: The Case of South African Gold Mining Finance 1886–1914*. 1979. p. 141.

Table 5.1 'Big Ten' mining groups at the JSE, 1890–1895

'Big Ten'	Highest ranking JSE representative
Wernher, Beit and the Eckstein Group	Friedrich Eckstein
Gold Fields	Francis Dormer
Barnato Group	Barney Barnato
Robinson Mines	Joseph Robinson
Farrar Deep-Level Investments	George Farrar
George Albu and General Mining	George Albu
Adolf Goerz and Company	Adolf Goerz
Sigismund Neumann and Company	Sigismund Neumann
Lewis and Marks Partnership	Samuel Marks
Abe Bailey and Company	Abe Bailey

Source JSEA. Members Roll Books 1895–1896; JSEA. Minutes of an Ordinary Meeting, 26 April 1893; JSEA. Minutes of an Ordinary Meeting, 24 April 1894

roof. By 1892, the Exchange was not only the financial organisation at the centre of Johannesburg's industrial transformation but, more importantly, an increasingly politicised organisation dictating the corporate identity of South Africa's gold industry. With most of their early outcrop competitors out of business or amalgamated into the group system's portfolios, the new corporate model would reshape not only the political evolution of the JSE, but also financial structures of South African gold mining in general.

The corporate and bureaucratic connections between the Randlords and the JSE were leveraged where company listing requirements were made, submitted, and approved. Floating a company in Johannesburg was a relatively simple administrative procedure made even more convenient by the fact that most members on the General Committee of the JSE were affiliated with the Corner House or other influential deep-level groups. As already illustrated with the case of Rand Mines Ltd., Hermann Eckstein's brother, Friedrich was a key member on the Exchange's General Committee and simultaneously the Director of the Johannesburg Estates Company.[110] The sub-committee for the *Quotation and Erasure of Companies,* that was established on 26 April 1892, was the proof of how the group system's Randlords had entrenched themselves inside the

[110] JSEA. *Minutes of an Ordinary Meeting,* 26 April 1892.

JSE's organisational structure.[111] Along with Friedrich Eckstein, W.H. Adler, J. Berlein, W. John Carr, C. Hanau, and G. Imroth were Johannesburg's greatest proponents of the deep-level transition, each acting on the boards of multiple JSE-listed companies.

The most important quantitative investigations into the capital formation and profitability of the Rand's deep-level transition were conducted by Rönnbäck and Broberg (2019), and Sally Herbert Frankel (1967) using varied data sources for mining companies listed in Johannesburg and London.[112] However, despite making a number of qualitative observations about the industry's corporate structures in its formative years, these studies focused on the mines' return on investments and profitability and did not explicitly intend to map the group system's corporate organisation in Johannesburg. According to Hobson, 'The names of the chief directors of the leading companies—Wernher, Beit, Eckstein, Rhodes, Rudd, Neumann, Rothschild, Albu, Goetz, Rouliot, Farrar, Barnato, Robinson—fairly indicates the distinctively international character of this financial power, as well as the closely-concentrated form which it has taken.'[113] Given that the data studied by Frankel inspired a whole generation of Marxist writings on the origins of financial capitalism in South Africa, its contribution to the outbreak of the South African War and the development of apartheid, using the same raw data source as Frankel[114]— a sample of all JSE-listed companies listed before the end of 1892, with nominal capital of at least £50 000—one can qualify and quantify the overwhelming participation of JSE members in the issue and directorships of the most capitalised public companies listed in the ZAR. The sample of the top 100 best-capitalised companies (out of a total of 150 companies on the JSE's Official List) concludes that 84% of the listed companies were chaired by JSE members. At an aggregate measure of all members of the boards of directors, 75% were members of the JSE. Even if the origin and quantity of capital invested in South African mines remain

---

[111] Ibid.

[112] Rönnbäck, Klas, and Oskar Broberg. *Capital and Colonialism: The Return on British Investments in Africa 1869–1969*. Springer. 2019.

Frankel, Sally Herbert. *Investment and the Return to Equity Capital in the South African Gold Mining Industry, 1887–1965: An International Comparison*. 1967.

[113] Hobson, John Atkinson. *Capitalism and Imperialism in South Africa*. 1900. p. 7.

[114] See: Goldman, Charles Sydney. *The Financial, Statistical, and General History of the Gold & Other Companies of Witwatersrand, South Africa*. 1892.

highly debatable, the highly representative sample brings to light the direct links between JSE members who were behind floating, managing, and marketing Johannesburg's most capitalized companies.

These findings confirm the importance of the JSE as an organisation serving the financial needs and operational demands of its members and, more significantly, the growing group system. As further outlined by Hobson in his interpretation of the group system's corporate organisation, even when a company's independent structure was preserved, the cross-ownership and distribution of financial capital by members of other companies in a particular holding group reduced the real economic independence.[115] The relationship between JSE members, their companies and the young gold industry is even more pronounced when considering that only three of the companies in the sample were not directly linked to gold mining. Although *Johannesburg City and Suburban Tramway*, *Johannesburg Waterworks and Exploration* and *Johannesburg Gas* were all public utilities companies, their JSE-dominated boards of directors also show a wider commitment to early industrialisation in Johannesburg through the group system.

Towards the Rand's Financial Internationalisation

Apart from the progress made in the gold industry's output and production efficiency during the period 1892–1893, the galvanisation of leading deep-level companies under the group system restructured the capital base of the industry in Johannesburg and Europe.[116] The most significant financial advantage of the group system was the improved access to European capital markets in London, Paris, and Berlin and, even more so, to large European banking houses, such as the Rothschilds, *Paribas*, and even the Ottoman Bank.[117] Even in the early period of South Africa's diamond industry, the financial successes of the De Beers, Kimberley Central, and the French Diamond Mining Company would have been impossible without the active participation of major European banks and

---

[115] Hobson, John Atkinson. *Capitalism and Imperialism in South Africa*. 1900. p. 7.

[116] "Long Expected Turn in the Market." *The Star*, 13 February 1892.

[117] Richardson, Peter and Jean-Jacques Van Helten. "The Gold Mining Industry in the Transvaal 1886–99." 1980. p. 28.

financiers in promoting their development.[118] The group system's international appeal lay in its growing London presence. Despite a general slump in the prices of most shares on the LSE's mining market between 1890 and 1893, the South African deep-level momentum was an exception to the rule.[119] Even if most London investors were aware of market manipulations by London-based representatives of South African mining groups, a gradual recovery of British banks facilitated new opportunities for international credit and stock market capitalisation.[120]

The London market for South African mining shares was however not as uniform as it appeared to many foreign financial commentators and came with numerous legal constraints, making the growing community of brokers and jobbers specialised in South African shares increasingly cunning in their conduct with the investing public.[121] Even in the mid-1890s, the great majority of all South African stocks in London were not traded on the LSE's official market.[122] The South African mining market gradually migrated from Hatton Garden to Throgmorton Street, displacing the American railway market to Broad Street.[123] There were more than 150 different South African securities traded on the unofficial market for the period 1891–94 (See Fig. 5.3), leaving many LSE brokers to believe that the Exchange Committee was working against its members to keep the South African mining market out of the Main House.[124]

According to Kynaston, the South African mining market in London transformed the cultural landscape of share trade on the LSE, with a sizable influx of American, German, and even South African-born jobbers unfamiliar with London finance's 'gentlemanly approach' using the experience on the curb market as a career development path to fixed

[118] Innes, Duncan. *Anglo: Anglo American and the Rise of Modern South Africa.* 1984. p. 71.

[119] "Financial History of the Year." *Investors Monthly Manual*, 31 December 1892. p. 621.

[120] Ibid.

[121] "Financial History of the Year." *Investors Monthly Manual*, 31 December 1892. p. 621.

[122] "The South African Boom." *The Economist*, 1 December. 1894. p. 1470.

[123] "Monstrous Growth of this Peculiar Market in Ten Years." *New York Times*, 31 May 1896. p. 22.
See also: "The Money Market." *The Times*, 24 April 1895. p. 4.

[124] Kynaston, David. *City of London: The History.* 2011. pp. 162–163.

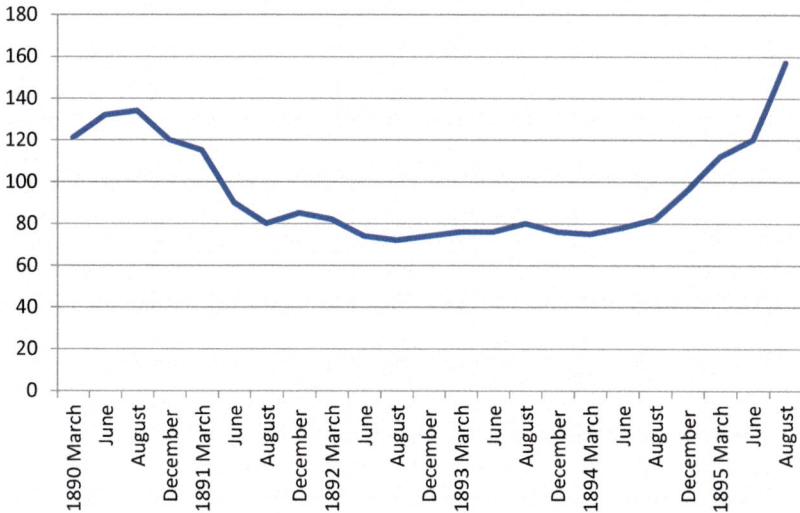

Fig. 5.3   No. of South African companies on London's unofficial market, 1890–1895 (*Source* 'Mining Market.' *The Financial Times.* 1890–1895)

positions with the City's best brokerage houses.[125] The high volume of complicated international settlements associated with the stream of South African stocks directly from Johannesburg put the LSE's General Committee under significant pressure to speed up transaction processing. Due to the increasingly international scope of orders on LSE-listed South African stocks, transactions needed to be double-checked and the identity of the foreign buyers and sellers confirmed before the accounts were officially cleared.[126] Furthermore, it was never clear if the shares traded on the floor of the LSE were smuggled inside from the unregulated curb market, forcing the clearing house to verify the origin of each share in mixed portfolios of deep-level companies.[127]

[125] Kynaston, David Thomas Anthony. *The London Stock Exchange, 1870–1914: An Institutional History.* Unpublished Dissertation. London School of Economics and Political Science (University of London). 1983. pp. 201–202.

[126] Ibid.

[127] "About Kafir Finance: Monstrous Growth of this Peculiar Market in Ten Years." *New York Times,* 31 May 1896. p. 22.

See also: Michie, Ranald C. *The London Stock Exchange: A History.* 1999. p. 87.

The LSE General Committee's reluctance allow significant numbers of South African shares onto the Official List was further justified by the ZAR's corporate law.[128] Stocks registered in the ZAR were not recognised under the Colonial Company Act of 1883, making trading disputes on the legality of South African stocks a further gamble. The greatest restriction on London-formed mining companies intending on operating in South Africa was the question 'whether or not the vendors' shares [were] transferable as fully-paid shares,' which was not fully regulated by the ZAR government.[129] Despite the Committee's unwillingness, towards the end of 1894, the LSE responded to the increase in shares trading on the unofficial market with the inclusion of numerous South African securities to the Official List (See Fig. 5.4).[130] The nominal capitalisation of British-registered Rand mining companies increased from £ 3.8 million in 1894 to £ 27.5 million in 1895.[131]

While the growth of a new pool of international investors presented the Randlords with rapid capitalisation of their deep-level projects, it severely limited their opportunities to control the international market for South African securities.[132] The most influential JSE members used their British and European continental connections to encourage buying at all exchanges where South African securities were on offer. The Barnatos, Goerz, Neumann, and Albu were the most successful JSE members and promoters of JSE-registered products on foreign markets, using the group system to diversify their mining portfolios between the exchanges and the deep-level/outcrop combinations of mining stocks they floated.[133] The ZAR was by then responsible for the production of nearly a quarter of the world's gold production, with the financial and administrative management of local companies revitalised by the international group system.[134] Although the amount and value of mining stocks listed on the JSE

[128] "The Constitution of the Mining Market." *The Economist*, 1 September 1894. p. 1069.

[129] "The Stock Exchange and Mining Shares." *The Economist*, 3 June 1893. p. 658.

[130] See: Kynaston, David. *City of London: The History*. 2011. pp. 160–164.

[131] Van-Helten, J. J. "Mining, Share Manias and Speculation: British Investment in Overseas Mining, 1880–1913." 1990. p. 175.

[132] Kubicek, Robert V. *Economic Imperialism in theory and Practice: The Case of South African Gold Mining Finance 1886–1914*. 1979. pp. 66–67.

[133] Klein, Harry. *The Story of the Johannesburg Stock Exchange, 1887–1947*. 1948. p. 46.

[134] Henry, James A. *The First Hundred Years of the Standard Bank*. 1963. p. 100.

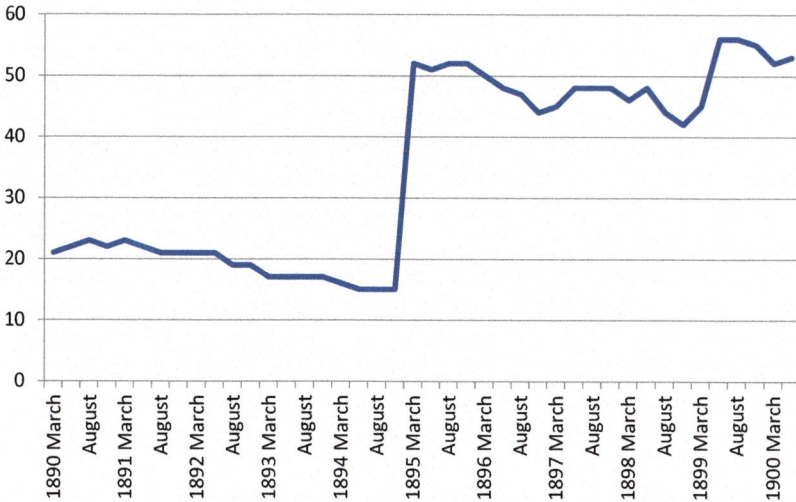

Fig. 5.4 No. of ZAR-registered companies on LSE's official list (*Source Investors Monthly Manual*, 1890–1900)

increased gradually throughout 1894,[135] it was in London and, indirectly, Paris where the rising demand for gold in the international monetary system ignited a new international boom and tested the Paris Bourse's duality between the *parquet's* regulated market where only authorised *agents de changes* could trade securities and the *coulisse* where brokers could participate relatively unhindered from government regulation.[136]

Although Paris's financial market was considerably smaller than London and the Paris Bourse's nominal value of listed shares was half as large as that of LSE at the end of the nineteenth century, the French capital was continental Europe's premier financial and commercial centre. Even though Van Helten, Kubicek, and Maubrey were able to document the evolution of French interests in South African financial products, their

[135] "A Cheerful Prospect." *The Star*, 7 January 1895. p. 5.

[136] Kynaston, David. *City of London: The History*. London: Random House. 2011. p. 161.

Lukasiewicz, Mariusz. "Bourses, Banks, and Boers: Johannesburg's French Connections and the Paris Krach of 1895." *Economic History of Developing Regions* 36, no. 2 (2021): 124–148.

studies were geared towards identifying London as the strategic intermediary in the South African share market, and largely overlooked direct connections to Johannesburg's financial organisations.[137] According to estimates by the *Banque de Paris et des Pays-Bas*, French investors held more than £ 100 million in South African mining stocks by 1895 and purchased more than 30% of all securities issued since 1887.[138] Paris was a crucial market for international mining securities and soon enough, became consumed by the ZAR's mining market and the Randlords. Paris-based investors became significant purchasers of South African securities during the early days of the Rand gold rush and the collapse of the 1889 boom in Johannesburg and London prompted French banks to actively support the formation of the new group system.[139] Unlike in London, but similar to Johannesburg, major French and international banks were allowed to establish offices inside the Bourse, giving them direct access to the brokers.[140] As was evident with South African mining stocks in Paris, the support of major retail banks was key to securing a listing and market on the *parquet*.[141]

After trades in foreign securities on the Paris Bourse were fully legalised in 1893, a boom began in South African gold mining stocks, focused

---

[137] Kubicek, Robert V. *Economic Imperialism in Theory and Practice: The Case of South African Gold Mining Finance 1886–1914*. 1979.

Van Helten, Jean Jacques. "La France et l'Or des Boërs: Some Aspects of French Investment in South Africa between 1890 and 1914." *African Affairs* 84, no. 335 (1985): 247–263.

Maubrey Michel. "Les Français et le veau d'or: la question sud-africaine (1896–1902)." In: Bach, Daniel, ed. *La France et l'Afrique du Sud. Histoire, Mythes et Enjeux Contemporains*. Paris: Karthala. 1990. pp. 37–63.

[138] PBA. Participation des capitaux français aurifere sud-africaine. *Banque de Paris et des Pays-Bas*. PTC/166/5, 6 July 1949. p. 1.

[139] PBA. Wernher, Beit et Cie to Banque de Paris et des Pays-Bas. 11DFOM/221/34, 10 July 1894.

[140] Michie, Ranald. *The Global Securities Market: A History*. 2007. p. 94.

Flandreau, M., and P. Sicsic. 2003. "Crédits à la spéculation et marché monétaire: le marché des reports en France de 1875 à 1914." In: O. Feiertag, and M. Margairaz, eds. *Politiques et pratiques des banques d'émission en Europe*. Paris: Albin Michel. pp. 197–222.

See also: Walker, Donald A. "A Factual Account of the Functioning of the Nineteenth-Century Paris Bourse." *European Journal of the History of Economic Thought* 8, no. 2 (2001): 186–207.

[141] See: Hautcoeur, P. C., Rezaee, A., and Riva, A. Competition Between Securities Markets: Stock Exchange Industry Regulation in the Paris Financial Centre at the Turn of the Twentieth Century. *Cliometrica*. 2022. pp. 1–39.

mostly on the coulisse.[142] According to the Paris-published *Revue Sud-Africaine*, by the end of May 1893 there were as many as 50 South African mining securities available on the coulisse.[143] The first significant South African mine that caught the attention of the Paris press was owned by Joseph Robinson. Shares in the Robinson Mine, the most capitalised of the outcrop mines on the Rand until 1890, were introduced to the coulisse with the help of the *Banque Russe et Française* in October 1889, and by 1892, nearly half of the mine's shareholders were based in France.[144] Although contemporary reports also document the availability of shares of Johannesburg-based mining companies such as Salisbury, City and Suburban, and Jumpers, there is only limited financial data that can be used to estimate the extent of their circulation on the coulisse and even less to base generalisations about the identities of French shareholders.[145] What can nonetheless be observed is that compared to London, Paris was a late entrant to the South African mining market, giving French speculators new opportunities to direct their investments away from sovereign bonds and in favour of private foreign securities.[146] A direct intermediary role in South African gold shares between Johannesburg and Paris can be traced back to the summer of 1894 and the establishment of the *Syndicat Sud-Africaine* as part of an international partnership between the Corner House and Paribas. By allocating portfolios of Rand shares among Parisian investment partners and establishing links with the coulissiers, the Corner House cooperated with several French banks and influential *agents de change* to publicise the merits of a new wave of South African deep-level mines.[147] Charles-Eugène Dutilleul and Henri-Jules Béjot were two

[142] Riva, A., and E. N. White. "Danger on the Exchange: How Counterparty Risk Was Managed on the Paris Exchange in the Nineteenth Century." Explorations in Economic History 48, no. 4 (2011): 478–493.

[143] "Transvaal Mines d'or." Revue Sud-Africaine, 11 June 1893. p. 3.

[144] "La Bourse." Le Figaro, 8 November 1889. p. 3.
See, also: Dupont, Henry. Les mines d'or de l'Afrique du Sud. 1890. pp. 91–94.

[145] Dupont, Henry. Les mines d'or de l'Afrique du Sud. 1890. pp. 91–94.

[146] Esteves, Rui. "The Belle Epoque of International Finance: French Capital Exports, 1880–1914." University of Oxford Department of Economics Discussion Paper Series. Nr. 534. November 2011. pp. 20–22.

[147] Kubicek, Robert V. Economic Imperialism in Theory and Practice: The Case of South African Gold Mining Finance 1886–1914. 1979. p. 180.

of the first Paris Bourse brokers in the new South African Syndicate.[148] Although Kubicek claimed that there might have been as many as 25 *agents de change* involved in the Syndicate, the figure was probably much smaller and constantly changing.[149] Nonetheless, the participation of just a few agents de change indicated the Syndicate's ability to infiltrate the organisational structures of the Paris Bourse. By the end of 1894, South African-registered and JSE-listed stocks were widely traded on the European continent. In addition to London and Paris, smaller exchanges in Hamburg, Frankfurt, Berlin, and Vienna also traded and held significant South African mining portfolios.[150] South African mining shares were not listed on the official list of any German exchange, but were actively traded on various markets across the German Empire from 1892 onwards.[151] According to contemporary German sources, the German investing public was attracted to the South African market through the intermediary role of the Ottoman Bank, which was managed by Sir Edgar Vincent,[152] and included the names of prominent European capitalists such as Hottinger, Mallet, Berger, Andres, Vernes and Heine.[153] Although significantly smaller than France, and with only a fraction of the activity in Britain, the spread of South African shares to the German Empire exemplified the transimperial entanglement of the gold mining market. The international mining boom of 1894/5 demonstrated that global security trading in

---

[148] PBA. SGY/B/154. Supplement a la circulaire hebdomadaire de la Compagnie française des mines d'or de l'Afrique du Sud.

[149] Kubicek, Robert V. *Economic Imperialism in Theory and Practice: The Case of South African Gold Mining Finance 1886–1914.* 1979. p. 183.

[150] "Kaffirs on the Continent." *Standard and Diggers News*, 21 December 1895. p. 3.

[151] Moos, Ferdinand. "Ursprung, Entwickelung und Zusammenbruch der Spekulation in Goldaktien.(Nach statistischen Quellen.)." *Jahrbücher für Nationalökonomie und Statistik/Journal of Economics and Statistics* 10, no. 6 (1895): 919.

[152] See: Auchterlonie, Paul. "A Turk of the west: Sir Edgar Vincent's career in Egypt and the Ottoman Empire." *British Journal of Middle Eastern Studies* 27, no. 1 (2000): 49–68.
Davenport-Hines, R. P. T., and Jean-Jacques Van Helten. "Edgar Vincent, Viscount D'Abernon, and the Eastern Investment Company in London, Constantinople and Johannesburg." *Business History* 28, no. 1 (1986): 35–61.

[153] Moos, Ferdinand. "Ursprung, Entwickelung und Zusammenbruch der Spekulation in Goldaktien.(Nach statistischen Quellen.)." *Jahrbücher für Nationalökonomie und Statistik/Journal of Economics and Statistics* 10, no. 6 (1895): 928.

South African mining shares was possible and profitable.[154] More significantly for the agency of the JSE, the internationalisation of the market for South African stocks created new economic opportunities and political responsibilities towards the local financial industry and the growing mining sector they were serving.

CONCLUSION

The years between 1889 and 1894 were marked by a structural shift in Johannesburg's gold and finance industries. The technological transformation to deep-level mining operations set Johannesburg on a new course of financial reorganisation. Although outcrop mining continued to yield the largest share of gold outputs in the early 1890s, it was soon evident that deep-level mining would become the dominant industrial method by which South Africa's gold would be produced. The JSE stood at the centre of this structural shift to capital-intensive mining and housed the main corporate stakeholders dependent on the capitalisation of new deep-level projects in an increasingly international market for ZAR shares. However, marred by problems of defaulting members, the Estate's persistent intervention, and futile attempts to reform the trade system, the JSE was far from ready to respond to the new industrial agenda and the demands of international capital.

This chapter has provided an outline of the core industrial and financial features of Johannesburg's gold industry in a changing local and international economic climate. In stressing the importance of the JSE in facilitating the groups system's capital formation process, this chapter connected the Exchange to the mines' financial amalgamation. By using the JSE to restructure who owned and controlled the means of production in deep-level mining, the group system's initiators, the Randlords, were able to establish and entrench themselves in an increasingly international capital market. Exposing the Randlords' corporate reorganisation on the JSE, this chapter served as a bridge between the failures of Johannesburg's market in 1889 and the internationalisation of South African mining securities in the mid-1890s. The expansion of old and new financial networks from Kimberley to Johannesburg contributed to a new social cohesion of the financial industry, using the JSE as a central financial

---

[154] Van, Helten J. J. "Mining, Share Manias and Speculation: British Investment in Overseas Mining, 1880–1913." 1990. p. 177.

intermediary for local and international capital. Through the evolution of the group system and the closer cooperation of the mining industry through the Chamber of Mines and its representatives inside the JSE, Johannesburg's financial sector entered a new period of international capital mobility.

The introduction of deep-level shares and the first generation of non-mining securities to the JSE's Official List defined Johannesburg's new corporate commitment to industrialisation. Using the JSE's social networks as an institutional platform for attracting increasingly international investors, the group system of holding companies coordinated a new wave of company amalgamations and financial portfolios. Although the capital needs and managerial structures of the new financial houses differed considerably, the largest and most influential groups were linked to the JSE. Not only did the new corporate organisation of the ZAR's mining sector rise out of the doldrums of Johannesburg's first financial crisis, the group system's entrenchment inside the JSE facilitated risk sharing between the local and international capital markets.

The migration of South African deep-level stocks to Europe throughout the early 1890s represented the rapid internationalisation of the ZAR's mining market and mining finance. Although much has already been written about how the City of London's financial and political intermediaries influenced the ZAR's political economy, this chapter was able to extend the analysis to continental Europe. Applying the central function of the JSE as a financial nexus, the analysis of Johannesburg's financial class and its interaction with the Parisian mining market exposed new evidence on the Randlords' international ambitions during South Africa's first era of financial globalisation. The 1894/5 boom in London that quickly spread to Paris confirmed that South African securities, both Johannesburg and London-listed, were finally accepted by the European investing public and financial networks, further extending the JSE's exposure to the forces of international capitalism.

CHAPTER 6

Finance and Imperialism at the Exchange: The JSE and the Jameson Raid

The internationalisation of the market for ZAR mining securities throughout the 1890s allowed the JSE, its products and personalities to establish themselves in a complex web of transimperial finance and politics. Johannesburg emerged as a global financial centre with numerous local, colonial, and international banks operating inside the ZAR, and many of their managers and employees functioning as JSE members.[1] More significantly for the location of the JSE, instead of the South African securities market gravitating to an urban centre in a British colony such as Cape Town or Pietermaritzburg, Johannesburg became internationally recognised as the dominant capital market in sub-Saharan Africa.[2] Soon enough, the Randlords' international financial aspiration and local political mobilisation set Johannesburg and Pretoria on a divergent path towards imperial aggression.

This chapter returns to the ZAR's political polarisation and explores how Johannesburg's position in international finance influenced southern Africa's colonial politics, culminating in the failed Jameson Raid that attempted to overthrow President Paul Kruger. The 1895 *Krach* of Paris' mining market demonstrated just how exposed the JSE was to the

---

[1] JSEA. *Minutes of an Ordinary Meeting*, 13 March 1894.

[2] Michie, Ranald. *The Global Securities Market: A History.* 2007. p. 108.

© The Author(s), under exclusive license to Springer Nature Switzerland AG 2024
M. Lukasiewicz, *Gold, Finance and Imperialism in South Africa, 1887–1902*, Cambridge Imperial and Post-Colonial Studies, https://doi.org/10.1007/978-3-031-51947-5_6

forces of international finance, and how events such as these could have severe political consequences for the ZAR. Leander Starr Jameson's incursion into the ZAR from the British South African Company' territories on 29 December 1895 exposed the direct connections between British imperialism and Johannesburg's financial community. Given the overlapping chronological development of the South African mining market in Europe, this chapter returns to Johannesburg at the beginning of 1895 to clearly outline the JSE's financial and political context in southern Africa.

For historians of British imperialism in Africa, the Jameson Raid has always been a subject of controversy and intense debate when assessing the motives for the South African War.[3] At the local and regional level, the Jameson Raid was largely the culmination of the activities of the Reform Movement, which a number of Johannesburg's Randlords initiated with considerable, but discreet, support from Rhodes.[4] At the British imperial level, much scholarly effort has gone into outlining a causal relationship between the change of government in London from Liberal to Conservative in June 1895, which put Joseph Chamberlain in charge of the British Colonial Office, and exposed government involvement in the planning of the Raid.[5] Additionally, much attention has also been paid to proving that Rhodes and his BSAC Administrator General of the Matabeleland, Leander Starr Jameson, had planned the incursion into the ZAR together,

---

[3] See for example: Phimister, Ian. "Markets, Mines, and Magnates: Finance and the Coming of War in South Africa, 1894–1899." *Africa: Rivista Semestrale Di Studi e Ricerche* 2, no. 2 (2020): 5–22.

Blainey, Geoffrey. "Lost Causes of the Jameson Raid." *The Economic History Review* 18, no. 2 (1965): 350–366.

Webb, Arthur. "Blainey and Early Witwatersrand Profitability Some Thoughts on Financial Management and Capital Constraints Facing the Gold Mining Industry 1886–1894." *South African Journal of Economic History* 12, no. 1–2 (1997): 128–152.

Katz, Elaine N. "Outcrop and Deep Level Mining in South Africa Before the Anglo-Boer War: Re-examining the Blainey Thesis." *The Economic History Review* 48, no. 2 (1995): 304–328.

Mendelsohn, Richard. "Blainey and the Jameson Raid: The Debate Renewed." *Journal of Southern African Studies* 6, no. 2 (1980): 157–170.

[4] Giliomee, Hermann Buhr and Bernard Mbenga. *New History of South Africa.* 2007. p. 200.

[5] See: Butler, Jeffrey. *The Liberal Party and the Jameson Raid.* 1968.

but it was ultimately Rhodes who pushed for the Johannesburg uprising and the Raid which it was meant to promote.[6]

Even more than a century after the political fiasco, especially after apartheid's demise and Britain's decline as a world power, historians continue to find new impulses and postcolonial theoretical perspectives with which to reassess the local, regional, and global historical significance of the Jameson Raid.[7] Despite the countless debates on the origins of the Jameson Raid, all have failed to notice and recognise the significant complicity of the JSE. However, and perhaps indicative of the manner in which how the JSE intended to portray its involvement in the growing Anglo-Afrikaner conflict, the official documentation points to the Exchange's active support and involvement in regional colonial politics. According to the records of all members from the *JSE Members Roll Books 1889–1899*, at least 40 of the 64 Reforms Committee members who were put on trial by the Pretoria Government in February 1896 were active members of the JSE. Once the overwhelming connection to Johannesburg's financial community was exposed, it was the JSE that rallied behind the *Uitlander* community of European immigrants when the Raid turned into an international embarrassment.[8] Given the broad multicausal approach of most investigations into the Jameson Raid, this chapter isolates the lacuna only as far as the JSE was involved and does not intend to debate the wider origins of Johannesburg's Reform Movement. The inclusion of the JSE in debates around the role of finance in the 'Scramble for southern Africa' provides an overdue contribution to the study of imperialism in Africa.

---

[6] Robert Rotberg. "Who was Responsible. Rhodes, Jameson, and the Raid." In: Brenthurst Press. *The Jameson Raid: a centennial retrospective*. Vol. 1. Johannesburg: Brenthurst Press. 1996. p. 131.

[7] See: Phimister, Ian. "Markets, Mines, and Magnates: Finance and the Coming of War in South Africa, 1894–1899." *Africa: Rivista Semestrale Di Studi e Ricerche* 2, no. 2 (2020): 5–22.
Brenthurst Press. *The Jameson Raid: A Centennial Retrospective*. 1996.

[8] *Uitlander* (Dutch: Foreigner) was the term given to all non-Afrikaner Europeans working and living in the ZAR.

CONVERGING FINANCIAL INTERESTS
IN A DIVERGING SETTLER SOCIETY

Despite the ZAR becoming the world's largest producer and exporter of gold during 1895,[9] the year got off to a relatively slow start for the JSE. The last quarter of 1894 was made up of small, albeit steady movements in prices and volumes of shares, largely due to the lack of initiative from London, where traders were recovering from the drop in prices of US railway stocks.[10] Johannesburg's implementation of telecommunication technology was very slow, and the JSE was the only large financial intermediary without its own functioning telephone.[11] Brokers in London and Paris used an extensive network of telegraph (and, increasingly, telephone) lines to trade in South African stocks across the Channel, with Johannesburg left behind and isolated due to limited technological advancement since the first boom of 1889.[12] The JSE's own telegraph office was operational, but persistent problems with the availability of a stable electricity supply made the service unpredictable and largely unreliable.[13] The diffusion of printed information from the Exchange was also limited due to the simple fact that *The Star* held a monopoly on the publishing and printing of all JSE price lists. With Barnato's Estate Company owning most of the shares in the Argus Printing Company, competing newspapers such as the *Standard and Diggers' News* and the new *Johannesburg Times*, had restricted access to the daily price summary of the Official List.[14] At Barnato's personal orders, the relationship with newspapers continued

---

[9] Curle, James Herbert. *The Gold Mines of the World: Containing Concise and Practical Advice for Investors Gathered from a Personal Inspection of the Mines of the Transvaal, India, West Australia, Queensland, New Zealand, British Columbia, and Rhodesia.* Waterlow and Sons Limited. 1899. pp. 23–24.

[10] "The Stock Exchange." *The Star*, 3 January 1895. p. 3.
See: "Financial History of the Year.' *Investors Monthly Manual.* 31 December 1894. p. 622.

[11] 'The Stock Exchange." *The Star*, 7 January 1895. p. 3.

[12] Ibid.

[13] : JSEA. *Minutes of an Ordinary Meeting of the Committee*, 30 July 1895.

[14] JSEA. *Minutes of an Ordinary Meeting of the Committee*, 12 March 1895.
See also: JSEA. *Minutes of an Ordinary Meeting of the Committee*, 30 January 1894.

to be constrained and only *The Star* was granted full publishing privileges and a permanent office inside the JSE building.[15]

Restrictions in telecommunication and access to financial information were not the only concerns of Johannesburg's financial community in 1895. In addition to the already apprehensive political mood on the Exchange, the rise in criminal activity throughout the first quarter of the year became a significant concern for the financial community.[16] Johannesburg had become an industrialising city with a thriving underworld of gang violence, illegal gambling halls, and prostitution, with most of the activities taking place in the back allies of Commissioner Street around the corner from the JSE.[17] The General Committee was increasingly distressed about the rising social class of poor European settlers and believed the JSE's location was a drawing force for troubled elements of Johannesburg's society that Pretoria took little notice of.[18]

The development of financial services had linked Johannesburg to the commercial capitals of Europe, but the increased dominance of the financial community gradually distanced it from Pretoria. The major shift from outcrop to deep-level mining contributed to the changing social relations between Afrikaners and the Rand's growing foreign-born population, known to the Pretoria government as the *Uitlanders*.[19] Despite its centrality, the Exchange was only important to a small, but well organised community of international financiers. The Rand's international capitalists were preoccupied with establishing strategic financial links across colonial Africa and Europe, but had little understanding of Kruger's policies for the ZAR. As an organisation, the JSE never hesitated to put the blame for commercial and political problems in Johannesburg on the government.[20] Although Pretoria tolerated Johannesburg's financial industry, it

[15] JSEA. *Minutes of an Ordinary Meeting of the Committee*, 30 January 1894.

[16] "Recent Murders." *The Star*, 11 March 1895.

[17] See: Van Onselen, Charles. *Studies in the Social and Economic History of the Witwatersrand 1886–1914. New Babylon.* 1982. p. 104.

[18] JSEA. *Minutes of an Ordinary Meeting of the Committee*, 25 March 1895.

[19] Katz, Elaine. "Outcrop and Deep Level Mining in South Africa Before the Anglo-Boer War: Re-examining the Blainey Thesis." *The Economic History Review* 48, no. 2 (1995): 305.

[20] See: JSEA. *Minutes of an Ordinary Meeting of the Committee*, 9 February 1895.

became increasingly concerned about how its cosmopolitan society could disrupt the Boers' authority over the Republic.[21]

The JSE's 1895 General Committee elections created a partisan dynamic within the local financial community. Barnato challenged the rise of the Corner House as the commercial leader of Johannesburg's mining capitalists and used the elections to expand the Estate's grip on the JSE and its political mobilisation. Barnato's cousin and Estate partner Solly Joel, won the presidential elections outright, with George Imroth, the co-founder of Barnato's Johannesburg Consolidated Investment Company, coming in second. Acknowledging his intention to regularly travel between Johannesburg and London, Joel convinced the General Committee to allow him to delegate his authority to Imroth.[22] With Barnato's two most trusted business partners at the helm of the JSE, the Exchange continued its development as the Estate's tool in supporting Barnato's personal ambitions of global financial expansion. Although the Estate was now in charge of the Exchange's presidency, the Corner House's representatives still dominated the seats on General Committee and many new sub-committees.[23] The Corner House would be subjected to Barnato's ownership and management of the Exchange, but with its established contacts in the Chamber of Mines, it was slowly able to use the JSE to further its growing political engagement in the ZAR. Otto Beit and Friedrich Eckstein, the two most senior directors in the Corner House's Johannesburg offices and Rhodes' most trusted partners in Johannesburg were already established members of the General Committee at the beginning of 1895. On 8 February Otto Beit, the mining group's stock market specialist,[24] accepted a seat on the quotation sub-committee and became the head of the JSE's Rules and Regulations Committee.[25] Later that year in October, Beit also became head of the Examining Committee, a position that made him responsible for

---

[21] Van Onselen, Charles. *Studies in the Social and Economic History of the Witwatersrand 1886–1914. New Babylon.* 1982. pp. 12–14.

[22] JSEA. *Minutes of an Ordinary Meeting of the Committee,* 23 April 1895.

[23] JSEA. *Minutes of an Ordinary Meeting of the Committee,* 7 May 1895.

[24] Alfred and Otto Beit. In: Rubinstein, William D., ed. *The Palgrave Dictionary of Anglo-Jewish History.* 2011. p. 66.

[25] JSEA. *Minutes of an Ordinary Meeting of the Committee,* 8 February 1895.

screening all companies requesting a listing on the Exchange.[26] With Beit in the Exchange, the Corner House's—and increasingly Rhodes'—interests in Johannesburg were firmly entrenched in the JSE's management and regulatory structures.

Using the Chamber of Mines and the JSE to coordinate its industrial and financial activities, the Corner House could now apply Rhodes' colonial authority in the Cape to launch numerous political attacks against the Pretoria government. With Rhodes acting as the Prime Minister of the Cape Colony, Chairman of De Beers, Chairman of Gold Fields, and managing director of the British South Africa Company, the Corner House forged a decisive partnership in its increasingly political activities against Kruger. Consolidated Gold Fields was formed at the end of 1892 as an amalgamation of the old London-based Gold Fields of South Africa and Rhodes' only other venture into deep-level mining, the African Estates Agency.[27] Floated in Johannesburg on 5 September 1893 on the same day as Rhodes' chartered the British South African Company,[28] Consolidated Gold Fields initiated Rhodes' return to the Rand and strengthened the bond with the Corner House. With Otto Beit controlling most of Gold Field's activities in Johannesburg through the Wernher & Beit partnership, Rhodes was slowly reintroduced to Johannesburg's finance and politics after ignoring the city since the late 1880s to focus on his efforts to the north of the ZAR.[29] Rhodes on the other hand saw his power in the Cape, the Matabeleland, and Mashonaland as the key to isolating Kruger in an increasingly British southern Africa. Any possible political organisation depended on the cooperation of the Corner House, and it became Rhodes' responsibility to convince Alfred Beit and Julius Wernher that their political and financial assistance was needed.[30]

---

[26] JSEA. *Minutes of an Ordinary Meeting of the Committee*, 1 October 1895.

[27] See: Kubicek, Robert V. *Economic Imperialism in Theory and Practice: The Case of South African Gold Mining Finance 1886–1914*. 1979. pp. 96–97.
"A South African Amalgamation." *The Economist*, 13 August 1892. p. 1039.

[28] JSEA. *Minutes of an Ordinary Meeting of the Committee*, 5 September 1893.

[29] According to Phimister, the Jameson Raid is the one notable exception to Rhodes' general disregard for the Rand.
See: Phimister, Ian R. "Rhodes, Rhodesia and the Rand." *Journal of Southern African Studies* 1, no. 1 (1974): 74–90.

[30] Cartwright, Alan Patrick. *The Corner House: The Early History of Johannesburg*. 1965. p. 146.

Aided by Lionel Phillips at the Chamber of Mines, 1895 was the year that the Corner House and its members inside the JSE sided with the imperial ambitions of Cecil Rhodes.[31]

MIXED CONFIDENCE AND RHODES' PLAN FOR THE RAND

Despite improving mining results throughout the first half of 1895,[32] the share market in Johannesburg was not as enthusiastic as in London and the JSE was challenged by growing pessimism in Paris.[33] The increased industrial capacity and financial legitimacy of many gold-producing mines in Johannesburg had a limited impact on the general perception of the mining market in Europe. The markets in London and Paris were still dominated by the group system's extensive portfolios of small subsidiary companies with little more than a land claim to justify their existence on Johannesburg's goldfields. In May, *The Economist* published a critical report by Victor-Stéphane Aubert, the French Consul General in Pretoria that questioned the ZAR shares' speculative market-making and international arbitrage:

> ...(South African) quotations are regulated not so much by the immediate and palpable results of the undertakings dealt in as by the more or less problematic hopes which the buyer entertains, by the more or less interested reports on which these hopes are founded, by the manoeuvres and of the promoters of these undertakings who understand how to create fictitious quotations by simulated sales and purchases as to simulate the bona fide purchases by the power wielded by the large shareholders and the blind confidence reposed in them by the small ones.[34]

The widely circulated report from the respected French authority on the gold industry in South Africa had an immediate negative effect on the Paris mining market.[35] Johannesburg financial commentators initially

---

[31] Van Onselen, Charles. *Studies in the Social and Economic History of the Witwatersrand 1886–1914. New Babylon.* 1982. pp. 12–13.

[32] "Mining Industry." *Standard and Diggers' News*, 18 December 1895. p. 3.

[33] See: "The Stock Exchange: Steady and Dull." *The Star*, 3 October 1895.

[34] "The Reaction in South African Shares." *The Economist*, 18 May 1895. pp. 645–646.

[35] "Some Phases of South African Speculation." *The Economist*, 17 August 1895. p. 1075.

played down the consul's report, arguing that the French investing public had attached an exaggerated value to financial intelligence from an official diplomatic mission in a country they knew very little about.[36] However, Johannesburg had limited power in influencing the opinions of the European investing public and the report served as a negative precedent for the investment climate on the JSE .

Although the mining markets in London and Paris made strong gains throughout the early part of 1895, Johannesburg lost much of the optimism that the city showed just a few months ago. Trade was only dominated by the large deep-level groups and outcrop companies lost most potential buyers.[37] Out of more than active 120 shares on the Official List, less than 30 were traded during the first week of June.[38] By the end of the month, the mood at the JSE had become so dull that brokers resorted to gambling with dice, just as in the aftermath of the 1890 slump.[39] With very few brokers even coming to the Exchange, it was suggested that the process of High 'Change should be moved to the late afternoon and shortened to only 30 minutes of trade between 4:00 and 4:30 p.m.[40] Although the General Committee commented on the numerous correspondences received from London praising the state of the market in Europe,[41] Johannesburg remained quiet and showed few signs of potential recovery beyond the Corner House's deep-level stocks such as Langlaagte, New Primrose, and Wolhuter.[42] Additionally, the continued technical problems with the JSE's telegraph service persisted throughout the year. Between March and August, the telegraph service provided inside the JSE was described as 'inadequate' and of great 'inconvenience' to the business needs of the members.[43] The London Stock Exchange grew weary of the constant communication breakdowns

---

[36] "The Shake Out." *The Star*, 10 June 1895. p. 3.

[37] "Suspended Animation." *The Star*, 4 June 1895. p. 3.

[38] "The Shake Out." *The Star*, 10 June 1895. p. 3.

[39] JSEA. *Minutes of an Ordinary Meeting of the Committee*, 25 June 1895.

[40] JSEA. *Minutes of an Ordinary Meeting of the Committee*, 23 July 1895.

[41] "The Stock Exchange." *The Star*, 4 July 1895. p. 3.

[42] "A Better Tendency." *The Star*, 8 July 1895. p. 3.

[43] JSEA. *Minutes of an Ordinary Meeting of the Committee*, 20 May 1895.

and requested a full investigation into how the JSE was intending to stay connected to the international markets for South African shares.[44]

A significant change in the JSE's outlook was, however, around the corner. As already emphasised, it was in mid-1895 that Rhodes intensified his commercial and political relationship with the Rand. Just a month after local investor confidence reached new lows, the Exchange was revitalised by a new issue of Rhodes' British South Africa Company shares. Strategically floated during the quiet market period on 17 June, the second BSAC flotation on the JSE reinvigorated market activity.[45] To most informed brokers it was reasonably clear that a political motive was behind the new Johannesburg shares. The new issue of Chartered shares was needed to finance what by July 1895 was rumoured to be potential political uprising against Kruger.[46] According to Rhodes' imperialist vision for southern Africa, a Johannesburg revolt against Kruger, followed by a federation of settler colonies, would create the political conditions for rapid capitalisation of the Chartered Company and the deep-level mining industry in southern Africa.[47] With the support of his BSAC administrator stationed in Matabeleland, Leander Starr Jameson, and his Johannesburg-based brother, Frank Rhodes, Cecil Rhodes was able to combine regional imperial ambitions with financial speculation.

The Company Law of the BSAC Charterland was adopted on 10 July 1895 and had an immediate effect on the company's share price in Johannesburg.[48] The new Company Law created much-needed corporate legislation for a set of Rhodesian shares prone to excessive speculation in a colonial territory with a previously undefined system of property rights.[49] The regulatory reforms were immediately felt, with a series of new listings of Rhodesian mining and exploration companies in London.[50] With the boom in South African stocks in London reaching new heights, investors

[44] JSEA. *Minutes of an Ordinary Meeting of the Committee*, 29 August 1895.

[45] "Renewed Activity at the Stock Exchange." *The Star*, 17 June 1895. p. 3.

[46] See: Kubicek, Robert V. "The Randlords in 1895: A Reassessment." *The Journal of British Studies* 11, no. 2 (1972): 99.

[47] Rosenthal, Eric. *On 'Change Through the Years; a History of Share Dealing in South Africa*. 1968. p. 186.

[48] BLA. *The British South African Company. Director's Report and Accounts for Period 31 March 1896–31 March 1897*. PAM 203.

[49] "Company Law in Charterland." *The Economist*, 24 August 1895. p. 1109.

[50] "South African Financial Methods." *The Economist*, 6 July 1895. pp. 876–877.

were easily persuaded that fortunes awaited them in BSAC territory north of the ZAR.[51] Rhodes was interested in keeping the price of the BSAC shares as high as possible and the prosperity of the Chartered Company's territory depended on the momentum of JSE-listed stocks. As illustrated in communications with Alfred Beit, Rhodes continued to prop up the price by placing high orders on BSAC shares with the help of Francis Dormer at *The Star*[52] (See Table 6.1).

The importance of stock exchanges in Rhodes' regional strategy was further pronounced by the opening of the Bulawayo Stock Exchange in late 1894.[53] Although it had been established the previous year, the Bulawayo Stock Exchange only announced its first High 'Change in July 1895 with the BSAC company being the first stock on its Official List, trading at £8 17s 6p.[54] The JSE's management saw the BSAC share and

Table 6.1 British South Africa Company Share Price 1895	Date	Share Price (in shillings)
	7 January	51
	13 May	86
	17 June	84
	23 July	95
	5 August	112
	12 August	145
	26 August	140
	16 September	176
	12 October	140
	25 November	85
	3 December	120
	30 December	97

Source "The Stock Exchange." *The Star*, 14 March 1896. p. 3

See also: Phimister, Ian. "Late Nineteenth-Century Globalization: London and Loma-gundi Perspectives on Mining Speculation in southern Africa, 1894–1904." *Journal of Global History* 10, no. 1 (2015): 27–52.

[51] Ibid. p. 33.

[52] BLA. Cecil John Rhodes to Alfred Beit. MS 114, August 1895.

[53] See: Karekwaivenani, George. "A History of the Rhodesian Stock Exchange: The Formative Years, 1946–1952." *Zambezia: The Journal of Humanities of the University of Zimbabwe* 30, no. 1 (2003): 15.

[54] Phimister, Ian. "Rhodes, Rhodesia and the Rand." *Journal of Southern African Studies* 1, no. 1 (1974): 81.

the simultaneous development of a share market in Rhodesian territories as a massive boost to the Exchange's regional and international reputation.[55] Stockbroking services were already available to European settlers in Matabeleland since 1891.[56] While little is known about the scope of Bulawayo Stock Exchange's early operations,[57] the JSE Committee sent its congratulations and encouraged deeper cooperation between the financial intermediaries.[58] More significantly for the political developments of that year, with Rhodes marketing his financial products in ZAR and Rhodesia, Johannesburg's politically agitated population saw their strategic link to international finance as a drawing card for British support against Kruger's administration.

THE PARIS *KRACH* AND ITS IMPACT

The peak of the Parisian boom in ZAR mining shares can be traced back to Barnato's operations in Paris during the first week of September. After revealing his plans for the Barnato Bank, Parisian brokers flooded the market with large quantities of mining stocks and land claims that, for the most part, were underdeveloped or not even in operation.[59] Using the slowdown in the share market during the Jewish New Year celebrations between 5 and 9 September, the *coulisse* was swarmed by new South African shares brought over from London or directly from Johannesburg[60] (See Fig. 6.1).

However, Barnato was not the only JSE member capitalising on Paris' increased interest in South African securities. Joseph Robinson's participation in the Parisian financial market went further back and was also linked

---

[55] JSEA. *Minutes of an Ordinary Meeting of the Committee*, 27 July 1895.

[56] Nyamunda, Tinashe. "Gold, Currency and Stamps: The Rejected Plans for a State and Public Bank in Early Colonial Zimbabwe (1896–1907)." In: Pallaver, Karin, ed. *Monetary Transitions: Currencies, Colonialism and African Societies*. Palgrave Macmillan. 2022. p. 117.

[57] See: Karekwaivenani, George. "A History of the Rhodesian Stock Exchange: The Formative Years, 1946–1952." *Zambezia: The Journal of Humanities of the University of Zimbabwe* 30, no. 1 (2003): 15.

[58] JSEA. *Minutes of an Ordinary Meeting of the Committee*, 3 September 1895.

[59] Kynaston, David. *City of London: The History*. 2011. p. 168.

[60] See: "La Bourse." *Le Figaro*, 7 September 1895. p. 3.

Black Reef Prop.	2 1/2	Knights.............	10 1/8
Buffelsd. consol..	2 7/8	Lo Magunda..,....	1 pr.
Bonanza...........	2 5/16	Luipaards Vlei...	29/»
Chartered	8 3/8	Mashonaland Ag.	3 13/16
Chimes West....	3 5/16	Modderfontein...	15 3/8
City and Suburb..	26 3/4	Nigel..	7 3/4
Crown Deep.....	13 1/2	Rand Mines	39 »/»
East Orion......	3/4	Rose Deep	6 1/2
East Rand Centr¹	3 5/8	Simmer and Jack.	21 3/4
East Rand	9 1/8	Transv. Gold Exp.	9 1/2
Eerste Fabrieken	4 9/16	Treasury........	3 5/8
Goldfields Deep..	10 7/8	Van Ryn	9 3/8
Geldenhuis Deep.	10 3/4	Village Mainreef.	8 3/8
Henry Nourse....	7 15/16	Western Nigel...	2 1/4
Hériot.............	11 »/»	West Rand Mines	3 5/16
Kleinfontein.....	6 »/»	Wolhuter........	10 5/8

Communiqué par MM. Lemaire, Dupont et Cⁱ,
18, r. du 4-Septemb. Négoc. spéc. de ces valeurs
etrenseigtˢ. Éditeurs de la *Revue Sud-Africaine*.

Fig. 6.1 South African Stocks on the Coulisse, 7 September 1895 (*Source* 'La Bourse.' *Le Figaro.* 7 September 1895. p. 3)

to Paris' largest banks, *Paribas* and *Société Générale*.[61] On 27 August 1895 Robinson registered the Robinson South African Banking Company in Paris.[62] Robinson's entry into the Paris market with the Robinson Bank was made possible by earlier connections to *Paribas* that helped introduce the Robinson Gold Mining Company to the *coulisse*. Thanks to his connections to members of the board of directors such as Baron Hély d'Oissel, vice-president of Société Générale at the time, Robinson's bank was quickly made welcome on the *parquet* in September.[63]

Back in the ZAR, the JSE was increasingly worried about the potential destabilising effect Paris' preoccupation with South African mining shares could have on London and Johannesburg if the mining market was

[61] PBA. Participation des capitaux français aurifere sud-africaine. Banque de Paris et des Pays-Bas. PTC/166/5, 6 July 1949. p. 4.

[62] Michelet, J. *Annuaire des mines d'or pour 1896.* Renseignements généraux sur les mines d'or et de métaux précieux du monde entier. 1896. p. 5.

[63] Lamy, C. *Annuaire Français des Mines D'Or: Transvaal, Sudafrique.* 1896. pp. 613–614.

to crash. The opinion in Johannesburg was that the Corner House and other deep-level groups would need to step in and support the market in Paris.[64] Even the financial analysis from the Chamber of Mines advised caution. In a letter to S.A. Ralli, a major ZAR mining shareholder in London, Lionel Phillips warned against any hasty purchases:

> An awful pike of rubbish has been foisted on the market (in Paris) and some people will bite their fingers when the mania subsides. I know it is unnecessary to warn you, as you would not blindly buy our stocks when you know that you can get reliable advice from me. Of course, this is confidential advice. I have often thought of trying to protect the public, but I cannot think of any practical way of doing so.[65]

The news coming out of Europe was probably not at all a surprise for Johannesburg's financial industry and the local press also expressed its scrutiny of the Parisian market. French investors had persistently ignored most warnings about many suspicious enterprises being established in Johannesburg and had become a key driver in the international market for South African securities.[66] September proved to be the most challenging time for South African stocks in circulation in Johannesburg, Paris and London. The Barnato-induced flood of mining stocks to the *coulisse* was a major failure and saturated the market, instead of providing a new pool of South African financial products to a growing French customer base. Most portfolios introduced to the market by Barnato, Robinson, and Farrar were ignored by the *coulissiers* who were now convinced that the Corner House had no serious intention to offer its best stocks to the Paris public.[67]

In comparison to London where the boom of 1894 tested the South African mining market balance between the Official List and the curb market, the Paris boom and *Krach* were largely restricted to the *coulisse*. The Parisian market took a plunge when the coulissiers discovered that the massive over-supply of South African stocks was managed by only

[64] "The Stock Exchange." *The Star*, 12 October 1895. p. 3.

[65] Phillips to S. A. Ralli. HE 147. Johannesburg, 23 August 1895. In: Fraser, Maryna, and Alan Jeeves, eds. *All That Glittered: Selected Correspondence of Lionel Phillips, 1890–1924.* 1977. p. 87.

[66] "Letter from Paris." *The Star*, 31 August 1895. p. 3.

[67] "La Bourse." *Le Figaro*, 20 October 1895. p. 3.

a few disinterested brokers. Although there were no South African mining stocks on the *parquet* in October 1895 (the only ZAR-registered company on the *parquet* at the time was the Robinson South African Banking Company), the outside mining market influenced the trade on the main floor. The financial panic had spread from the *coulisse* to the *parquet* where, according to some initial calculations by White, the total value of the Bourse's share index declined by just over 1% in October and the huge sell-off on the *coulisse* was held to be the negative driving force.[68] Bankruptcy was on everyone's lips and soon enough brokers were selling whole South African portfolios on the *coulisse*.[69] The direct involvement of French banks turned the mining crisis into a banking debt crisis.[70] With the *Banque de France* leading the negative sentiments, the *Société Générale* and *Banque Ottoman's* involvement in the South African market was quickly exposed, depreciating their already lowered share prices.[71] It was also widely acknowledged that the French government would have to step in sooner than later to consolidate the floating debts, and advised local banks to stay clear of the Bourse.[72]

The JSE and the whole Johannesburg financial community observed the events in Paris with disbelief. When the rapid fall of prices continued into October it became reasonably clear that a *Krach* in Paris might easily entail the downfall of the international market for South African mining shares and, just as in 1889, leave Johannesburg's mines and financial sector in another long-term crisis.[73] Aware of Barnato's intervention in Europe, the JSE's General Committee was in constant communication with the Johannesburg Estate, waiting for orders from the landlord.[74] Despite frantic efforts to communicate directly with Barnato, the General

[68] White, Eugene N. *The Crash of 1882, Counterparty Risk, and the Bailout of the Paris Bourse.* 2007. p. 34.

[69] "La Bourse." *Le Figaro*, 1 October 1895. p. 3.

[70] See also: Flandreau, Marc and Pierre Sicsic. "Crédit à la speculation et marché monétaire: Le marché des report en France de 1875 à 1914." In: Olivier Feiertag and Michel Margairaz, eds. *Politiques et pratiques des banques d'émission en Europe.* 2003. pp. 213–214.

[71] "La Bourse." *Le Figaro*, 11 October 1895. p. 3.

[72] Kubicek, Robert V. *Economic Imperialism in Theory and Practice: The Case of South African Gold Mining Finance 1886–1914.* 1979. p. 185.

[73] "The French Market." *The Star*, 11 October 1895. p. 3.

[74] JSEA. *Minutes of an Ordinary Meeting of the Committee*, 19 October 1895.

Committee was left to read daily reports from London and Paris brokers, with no news filtering through about the whereabouts of the JSE's owner.[75] The largest losses during October were suffered by the Barnato group of companies. Along with Robinson and Farrar, it was Barnato who had created the bubble by flooding the market with 'rubbishy' stocks[76] (Table 6.2).

What followed confirmed the by then interconnected dynamics of the globalised market for South African gold securities. The fall in prices triggered more tension within the already political situation in the ZAR and put the JSE under severe pressure to find a common rescue strategy with Barnato's Estate.[77] The only stock that made solid share price gains in Johannesburg during October was Rhodes' BSAC. The financial crisis provoked the ZAR's mining community to threaten Pretoria's authority

Table 6.2   South African stocks on the Coulisse

Company	Price 17 October (Fr.)	Price 24 October (Fr.)	Change (Fr.)
Tharsis	127.49	125.62	−1.87
Cape Copper	66.24	65.62	−0.62
British SA Chartered Co	160.00	148.75	−11.25
Bechuanaland Exploration	70.00	60.00	−10.00
Transvaal Land	71.30	71.25	−0.05
Buffelsdoorn	181.44	174.37	−7.07
Ferreira	480.00	466.25	−13.75
Geldenhuis	141.25	140.00	−1.25
Sheba	45.62	43.12	−2.50
Oceana	66.25	56.25	−10.25
Simmer and Jack	667.50	635.00	−32.50
Robinson Mines	262.49	260.62	−1.87
Consolidated Gold Fields	447.50	431.25	−16.25
East Rand Proprietary	243.75	218.75	−25.00
Robinson Bank	210.00	185.00	−25.00
Langlaagte Estate	152.50	**155.00**	**+2.50**
French Mines d'Or	150.00	**152.50**	**+2.50**

Source "France." *The Economist*, 26 October 1895. p. 1403

[75] JSEA. *Minutes of an Ordinary Meeting of the Committee*, 12 October 1895.

[76] Wheatcroft, Geoffrey. *The Randlords*. 1987. p. 170.

[77] JSEA. *Minutes of an Ordinary Meeting of the Committee*, 29 October 1895.

in Johannesburg by claiming that the leaders of the gold industry would not be content to remain politically marginalised in the Republic which had become wealthy as a result of their efforts.[78] With clear crisis-induced political mobilisation among the *Uitlanders* in Johannesburg further contributing to the antagonism against Pretoria, the JSE would again be tested in its uniting role between finance and industry.

THE POLITICS OF DISCONTENT AND THE RAID

The failures of the international mining market in Paris and London had a direct impact on South Africa's colonial politics.[79] By the end of September, Rhodes, fearing an escalation of Kruger's anti-British policies and his neglect of the *Uitlanders'* demands of extending the franchise to non-Afrikaners residing in the ZAR, began to actively plan the downfall of the Republic.[80] The outright objective of the BSAC was to dismantle the ZAR's government and restore the political supremacy of the Cape Colony in a British-dominated southern Africa. After the British liberal government fell in June, Rhodes visited the newly-elected Colonial Secretary Joseph Chamberlain to obtain full control of Bechuanaland for the BSAC and suggested a potential military campaign into the ZAR.[81] Rhodes saw his regional power in the Cape, the Matabeleland, and Mashonaland as the key to exerting political pressure on Kruger's government, but needed the support of all economic stakeholders in Johannesburg and London for any plan to work.[82]

Although initially beyond the interest of JSE's General Committee, the main direct economic and political threat to Johannesburg's commercial development throughout 1895 was the Drifts Crisis.[83] As soon as

---

[78] Klein, Harry. *The Story of the Johannesburg Stock Exchange 1887–1947.* 1948. p. 49.

[79] Blainey, Geoffrey. "Lost Causes of the Jameson Raid." *The Economic History Review* 18, no. 2 (1965): 361.

[80] Lang, John. *Bullion Johannesburg: Men, Mines and the Challenge of Conflict.* 1986. p. 82.

[81] Ibid. p. 91.

[82] Cain, Peter J. and Anthony G. Hopkins. *British Imperialism: 1688–2000.* 2002. p. 324.

[83] See: Wilburn, Kenneth. "The Drifts Crisis, the 'Missing Telegrams', and the Jameson Raid: A Centennial Review." *The Journal of Imperial and Commonwealth History* 25, no. 2 (1997): 219–239.

the new 52-mile railway line connecting the Vaal River to Johannesburg was opened for service on 1 January 1895, the government in Pretoria trebled the duty charges for transporting goods in and out of Johannesburg.[84] In a desperate attempt to boycott the government's railway charges in September, more than 100 ox-wagons a day would cross the Vaal River at various fords, known as drifts.[85] Using the railway embargo as a pretext for an incursion into the Republic, the plan and base for a potential military intervention to the economic blockade on rail goods were already decided in early October after Pitsani, a small area of six miles on the ZAR's western border was transferred to the BSAC.[86] Although all railway tariffs in the Republic were quickly lowered to 1894 levels, Johannesburg's industrial community viewed the railway crisis as a further sign of explicit discrimination against the city's economy and population. Most importantly, with Chamberlain's imperial endorsement, greater industrial cooperation in Johannesburg, and Jameson mobilising military resources in Pitsani, Rhodes was now firmly set on a takeover of the Rand.[87]

Spurred on by the negative political, economic, and financial changes, Johannesburg's reformers began to embrace drastic measures to bring about future stability. The political problems of the Rand had been exposed to the global financial community and little could be done in Johannesburg to alleviate the worries of an increasingly pessimistic mining market after the September Paris *Krach*.[88] According to Hobson, the Chamber of Mines was still the main concentration of economic power in Johannesburg of 1895, and took on the leading role in preparing the mining industry for an eventual raid on the city.[89] Continuity of the close relationship between the JSE and the Chamber was clearly evident at the beginning of 1895, and the two organisations worked together beyond their official mandates to encourage political reforms. The Chamber was still located only a few metres from the JSE, in the Bettelheim Building,

[84] Ibid. p. 222.

[85] Leasor, James. *Rhodes & Barnato: The Premier and the Prancer.* 1997. p. 185.

[86] Meredith, Martin. *Diamonds, Gold, and War: The Making of South Africa.* 2008. p. 318.

[87] See: Holli, Melvin G. "Joseph Chamberlain and the Jameson Raid: A Bibliographical Survey." *The Journal of British Studies* 3, no. 2 (1964): 152–166.

[88] "Kaffirs on the Continent." *Standard and Diggers' News*, 21 December 1895.

[89] Hobson, John Atkinson. *Capitalism and Imperialism in South Africa.* 1900. p. 26.

and was conveniently owned by prominent JSE founding member and honorary Ottoman Empire Consul, Henry Bettelheim.[90] Just about all the seats on the Executive Committee of the Chamber were occupied by members of the JSE. With the notable exception of the Chamber's President Lionel Phillips and James Tudhope, all the members of the Executive Committee were concurrently influential members of the JSE's General Committee[91] (Table 6.3).

Although Lionel Phillips was never a member of the JSE, his position as president of the Chamber and Johannesburg's representative of the Corner House put him at the centre of ZAR's gold mining industry. Initially politically disengaged and mistrusting, Phillips was regularly criticised by *The Star* for not using his strategic position at the head of the mining industry to diffuse the political agitation of the *Uitlanders*.[92] The opening of the Chamber's new headquarters, however, came at a time of significant financial tension on the international mining market and would serve as an ideal platform upon which to proclaim the Chamber's political ambitions for Johannesburg. In his infamous inauguration speech to a partisan audience of more than 300 mining representatives and financiers, Phillips, by then fully behind the *Uitlanders* and confident in Rhodes' plan for a potential uprising, delivered a formal declaration of the Chamber's unity behind the Reformers in Johannesburg:

Table 6.3 Witwatersrand Chamber of Mines Executive Committee at the end of 1894

Lionel Phillips (President)	**G.H. Farrar**
Carl Hanau (Vice-President)	**S.B. Joel**
James Hay (Vice-President)	**G.H. Goch**
F. Lowrey	**W.H. Rogers**
J.B. Taylor	**J.W.S Langerman**
J. Ballot	**A. Goerz**
W. St. John Carr	J. Tudhope

Names in bold JSE members
Source South African Chamber of Mines. *Annual Report for the year ending 1894*. 1895. p. 1

[90] Van der Waal, G.-M. *From Mining Camp to Metropolis: The Buildings of Johannesburg, 1886–1940*. Pretoria: Human Sciences Research Council. 1987. p. 22.

[91] JSEA. *Minutes of an Ordinary Meeting of the Committee*, 14 August 1895.

[92] Lang, John. *Bullion Johannesburg: Men, Mines, and the Challenge of Conflict*. 1986. p. 87.

Nothing is further from my heart than the desire to see an upheaval which would be disastrous from every point of view, and which would probably end in the most horrible of all endings, in bloodshed, but I would say this that it is a mistake to imagine that this much maligned community which consists anyhow of a majority of men born of freemen will consent indefinitely to remain subordinate to the minority of this country, and that they will forever allow their lives, their property, and their liberty to be subject to its arbitrary will.[93]

Although a substantial majority of the *Uitlanders* disapproved of Kruger's policies, some Randlords were very much against any potential military aggression against Kruger's state, and distanced themselves from any association with the Chamber and further links to Rhodes.[94] Joseph Robinson and Sammy Marks, both influential members of the Exchange, worked closely with Kruger throughout the 1890s and eventually warned him about a potential raid on Johannesburg in the final days of 1895.[95] Despite the central involvement of JSE members in the plot, it was Rhodes who feared the political participation of the conspirators most closely associated with the Exchange. Robinson, Barnato, Lippert, and Albu were all prominent members of the JSE, but acted as an obstruction to Rhodes' political plans for a successful Raid.[96]

The planning and execution of a potential rebellion was to be carried out by Leander Starr Jameson and his BSAC administration in Matabeleland. Meanwhile, the Johannesburg Reformers would recruit a local militia of 7 500 volunteers and prepare to join Jameson and his troops at the outskirts of the city.[97] Although the arms and ammunitions were smuggled into the ZAR by a small group of American engineers led by

[93] "Mr. Phillips Speech." *The Star*, 23 November 1895. p. 1.

[94] Kubicek, Robert V. "The Randlords in 1895: A Reassessment." *The Journal of British Studies* 11, no. 2 (1972). p. 99.

[95] Hammond, John Hays and Alleyne Ireland. *The Truth About the Jameson Raid.* Boston: Marshall Jones Company. 1918. pp. 30–31.

[96] Kubicek, Robert V. "The Randlords in 1895: A Reassessment." *The Journal of British Studies* 11, no. 2 (1972): 99–101.

[97] Meredith, Martin. *Diamonds, Gold, and War: The British, the Boers, and the Making of South Africa.* 2008. p. 322.

John Hays Hammond,[98] George Farrar, permanent member of the JSE General Committee since late 1888, was one of the key figures behind delivering the consignment of arms further to Johannesburg. In early December, Farrar even arrived at the meeting of the Reform Committee covered in oil, having personally assisted in the unpacking of rifles that were secretly hidden in large oil drums.[99] Although not acting in unison, the Reformers, mostly made up of JSE members, were ready to seize Johannesburg from the ZAR's control.

The final events of the conspiracy moved very quickly. A letter was drafted by Charles Leonard, the leader of the Transvaal National Union, to be handed over to Jameson on his visit to Johannesburg in late November. It was in fact Jameson who insisted on the letter as evidence to justify his actions to the BSAC administrators in Matabeleland and Cape Town.[100] The letter was to be used as an invitation for Jameson to 'aid' Johannesburg's Reformers in a takeover of the city:

> It is under these circumstances that we feel constrained to call upon you to come to our aid, should a disturbance arise here. The circumstances are so extreme that we cannot but believe that you and the men under you will not fail to come to the rescue of people who will be so situated. We guarantee any expense that may reasonably be incurred by you in helping us, and ask you to believe that nothing but the sternest necessity has prompted this appeal.[101]

The five conspirators who signed the letter in the name of the Reform Committee were Charles Leonard, Cecil Rhodes' brother, Colonel Frank Rhodes, John Hays Hammond, Lionel Phillips, and George Farrar.[102] Although the role of the JSE was not directly included in the plans, official communication in the General Committee's minutes pointed to knowledge of an uprising and the active participation of key members.

[98] See: Katz, Elaine. "The Role of American Mining Technology and American Mining Engineers in the Witwatersrand Gold Mining Industry 1890–1910." *South African Journal of Economic History* 20, no. 2 (2005): 48–82.

[99] Rosenthal, Eric. *Gold! Gold! Gold!* 1970. p. 281.

[100] Meredith, Martin. *Diamonds, Gold, and War: The British, the Boers, and the Making of South Africa.* 2008. p. 325.

[101] Quoted in: Fitzpatrick, Percy. *The Transvaal from Within: A Private Record of Public Affairs.* 1899. p. 126.

[102] Leasor, James. *Rhodes & Barnato: The Premier and the Prancer.* 1997. p. 189.

Throughout December a number of prominent members announced their leave from all JSE duties for a temporary period.[103] Along with the JSE Chairmen Solly Joel and George Imroth, other influential members such as Edward Solomon and William Dettelbach announced their immediate leave from all General Committee duties for an indefinite period.[104] The more significant connections to the Reform Movement were exposed by members who chose to remain in Johannesburg in the final days of the year. Three of the members present at December's final meeting of the General Committee were committed Reformers who, by then, were aware of the imminent uprising: Colonel Rowland Albermarle Bettington who was responsible for coordinating the military uprising in Johannesburg, William Rogers and Andrew Mackie Niven.[105]

The final week of the year on the Exchange did indeed expose the politicisation of Johannesburg's capital market.[106] Although there was no mention of the uprising, the Committee reported on the great political unrest inside the Exchange Hall with significant 'political harangue' by some members disrupting the proceedings of High 'Change.[107] The General Committee was required to investigate the political debates obstructing the course of daily trade, but no further details on the exact reasons behind the heightened tension were presented.[108] Additionally, a rather absurd piece of evidence points to the JSE's complicity in the Raid. Already anticipating a successful uprising in Johannesburg, JSE's General Committee approved an official application by Lionel Phillips to use the Exchange Hall for a 'New Year celebration.'[109] Knowing that the Raid would take place in the final days of the year, Phillips was clearly preparing to celebrate the potential breakaway of Johannesburg from the Republic inside the JSE.

The final planning and execution of the uprising exposed Rhodes' misjudgement of both political situation in Johannesburg and the BSAC's

[103] JSEA. *Minutes of an Ordinary Meeting of the Committee*, 19 December 1895.

[104] JSEA. *Minutes of an Ordinary Meeting of the Committee*, 24 December 1895.

[105] Ibid.

[106] JSEA. *Minutes of an Ordinary Meeting of the Committee*, 19 December 1895.

[107] Ibid.

[108] JSEA. *Minutes of an Ordinary Meeting of the Committee*, 24 December 1895.

[109] JSEA. *Minutes of an Ordinary Meeting of the Committee*, 19 December 1895.

readiness. In the final two weeks of the year, members of the Bechuanaland Border Police and further European volunteers from Matabeleland
and Mashonaland were transferred to the BSAC police camp in Pitsani.[110]
On Sunday 29 December, Jameson crossed into the ZAR with the
majority of BSAC's police force hurrying to reach Johannesburg and join
up with the volunteers from the Reform Movement.[111] In an attempt
to break the communication network between the BSAC territories, the
Cape Colony, and the ZAR, Jameson's militia cut the telegraph wires
to Cape Town, but had completely ignored to cut the communication
line to Pretoria.[112] Not surprisingly, news of the uprising reached President Kruger before Rhodes knew that Jameson had crossed the border.
Informed about the BSAC's plan, Jameson's armed column was followed
by Kruger's forces from the moment it entered the ZAR.[113]

It was, however, only on 30 December, a day after Jameson crossed
the border that Johannesburg Reform Committee formally expanded
into a larger body, which in a matter of hours included 'about seventy–
five of the most prominent men on the Rand.'[114] Colonel Bettington,
JSE director and chairman of the JSE Brokers' Association, made a late
attempt to link a small group of Johannesburg's Reformers with Colonel
Frank Rhodes' troops west of Johannesburg[115] before they were finally
defeated by Kruger's army at Krugersdorp on 31 December.[116] On 2

---

[110] Wilburn, Kenneth. "The Drifts Crisis, the 'Missing Telegrams', and the Jameson
Raid: A Centennial Review." *The Journal of Imperial and Commonwealth History* 25, no.
2 (1997): 230.

[111] "The Crisis. The Jameson Expedition." *Standard and Diggers' News*, 2 January
1895. p. 3.

[112] Parsons, Neil. "The 'Victorian Internet' Reaches Halfway to Cairo: Cape Tanganyika
Telegraphs, 1875–1926." 2012. p. 97.
See also: Schreuder, Deryck and Jeffrey Butler, eds. *Sir Graham Bower's The History
of the Jameson Raid and the South African Crisis, 1895–1902.* 2002. p. 79.

[113] Schreuder, Deryck and Jeffrey Butler, eds. *Sir Graham Bower's the History of the
Jameson Raid and the South African Crisis, 1895–1902.* 2002. p. 172.

[114] Hammond, John Hays and Alleyne Ireland. *The Truth About the Jameson Raid.*
1918. p. 32.

[115] Fitzpatrick, Percy. *The Transvaal from Within: A Private Record of Public Affairs.*
1899. p. 201.

[116] "Fighting near Krugersdorp." *Standard and Diggers' News*, 2 January 1895. p. 3.
Rosenthal, Eric. *On 'Change Through the Years; a History of Share Dealing in South
Africa.* 1968. p. 186.

January, Jameson and his remaining BSAC troops were surrounded by ZAR forces under Commandant Piet Cronje at Doornkop, just 15 km west of Johannesburg.[117] The whole rebellion was broken up quickly and the centre of Johannesburg was occupied by Kruger's ZAR forces. With limited exchanges of fire, Jameson's force suffered 18 casualties and around 40 wounded.[118] Cronje's force, on the other hand, suffered 4 casualties.[119]

The Jameson Raid was a disaster for Rhodes and his BSAC administrators. Responding to the numerous telegrams from his Cape Town residence at Groote Schuur, Rhodes knew his financial and political career was on the line. Facing ruin and expecting to lose the charter for his BSAC territories, Rhodes handed in his resignation as Prime Minister of the Cape Colony on 1 January 1896.[120] Rhodes might have been essential to the organisation of the Raid, but was ultimately unable to understand Johannesburg's political needs, instead relying on his own imperial convictions.[121]

THE RAID'S FAILURE AND IMPLICATIONS

The Jameson Raid further polarised southern African settler societies along ethnolinguistic lines.[122] In all likelihood, the uprising disintegrated in Johannesburg because a significant portion of the city's population was not convinced by the prospects of British annexation and preferred to settle for a reformed republican state.[123] At an imperial level, the

[117] "The Crisis. The Jameson Expedtion." *Standard and Diggers' News*, 2 January 1895. p. 3.
Hammond, John Hays, and Alleyne Ireland. *The Truth About the Jameson Raid.* 1918. p. 36.

[118] Fitzpatrick, Percy. *The Transvaal from Within: A Private Record of Public Affairs.* 1899. p. 224.

[119] Ibid.

[120] See: "Rhodes Resigns." *Standard and Diggers' News*, 1 January 1896.

[121] Trapido, S. "Imperialism, Settler Identities, and Colonial Capitalism: The Hundred-year Origins of the South African War." 2011. p. 92.

[122] Marks, Shula. *Class, Culture and Consciousness in South Africa, 1880–1899.* In: Ross, Robert, Anne Kelk Mager, and Bill Nasson, eds. *The Cambridge History of South Africa: Volume 2, 1885–1994.* 2011. p. 148.

[123] Trapido, S. "Imperialism, Settler Identities, and Colonial Capitalism: The Hundred-year Origins of the South African War." 2011. p. 84.

situation was anything but stable, forcing Chamberlain to fight for his political life.[124] Although the British government did not act as an instrument of Johannesburg's mining magnates, nor did British capitalists in London want to fund Rhodes' imperial projects in southern Africa, the Raid confirmed that all parties were involved and mostly supportive of expanding British colonial rule into the Boer republics.[125] The influence of Johannesburg's Randlords was probably much less pronounced than has hitherto been assumed, with Robinson and Gallagher even dismissing their own theory on the imperial influence of Johannesburg's capitalists, by stating that neither Salisbury nor Chamberlain trusted the mining magnates to cooperate with imperial policy and authority.[126] The problem for British imperial interests was not one of promoting trade and investments in the ZAR, but rather one of pushing through their political design.[127] Johannesburg's diverse community of *Uitlander* financiers and mining prospectors was still too fragmented to actively contribute to the British imperial project.

The Raid's economic implications also raised the risk of further operational instability for the JSE. Most of the mines were already closed on 30 December 1895 and mine owners remained unsettled about how African workers would react to the political uprising.[128] References to the Jameson Raid were conveniently left out of the internal documentation, but several important details were officially recorded to explain how the Exchange dealt with the political crisis. In a hastily-written statement on 2 January, the General Committee declared that due to 'the present condition of public affairs, Friday and Saturday, the 3rd and 4th of January 1896, be treated as dealers' holidays.'[129] A few days later the "holidays" were scrapped and the Exchange was closed for

---

[124] See: Winkler, Henry R. "Joseph Chamberlain and the Jameson Raid." *The American Historical Review* 54, no. 4 (1949): 841–849.

[125] Cain, Peter J. and Anthony G. Hopkins. *British Imperialism: 1688–2000.* 2002. pp. 324–325.

[126] Robinson, Ronald, James Gallagher and Alice Denny. *Africa and the Victorians: The Official Mind of Imperialism.* London: Macmillan. 1981. p. 429.

[127] Ibid.

[128] Hammond, John Hays and Alleyne Ireland. *The Truth About the Jameson Raid.* 1918. p. 33.

[129] JSEA. *Minutes of an Ordinary Meeting of the Committee,* 2 January 1896.

all trade[130] with the building remaining open for members wishing to access their offices.[131] On 8 January the sixty-four members of Johannesburg's Reform Committee were officially arrested and transferred to the ZAR government's jail in Pretoria. The international group of prisoners represented Johannesburg's top financiers, lawyers, engineers, and local politicians. Out of the 64 arrested, 35 were British subjects, 16 ZAR citizens, 8 US Americans, 2 Germans, 1 Dutch national, 1 Turkish subject, and one 1 Swiss citizen.[132] Most importantly for the direct link to the JSE, 40 of the arrested were JSE members at the time of the Raid. (See Table 6.4

Once share trade was eventually restored on 8 January, all the shares belonging to the arrested members were suspended and banned from the trading floor.[133] Since many transactions from December had not yet been cleared, a state attorney from Pretoria was invited to discuss the legality of the unsettled business.[134] The government officials immediately ordered that all pending share transactions from arrested members were to be put on hold and their Johannesburg bank accounts frozen.[135] The ZAR's High Court also requested the names and files of all the companies owned by the Reformers that were to be used as evidence during the Pretoria trial.[136] The international markets followed the legal proceedings with great urgency and alarm.[137] The LSE was particularly concerned about the legal status of JSE-listed stocks circulating in London and enquired about the legality of all securities associated with the Reformers.[138] London traders continued to be suspicious of the trade

---

[130] JSEA. *Minutes of an Ordinary Meeting of the Committee*, 6 January 1896.

[131] Ibid.

[132] Rosenthal, Eric. *Gold! Gold! Gold!* 1970. p. 293.

[133] JSEA. *Minutes of an Ordinary Meeting of the Committee*, 8 January 1896.

[134] JSEA. *Minutes of an Ordinary Meeting of the Committee*, 21 January 1896.

[135] Ibid.
  See also: Henry, James A. *The First Hundred Years of the Standard Bank*. 1963. pp. 130–133.

[136] JSEA. *Minutes of an Ordinary Meeting of the Committee*, 18 February 1896.

[137] *The Illustrated London News*, 11 January 1896. p. 1.

[138] Ibid.

Table 6.4 Arrested members of the Reform Committee and JSE affiliation 1895–1896

1. Lionel Phillips	17. D.F. Gilfillan	33. Dr. R.P. Mitchell	49. W.B. Head
2. Colonel F.W. Rhodes	18. C.H. Mullins	34. **Dr. Hans Sauer**	50. V.M. Clement
3. **George Farrar**	19. **E.O. Hutchinson**	35. **Dr. A.P. Hillier**	51. **W. Goddard**
4. J.H. Hammond	20. W. van Hulsteyn	36. **Dr. D.P. Duirs**	52. **J.J. Lace**
5. J.P. FitzPatrick	21. A. Woolls-Sampson	37. Dr. W. Brodie	53. C.A. Tremeer
6. **S.W. Jameson**	22. **H.C. Hull**	38. **H.J. King**	54. **R.G. Fricker**
7. **G. Richards**	23. Alf. Brown	39. **A. Bailey**	55. J.M. Buckland
8. **J.L. Williams**	24. **C.L. Andersson**	40. Sir Drummond Dunbar	56. J. Donaldson
9. G. Sandilands	25. **M. Langermann**	41. **H.E. Becher**	57. **F.H. Hamilton**
10. **F. Spencer**	26. **W. Hosken**	42. **F. Mosenthal**	58. **P. du Bois**
11. **R.A. Bettington**	27. **W. St. John Carr**	43. **W. H. Rogers**	59. H.B. Marshall
12.J.G. Auret	28. **H.F. Strange**	44.C. Butters	60. **S.B. Joel**
13. **E.P. Solomon**	29. C. Garland	45. **Walter D. Davies**	61. **A.R. Goldring**
14. **J.W. Leonard**	30. **Fred Gray**	46. **H. Bettelheim**	62. **J.A. Roger**
15. **W.H.S. Bell**	31. **A. Mackie Niven**	47. F.R. Lingham	63. **Thomas Mein**
16.**W.E. Hudson**	32. **Dr. W.T.F. Davies**	48. **A.L. Lawley**	64. J.S. Curtis

Names in bold are those of JSE members
Source JSEA. *JSE Members Roll Books 1895–1896*

on the JSE and how members' links to the political situation might influence the future of share trading in Johannesburg[139] (Fig. 6.2).

After capture, Jameson and all BSAC administrators involved were handed over to the British authorities in Cape Town and sent back to London for an official trial and imperial investigation. The 'Jameson Raiders' arrived in England at the end of February to face prosecution under the Foreign Enlistment Act of 1870 that prevented British soldiers

[139] "The Stock Exchange: Uncertain." *The Star*, 4 March 1896. p. 3.
See also: Duguid, Charles. *The Story of the Stock Exchange: Its History and Position.* 1901. pp. 338–340.

Fig. 6.2 The JSE after the Jameson Raid (*Source The Illustrated London News.* 11 January 1896. p. 1)

from acting as mercenaries in non-British territories.[140] All were officially charged with 'unlawfully preparing a military expedition to proceed
against the dominions of a certain friendly state, to wit, the South African
Republic, contrary to the provisions of the Foreign Enlistment Act.
1870.'[141] Despite the serious allegations, and the significant publicity
they received, Jameson's sentence of fifteen months imprisonment was
amended to a stay in a private hospital.[142] In Johannesburg, the situation
for the local Reform Committee, especially those linked directly to the
JSE, would be very different.

Many members were forced or, as in the case of Colonel Bettington,
strongly encouraged to resign from the General Committee and revoke
their membership.[143] Although Bettington and many others involved in
the Raid suspended their JSE memberships for the first quarter of the year,
by April 1896 most had renewed their subscriptions.[144] Large numbers
of members also left Johannesburg without announcing their leave, but
still chose to pay their quarterly subscription.[145] In all, as many as 70
members resigned from the JSE in the first two months of 1896.[146] By
the end of March, however, new applications were once again allowed
and the General Committee approved as many as 90 members within the
month.[147] The total membership numbers stabilised at 555 members and

[140] "Dr. Jameson's Return." *The Times*, 24 February 1896. p. 6.
  See: Van Heyningen. "Leander Starr Jameson." In: Brenthurst Press. *The Jameson
Raid: a centennial retrospective*. 1996. pp. 184–188.

[141] Quoted in: King, James. *Dr. Jameson's Raid: Its Causes and Consequences*. London:
Routledge & Sons. 1896. p. 138.

[142] "The Trial Of Dr. Jameson." *The Times*, 28 July 1896. p. 4.
  See also: Van Heyningen. "Leander Starr Jameson." In: Brenthurst Press. *The Jameson
Raid: A Centennial Retrospective*. 1996. pp. 184–188.
  "Dr. Jameson was released from Holloway Prison late on Wednesday." *The Spectator*,
5 December 1896. p. 17.

[143] JSEA. *Minutes of an Ordinary Meeting of the Committee*, 12 March 1896.

[144] JSEA. *JSE Members Roll Books 1895–1896*.
  JSEA. *Minutes of an Ordinary Meeting of the Committee*, 14 April 1896.

[145] See: JSEA. *Minutes of an Ordinary Meeting of the Committee*, 7 April 1896.

[146] JSEA. *JSE Members Roll Books 1895–1896*.

[147] JSEA. *Minutes of an Ordinary Meeting of the Committee*, 12 March 1896.

the Raid did not lead to a mass exodus as the financial crisis in 1889/90 did.[148]

All the Reform Committee prisoners were released on bail on 26 January with the notable exception of the Committee's leaders, Lionel Phillips, George Farrar, Colonel Frank Rhodes, Percy Fitzpatrick, and John Hays Hammond.[149] The official treason trial began in Pretoria on 3 February, and lasted until 12 February, with all but one of the sixty-four accused present.[150] After paying fines of £2 000 each, most of the Reformers had returned to Johannesburg or left the ZAR by the end of February.[151] The JSE became the central meeting place for crowds of Johannesburg's *Uitlanders* when the Reform Committee leadership was put on trial for high treason in Pretoria in April. The JSE stood in full solidarity with the original five who had signed the declaration letter inviting Jameson to Johannesburg, and began to mobilise political resources in order to potentially change the outcome of the trial.[152] The JSE also sent out an urgent telegram to the LSE asking their London colleagues to use their contacts in the City to initiate a diplomatic effort to mitigate the Reformers' punishment.[153] Despite the international solidarity and the JSE's direct efforts in Pretoria, at the end of the trial on 24 April 1896 Lionel Phillips, George Farrar, Frank Rhodes, John Hays Hammond, and Percy Fitzpatrick were presented with the official court verdict and sentence that needed no English translation: '*hangen bij den nek.*'[154]

---

[148] See: JSEA. *Minutes of an Ordinary Meeting of the Committee*, 14 April 1896.

[149] Hammond, John Hays, and Alleyne Ireland. *The Truth About the Jameson Raid*. 1918. p. 38.

[150] Ibid. p. 40.
See also: King, James. *Dr. Jameson's Raid: Its Causes and Consequences*. 1896. pp. 112–126.
For comprehensive documentation of the Jameson Raid trial, see: Krout, Mary Hannah. *A Looker on in London*. New York: Dodd, Mead and Company. 1899.

[151] "The Trial of the Reform Committee." *The Times*, 8 February 1896. p. 5.
See: Rosenthal, Eric. *Gold! Gold! Gold!* 1970. p. 301.

[152] JSEA. *Minutes of an Ordinary Meeting of the Committee*, 29 April 1896.

[153] Ibid. 29 April 1896.
See also: "Message from the Johannesburg Exchange." *Financial Times*, 30 April 1896. p. 5.

[154] Wheatcroft, Geoffrey. *The Randlords*. 1987. p. 183.

As the landlord and operator of the JSE, the Johannesburg Estate needed to take responsibility and action on the political crisis. Barney Barnato was in London at the time of the Raid and was inundated with hundreds of requests from British investors demanding the return of their investments in the Barnato's Bank in the first weeks of 1896.[155] Barnato spent a sizable portion of his personal fortune in an attempt to prop up the international market and would later be recognised by the Mayor's office where he bestowed with the title of *Lieutenant of the City of London* in November 1896.[156] Despite his official disassociation with Johannesburg's Reformers, it was Barnato who literally saved the five leaders from the noose.[157] While Rhodes saw Kruger as an enemy of the British Empire, Barnato had realised very early in his ZAR financial ventures the importance of staying on good terms with the President.[158] Kruger suspected that Barnato had not been involved in the Raid and was not a member of the Reform Committee.[159] After a long sequence of telegrams and meetings with Kruger between January and early May, Barnato was able to influence the appeal and even threatened Kruger that he and many other Randlords would take their capital out of the ZAR if the last prisoners were not released.[160] Barnato was eventually able to convince Kruger to change each of the death sentences to £20 000 fines which were later paid by Cecil Rhodes and Alfred Beit from a special fund they established with the BSAC.[161] Rhodes took on most of the fines and altogether, paid out more than £300 000 in consequence of the

---

[155] Leasor, James. *Rhodes & Barnato: The Premier and the Prancer.* 1997. p. 197.

[156] "Rand Gold Shares." *The Economist*, 18 January. 1896. pp. 67–68.
"The Barnato Burlesque." *The Economist*, 18 January 1896. pp. 66–67.
Kynaston, David. *City of London: The History.* 2011. p. 171.
The London Gazette, 27 November 1896. p. 6916. https://www.thegazette.co.uk/London/issue/26798/page/6916.

[157] See: "The Transvaal Prisoners and the Mines." *The Economist*, 23 May 1896. p. 656.

[158] Leasor, James. *Rhodes & Barnato: The Premier and the Prancer.* 1997. p. 199.

[159] Ibid. p. 201.

[160] Coulson, Michael. *The History of Mining: The Events, Technology and People Involved in the Industry that Forged the Modern World.* 2012 p. 91.

[161] Smith, Ian. "A Century of Controversy Over Origins." In: Lowry, Donal, ed. *The South African War Reappraised.* Manchster: Manchester University Press. 2000. pp. 32–35.
See also: BLA. BSAC. Memoranda of Accounts to 31 March 1896. MS 355/3/2. Salisbury, 22 March 1897.

Raid.[162] As confirmed by the confidential 'Memoranda of Accounts to 31 March 1896,' Rhodes was even able to claim the costs of the Raid and the trials from the BSAC.[163] Barnato was carried shoulder high into the JSE after arriving back from Pretoria with the General Committee sending a telegram to President Kruger thanking him for releasing the Reformers:

> At an enthusiastic meeting of the Johannesburg Stock Exchange held immediately on receipt of the announcement of the decision by the Honourable the Executive Council it was unanimously resolved to convey to your Honour and the Honourable Executive Council their warmest and heartiest expressions of thanks for your magnanimous and generous decision in regard to the release of the Reform Prisoners. Your decision cannot but have the most beneficial far reaching effects upon the whole of South Africa; and the members feel sure that the same magnanimity which prompted your action will be extended to those still under sentence.[164]

The Chamber of Mines was the commercial organisation most affected by the Raid. The Chamber's direct association with the Reformers discredited the organisation as an industrial body.[165] 23 member mining companies broke official ties with the Chamber in the first two weeks of 1896, justifying their decisions by stating that given the heightened political crisis, the Chamber was not able to provide adequate representation for Johannesburg's mining industry.[166] The disgruntled companies that left the organisation in January suggested that the Chamber was now only concerned with the negative political impact of the Raid on the few large groups dominating the leadership of the Chamber.[167] There was little doubt that Wernher, Beit and Co. were involved in the Raid. Despite the blatant discrepancies pointing to an extensive cover-up of the Corner House's participation in the Raid, no primary documentation exists to

[162] Wheatcroft, Geoffrey. *The Randlords*. 1987. p. 184.

[163] BLA. BSAC. Memoranda of Accounts to 31 March 1896. MS 355/3/2. Salisbury, 22 March 1897.

[164] JSEA. *Minutes of an Ordinary Meeting of the Committee*, 30 May 1896.

[165] Lang, John. *Bullion Johannesburg: Men, Mines, and the Challenge of Conflict*. 1986. p. 102.

[166] SACMA. *South African Chamber of Mines Annual Report for the year ending 1896*. 1897. p. 3.

[167] Lang, John. *Bullion Johannesburg: Men, Mines, and the Challenge of Conflict*. 1986. p. 102.

suggest this was true.[168] Just as in the case of the JSE, the Chamber of Mines and the Corner House group were very careful not to disclose official details of their support and participation in the Raid.

CONCLUSION

The Jameson Raid was a culminating point in Johannesburg's early political and economic history. It marked an important milestone in the development of South Africa's gold mining industry and showed the extent to which the city's financial community became involved in a complex web of regional and imperial politics. The British financial public viewed the Raid with a lot of excitement, but in official imperial circles the attempted military takeover of Johannesburg turned out to be a great embarrassment.[169] The JSE's association with the Chamber of Mines and the Reform Movement constituted a strategic imperial partnership that exposed Johannesburg's capital market to Rhodes' plot against President Kruger's government.

This chapter has shown that as a financial and increasingly political intermediary, the critical year of 1895 presented the Exchange with numerous local and international opportunities, but, more importantly, revealed significant weaknesses in the legitimacy and viability of the ZAR's mining market. Despite technological constraints and a generally subdued local market, a small number of deep-level mining stocks and Rhodes' BSAC were able to revive Johannesburg's increasingly politicised capital market. The sudden boom and abrupt *Krach* of Paris' mining market exposed the interference of Johannesburg capitalists such as Barnato and Robinson, thus worsening the reputation of the JSE and its products in Europe. The September market collapse in Paris and London dashed most hopes of any significant positive changes, adding to the already heightened political tensions among the city's *Uitlander* community. With Rhodes using his BSAC administration in Bechuanaland and Matabeleland to influence the Corner House, the Chamber of Mines, and many influential members of the JSE, the scene was set for a confrontation

[168] See: Fraser, Maryna, and Alan Jeeves. *All that Glittered: Selected Correspondence of Lionel Phillips, 1890–1924.* 1977. pp. 99–101.

[169] See: Duguid, Charles. *The Story of the Stock Exchange: Its History and Position.* 1901. pp. 338–340.

between Johannesburg's mining capital, British imperialism, and Kruger's republicanism.

Although the exact nature of the *Uitlanders'* political grievances and their contribution towards the Jameson Raid was not at the core of the argument, the evidence presented connects leading JSE members to the establishment of Johannesburg's Reform Committee and their participation in the Raid. General Committee members George Farrar, Colonel Rowland Bettington, and the JSE's chairman Solly Joel were all involved in the Raid's planning and participated in the failed uprising. With 40 out of the 64 Reformers arrested being JSE members, the Exchange was overwhelmingly implicated in the Raid. It was however the Pretoria trial in April 1896 that confirmed any doubts regarding the involvement of the Exchange. Having just returned to Johannesburg from working to stabilise the South African mining market in Europe, as chairman of the Johannesburg Estate Company, it was Barney Barnato who stood in solidarity with the Reformers and convinced President Kruger to free all the remaining prisoners, including his cousin and JSE chairman, Solly Joel. Although most of the prisoners' fines paid to the Pretoria government were settled by Rhodes, it was Barnato who hosted the celebration for the prisoners' release inside the JSE's Exchange Hall. Even if most of the Exchange's official positions on the Raid were left unrecorded, the original evidence presented in this chapter exposed the agency of numerous prominent members in a complex entanglement of British imperialism and international finance.

CHAPTER 7

A Modernising Exchange and the South African War

With the nineteenth-century drawing to a close, it became reasonably clear that Johannesburg and Pretoria were influencing local, regional, and global politics in very different ways. As all the political power of the ZAR resided in Pretoria's government institutions, just about all the economic and financial potential was firmly established in Johannesburg.[1] Despite the fact that the JSE made significant attempts to reach out to President Kruger's government in the aftermath of the Jameson Raid, the organisational restructuring created a very different financial intermediary in an increasingly hostile political environment. Recognising the intertwined relationship of the two cities, Kruger's government was prepared to offer Johannesburg's Randlords a set of financial and commercial reforms in return for a political settlement on the extension of the franchise.[2] However, and to the disappointment of most international mining investors,[3] Kruger's re-election win in February 1898 over the progressive Piet Joubert who campaigned for more generous

---

[1] Stephens, John. *Fuelling the Empire: South Africa's Road to War*. 2003. p. 180.
[2] Trapido, S. "Imperialism, Settler Identities, and Colonial Capitalism: The Hundred-year Origins of the South African War." 2011. p. 98.
[3] "President Kruger and the Banks." *The Economist*, 21 May 1898. pp. 766–767.

© The Author(s), under exclusive license to Springer Nature
Switzerland AG 2024
M. Lukasiewicz, *Gold, Finance and Imperialism in South Africa,
1887–1902*, Cambridge Imperial and Post-Colonial Studies,
https://doi.org/10.1007/978-3-031-51947-5_7

policies towards the Republic's *Uitlanders* and, especially, Johannesburg's financial community, increased the political agitation between the two cities. After President Kruger's swearing-in in May, many Johannesburg residents believed that stronger political links with the new High Commissioner for Southern Africa, Alfred Milner, in the Cape, had become a necessity.[4] By the end of the nineteenth century, JSE became a modern financial organisation increasingly preferring the Victorian model over Kruger's republicanism.

The causality of the events that took place between the Jameson Raid and the outbreak of the Anglo-Boer War, now known more commonly as the South African War, on 11 October 1899 has become an issue of much controversy and debate for scholars of African and imperial history alike.[5] Although the South African War has attracted more attention from historians than any other nineteenth century event in Southern African history,[6] the role of finance, and its institutions inside the ZAR, has been divided by opposing theoretical debates, leaving little room for the study of financial intermediaries and their specific roles in South Africa's international mining market.[7] Kubicek may have been fascinated by the social backgrounds of the shareholders in South Africa's gold mines residing in Europe, but never attempted studying the objectives of the financial intermediaries in southern Africa where these shares were traded before the outbreak of the War.[8] Although the recurring historiographical theme for studies of Anglo-African-Afrikaner relations has always been to establish connections between British territorial expansionism and the

---

[4] See: Cain, Peter J. and Anthony G. Hopkins. *British Imperialism: 1688–2000.* 2002. p. 326.

[5] For recent British perspective, see: Donaldson, Peter. *Remembering the South African War: Britain and the Memory of the Anglo-Boer War, from 1899 to the Present.* 2013.

For South African view, see: Nasson, Bill. "Commemorating the Anglo-Boer War in Post-Apartheid South Africa." *Radical History Review* 78 (2000): 149–165.

[6] See: Porter, Andrew. "The South African War and the Historians." *African affairs* 99, no. 397 (2000): 633–648.

[7] See: The Debate about South Africa. In: Lipton, Merle, ed. *Capitalism and Apartheid: South Africa, 1910–1986.* 1986. pp. 2–13.

[8] Kubicek, Robert V. *Economic Imperialism in Theory and Practice: The Case of South African Gold Mining Finance 1886–1914.* 1979. p. 31.

South African War, the JSE's position as Johannesburg's premier financial intermediary remains obscure.[9]

This final chapter investigates the social, economic, and political position of Johannesburg's financial sector and the JSE on the eve of the South African War. The objective is to connect the context of the war to the previously ignored agency of the Exchange and its members. Documenting the convergence of imperial connections between Johannesburg, London and Cape Town, this chapter exposes the JSE's deepening support for the British invasion of the ZAR. Additionally, and perhaps most interestingly, the chapter shows how the JSE prepared its members, operations, and physical property for the eventual outbreak of war and the duration of hostilities. With the explicit backing and support of the new British administration in South Africa after Johannesburg's surrender in May 1900, the JSE was poised to become the main capital market of a new colonial economy.

VICTORIA AT THE EXCHANGE

The JSE might seem an unlikely place to study Victorianism and its cultural manifestations. In comparison to other dominions in Australia, Canada, and New Zealand, by the end of the nineteenth-century Southern Africa was the least anglicised and the most politically volatile.[10] Although cultural accounts of social links between the colonial state, colonisers, and settlers are a major theme of Victorian Studies,[11] the case of Johannesburg, a city in an independent, albeit settler, republic in Africa, created an unusual affection for the new generation of London's gentlemanly capitalists.[12] It was due to this contrast that Johannesburg's

[9] See: Smith, Ian. "A Century of Controversy Over Origins." In: Lowry, Donal, ed. *The South African War Reappraised*. 2000. pp. 24–26.

[10] Dubow, Saul. "How British was the British World? The Case of South Africa." *Journal of Imperial and Commonwealth History* 37, no. 1 (2009): 4.
See, also: Darwin, John. *The Empire Project: The Rise and Fall of the British World-system, 1830–1970*. 2009. pp. 216–220.

[11] See: Schmitt, Cannon, Nancy Henry and Anjali Arondekar. "Introduction: Victorian Investments." *Victorian Studies* 45, no. 1 (2002): 7–16.

[12] See: Van der Waal, G-M., Wilhelm Grütter, and Anna Jonker. *Early Johannesburg, its Buildings and its People*. Human & Rousseau. 1986. pp. 20–25.

financial sector turned into a unique expression of Victorian commerce and culture.[13]

Johannesburg played an important part in the political imagination of Victorian era intellectuals. Anthony Trollop, Henry Rider Haggard, John Atkinson Hobson, Randolph and Winston Churchill, Rudyard Kipling, Mark Twain and even Mahatma Gandhi spent time in Johannesburg at some point during the last two decades of the nineteenth century, using their experiences in the city of gold to shape many of their ideas on global politics that were later disseminated throughout the English-speaking world. The Victorianism of the JSE was at the centre of a much greater cultural phenomenon. The emergence of South African gold mining securities in Britain and Johannesburg in the mid-1880s was a huge moral test for Victorian capitalism.[14] The South African gold mining share booms provided the ultimate insight into the operations of the late Victorian capital market.[15] It was in this role of finance that Victorian society imagined British engagement in the ZAR.[16]

Although already displayed in Kimberley in the early 1880s, Johannesburg's financial frontier was particularly unique in its cultural adaptation of European *haute finance*.[17] The JSE's international pool of brokers, bankers, and miners exemplified financial globalisation at the periphery. The hazardous efforts of the General Committee and its members contributed in a large measure to the recognition of Johannesburg's

---

[13] See: Michie, Ranald. *The Global Securities Market: A History.* 2007. p. 108.

[14] Johnson, Paul. *Making the Market: Victorian Origins of Corporate Capitalism.* Cambridge: Cambridge University Press. 2010. pp. 208–211.

Michie, R. C. *Guilty Money: The City of London in Victorian and Edwardian Culture, 1815–1914.* 2016. p. 133.

[15] Van Helten, Jean Jacques "Mining, Share Manias and Speculation: British Investment in Overseas Mining, 1880–1913." 1990. p. 170.

Robinson, R., J. Gallagher and A. Denny. *Africa and the Victorians: The Official Mind of Imperialism.* 1981. p. 429.

See also: Phimister, Ian. "Late Nineteenth-Century Globalization: London and Lomagundi Perspectives on Mining Speculation in Southern Africa, 1894–1904." *Journal of Global History* 10, no. 1 (2015): 27–52.

[16] Daunton, Martin J. *State and Market in Victorian Britain: War, Welfare and Capitalism.* London: Boydell Press. 2008. pp. 161–164.

[17] See: Rosenthal, Eric. *On 'Change Through the Years; a History of Share Dealing in South Africa.* 1968. pp. 143–144.

economic potential and political vulnerability. As much as Johannes-burg resembled a provincial Victorian town in its architecture,[18] it was for the Victorian 'art of the puff' that Johannesburg received the most public attention in London and Paris.[19] With London playing the critical capital link in the popularity and expansion of the South African mining market, the social life of the JSE replicated the commercial passions of Victorian Britain.[20] Realising the Victorian dream of financial fortunes became the very idea on which the JSE was developed and continu-ously expanded.[21] As represented by the suspicious death of Barnato in 1897, the JSE was also where many of these Victorian dreams came to die.[22] As already documented earlier in the previous chapter, the increased mobility of defaulting brokers between the JSE and the LSE posed a reputational threat to both organisations, prompting chairmen Solomon and Burdett to increasingly cooperate in exchanging information on their respective organisation's members and regulations.[23] On the LSE, the Randlords and the members of the Johannesburg Reform Committee became celebrities for the City's financial class after the Jameson Raid. Leander Starr Jameson, Abe Bailey, and Barney Barnato all graced the pages of London's Vanity Fair in 1896 and 1897. At the same time, as some JSE members were awaiting their Jameson Raid trial in Pretoria, LSE members were enacting theatrical scenes of the Raid on the trading

---

[18] Murray, Martin J. *City of Extremes: The Spatial Politics of Johannesburg*. 2011. pp. 47–48.

[19] Hobson, John Atkinson. *The War in South Africa: Its Causes and Effects*. 1900. p. 11.

For Victorian 'Art of Puff' see: Flandreau, Marc. *Anthropologists in the Stock Exchange*. 2016. p. 8.

[20] For cultural significance of the stock exchange in Victorian Britain See: Itzkowitz, David C. "Fair Enterprise or Extravagant Speculation: Investment, Speculation, and Gambling in Victorian England." *Victorian Studies* 45, no. 1 (2002): 121–147.

[21] For excellent study on the relathionship between psychology and economics in Victo-rian intellectual tradition, see: Kornbluh, Anna. *Realizing Capital: Financial and Psychic Economies in Victorian Form*. 2013.

[22] 'The Death Of Mr Barnato.' *The Economist*. 19 June 1897. p. 875. *The Story of 'Johnnies', 1889–1964: A History of the Johannesburg Consolidated Investment Co. Ltd*. 1965. p. 26.

[23] JSEA. *Minutes of an Ordinary Meeting of the Committee*, 13 December 1897.

floor.[24] A few of the Reformers who took part in the Raid caused great celebrations and amazement when they visited the LSE in the early months of 1896.[25]

A year after the Raid, some of the most influential gold producers were again protesting the ZAR government's policies that were seen as a great hurdle to the sustainable growth of the gold mining industry.[26] Despite the JSE General Committee's clear intentions to improve relations with Pretoria in the aftermath of the Raid, most of the members of the Exchange were staunchly opposed to Kruger's republican government. The resentment for Kruger was expressed in support for Britain and her empire. In March 1897 the General Committee established the Victoria Commemoration Committee to coordinate the planning of events celebrating Queen Victoria's Diamond Jubilee.[27] It was also resolved that on 22 June, the Queen's Jubilee be observed as an official stock exchange holiday, and all transactions falling on that date would be settled and cleared on 23 June.[28]

The great majority of Johannesburgers enthusiastically joined in the celebrations of Queen Victoria's sixtieth jubilee, in part as a form of protest against Kruger's government in Pretoria.[29] Johannesburg's residents used the celebration as an opportunity to encourage anti-republican demonstrations, waving British flags as a gesture to the Queen, but more importantly, to emphasise that they were denied the right to ZAR citizenship.[30] According to Rosenthal, few places in the British Empire flew more Union Jacks and formed longer processions than Johannesburg.[31] The JSE was closed for all business, but many members congregated around the Exchange Hall to sing 'God Save the Queen,' and joined

---

[24] Duguid, Charles. *The Story of the Stock Exchange: Its History and Position.* 1901. pp. 338–339.

[25] Ibid. p. 338.

[26] Trapido, S. "Imperialism, Settler Identities, and Colonial Capitalism: The Hundred-year Origins of the South African War." 2011. p. 96.

[27] JSEA. *Minutes of an Ordinary Meeting of the Committee*, 9 March 1897.

[28] JSEA. *Minutes of an Ordinary Meeting of the Committee*, 15 June 1897.

[29] Rosenthal, E. *Gold! Gold! Gold!: The Johannesburg Gold Rush*, 1970. p. 312.

[30] Ibid.

[31] Ibid.

the rest of the city in extensive celebrations on the Market Square.[32] The Jubilee commemorations included a procession on Commissioner Street, showing off nine gilded spheres carried on separate horse-drawn lorries, representing each year's gold output from Johannesburg's mines.[33] Although President Kruger sent a telegram with his congratulations to Buckingham Palace, unlike the festive scenes outside the JSE, Pretoria hosted no event to mark the Queen's jubilee.[34]

Yet, the most significant aspect of the JSE's support for the imperial project in southern Africa after the Jameson Raid came from the Victoria chartered British South African Company in Rhodesia. The JSE kept very close ties with the BSAC administration and the Rhodesian exchanges in regularly sending delegations to compare local rules and regulations.[35] In 1897 the JSE's General Committee was even elevated to diplomatic status by the BSAC when an official JSE delegation was sent to Rhodesia for the opening of the Bulawayo railway line.[36] Despite the condemnation of the Raid, the JSE hosted many Bulawayo Stock Exchange directors for regular discussions on the development of the share trade in southern Africa throughout the late 1890s.[37]

As much as the JSE's General Committee cooperated with the BSAC since 1889 and the BSE since 1894, members of the Exchange were far more interested in the trade in BSAC shares, which dominated the JSE's market throughout 1897.[38] The BSAC shares were listed on the LSE,

[32] See: Jim Davidson. "Also Under the Southern Cross: Federation Australia and South Africa — The Boer War and Other Interactions. The 2011 Russell Ward Annual Lecture." *Journal of Australian Colonial History* 14 (2012): 183–204.

[33] Fraser, Maryna. *Johannesburg Pioneer Journals, 1888–1909.* 1985. p. 57.

[34] Rosenthal, E. *Gold! Gold! Gold!* 1970. p. 313.

[35] Karekwaivenani, George. "'A History of the Rhodesian Stock Exchange: The Formative Years, 1946–1952." *Zambezia: The Journal of Humanities of the University of Zimbabwe* 30, no. 1 (2003): 13.

[36] JSEA. *Minutes of an Ordinary Meeting of the Committee,* 7 September 1897.

[37] JSEA. *Minutes of an Ordinary Meeting of the Committee,* 13 April 1897.
JSEA. *Minutes of an Ordinary Meeting of the Committee,* 1 February 1898.
JSEA. *Minutes of an Ordinary Meeting of the Committee,* 12 June 1898.
See also: Karekwaivenani, George. "A History of the Rhodesian Stock Exchange: The Formative Years, 1946–1952." *Zambezia: The Journal of Humanities of the University of Zimbabwe* 30, no. 1 (2003): 15.

[38] JSEA. *Minutes of an Ordinary Meeting of the Committee,* 23 November 1897.
See also: "The Stock Markets." *The Economist,* 1 January 1898.

BSE, and JSE. Towards the end of 1897 the market had turned and scrip for delivery in London was actively traded between Johannesburg and Bulawayo.[39] There was no single company listed on the JSE that received such a great deal of attention in meetings and communications in the final years of the nineteenth century. The BSAC was regularly consulted on its flotation plans in Johannesburg and any potential irregularities were always solved amicably, with the JSE holding the BSAC administration in its highest esteem.[40] Furthermore, several JSE and Bulawayo brokers were involved in a BSAC trading syndicate that was eventually broken up once the brother of Dr. Leander Starr Jameson, Samuel William Jameson, was expelled from the JSE.[41]

By the end of 1898, Johannesburg's preference for Victorianism, driven by a financial system centred on the JSE, highlighted the city's growing incompatibility with Pretoria's conservative republicanism and Afrikaner cultural identity. Although Kruger still saw opportunity over threat in the city's expanding industries, his tolerance was wearing thin. A similar view was also held in London. The British cabinet mistrusted Johannesburg's population and seriously doubted whether their renewed British loyalties were genuine since Kruger made repeated attempts to secure some economic and political autonomy for the city.[42] With the Union Jack rather than the ZAR's *vierkleur* being more visible in Johannesburg, the city of gold was about to become a bargaining chip in worsening Anglo-Afrikaner diplomatic relations.

PREPARING FOR WAR

The British government and colonies in southern Africa had for a long time tolerated and respected many of the Afrikaner diplomatic attempts to avert conflict, but time began to run out for the ZAR.[43] Outside the JSE, the political situation was deteriorating by the day. By the second half of 1899, the British government and Afrikaner republicans had come

---

[39] JSEA. *Minutes of an Ordinary Meeting of the Committee*, 1 February 1898.

[40] JSEA. *Minutes of an Ordinary Meeting of the Committee*, 12 January 1899.

[41] JSEA. *Minutes of an Ordinary Meeting of the Committee*, 19 August 1898.

[42] Robinson, R., J. Gallagher and A. Denny. *Africa and the Victorians: The Official Mind of Imperialism*. 1981. p. 459.

[43] "The Transvaal Crisis." *The Times*, 13 October 1899. p. 10.

to a political stalemate, leaving Lord Milner to resort to a military solution in South Africa. Chamberlain had stressed that peace in South Africa was of the greatest importance for the stability of the Empire in southern Africa and urged Milner to follow a careful and passive stance towards Kruger's policies in the ZAR.[44] President Kruger managed to persuade Milner to meet for talks to work on a potential franchise for *Uitlanders* on neutral ground in Bloemfontein. However, as negotiations after negotiations broke down, all the policies of compromise were abandoned. Having successfully persuaded the British cabinet to accept the prospects of another war in Africa,[45] the British War Office mobilised 10 000 troops to protect strategic military and economic positions in Natal.[46] Chamberlain went as far as taking a possible war far into all corners of the Empire by securing offers of military assistance from Canada, New Zealand, West Africa, the Malay States, Victoria, New South Wales, and Queensland.[47]

As talk of the possibility of war swept across southern Africa, the JSE General Committee was about to elect a new chairman. Acting in the position since Solomon's departure, Andrew Mackie Niven was officially reappointed as chairman on 18 April 1899. Despite coming third in the elections, Alfred Spring and Edward Berlandina relinquished their positions to allow Mackie Niven to continue with his chairmanship.[48] Mackie Niven, a deeply religious Protestant from Glasgow, was an unusual choice, but his selection proved how desperate the JSE was for a morally strong character to lead the JSE through the oncoming crisis. More importantly for the political reputation of the Chairman, Niven had been part of the Reform Committee and was arrested along with Jameson in the Raid. His credentials were considered ideal for the complexities of Johannesburg's political situation.

The new chairmanship came at a very difficult time for the Exchange and Johannesburg as a city. The 1899 General Committee elections were supposed to restore some confidence in a fragile share market and political

[44] JSEA. *Minutes of an Ordinary Meeting of the Committee*, 12 September 1899.

[45] "The Government and the War." *The Times*, 26 October 1899. p. 11.

[46] See *Preparing for a small war* in: Pakenham, Thomas. *The Boer War*. 1979. pp. 82–99.

[47] Ferguson, Niall. *Empire: The Rise and Demise of the British World Order and the Lessons for Global Power*. New York: Basic Books. 2003. p. 272.

[48] JSEA. *Minutes of an Ordinary Meeting of the Committee*, 18 April 1899.

system, but achieved very little in attracting brokers back to the Exchange Hall. Attempting to turn the crisis into an opportunity, the JSE took on another gamble. Although cautious and prudent, Mackie Viven believed that the political crisis could be used to purchase a property for the new Exchange building at a much lower rate than Solomon had budgeted. The new plot was situated on Commissioner Street, about 200 metres away from the current building. The proposed site, a 50 by 150 feet plot previously used as a field for auctions, was approved for sale by the government to the JSE at a price of £15 000 on 18 July.[49] It appeared that apart from the JSE, no one in the city was prepared to buy any land or buildings.[50]

The decision to purchase the site and commit to the construction of a new Exchange building came at the worst political time in Johannesburg's young history. With no political compromise between Pretoria and London in sight, by the end of July it had become clear that most interest in the JSE's share market was abandoned.[51] The decision to erect a new Exchange building installed no confidence in the members and had exactly the opposite effect. Throughout August and September, most of Johannesburg's financial professionals began to leave for Natal and the Cape Colony.[52] Despite the official approval of the General Committee, most members believed the decision proved how short-sighted the JSE was and ignored the realities of the share market, which had reached the lowest level since the Jameson Raid.[53] Out of the 571 JSE members at the end of June, only 40 members had paid their subscription fees for the final quarter.[54]

The London market had also come to accept the prospects of war despite a number of dealers still believing Kruger's government would be forced into submission.[55] On the other hand, London brokers were

---

[49] JSEA. *Minutes of an Ordinary Meeting of the Committee*, 6 June 1899.

[50] *The Story of 'Johnnies', 1889–1964: A History of the Johannesburg Consolidated Investment Co. Ltd.* 1965. p. 32.

[51] SBA. GMO 3/2/1/2, 8 August 1899. p. 85.

[52] Henry, J.A. *The First Hundred Years of the Standard*, 1963. p. 137.

[53] SBA. GMO 3/2/1/2, 8 August 1899. p. 84.

[54] JSEA. *JSE Members Roll Books for Year Ending 1899 and 1900.*

[55] Kynaston, David. *City of London: The History.* 2011. p. 180.
See also: "Progress of the Negotiations." *The Financial Times,* 1 September 1899. p. 3.

ready to support a military conflict in the ZAR, as a final political settlement to the problems of the *Uitlanders* in Johannesburg.[56] LSE members were generally convinced that whatever a British military intrusion into the Republic might result in, it would ultimately lead to an improvement of the conditions under which the gold mining industry was operating.[57] With many South African mining houses now operating out of offices in Cape Town, an increasing amount of telegraph traffic in the Cape Colony was directed to the LSE. London's South African mining market had, however, reached its lowest price levels of the year and remained quiet amidst rising press hysteria on the possibilities of war.[58] Shareholders in London and Europe were increasingly questioning the immediate operational future of Johannesburg's mines, leading to a constant flow of scrip to the market.[59]

The major concern in Johannesburg and London, however, remained over the legal status of open transactions that would be affected by the outbreak of war.[60] Official agreements were quickly reached with the Cape Town and Pietermaritzburg stock exchanges to facilitate trade in JSE-listed stocks in the event of the Exchange having to close due to an outbreak of war.[61] Even if the General Committee was convinced that the official declaration of war would suspend the civil process of all the courts, the ZAR's law was not clear on how commercial contracts were to be recognised.[62] Although the JSE General Committee remained deeply concerned about the potential legal changes that the ZAR government could implement without any prior consultation, an official position of the Exchange was drafted to dismiss some uncertainty. All calls on shares were to be suspended during a moratorium, even if no martial law would be declared. All time bargains, described, as 'shares sold on time,' would

[56] Kynaston, David. *City of London: The History*. 2011. p. 180.

[57] "Financial History of the Year." *Investors Monthly Manual*, 31 December 1899. pp. 669–670.

[58] See: "The Mining Market." *Investors Monthly Manual*, 30 September 1899. pp. 503–504.
See, also: "The Transvaal Situation." *The Economist*, 23 September 1899. p. 1354.

[59] "Financial History of the Year." *Investors Monthly Manual*, 31 December 1899. pp. 669–670.

[60] "The Johannesburg Stock Exchange." *The Financial Times*, 18 October 1899. p. 5.

[61] Klein, Harry. *The Story of the Johannesburg Stock Exchange, 1887–1947*. 1948. p. 56.

[62] JSEA. *Minutes of an Ordinary Meeting of the Committee*, 19 September 1899.

not mature during the moratorium, even if officially transferred by the JSE to any other stock exchanges in Natal, the Cape Colony, or Rhodesia. A special instruction was also given to French brokers in the case of contracts made with French financial intermediaries payable in a neutral place, the doctrine of viz *major* would still make the right to payment valid.[63]

With the legal strategy confirmed and approved by the General Committee, the final preparations were made for the potential closure of the JSE building. Special precautions were immediately taken to arrange the safekeeping of minute books, company annual reports, surety bonds, and fixed deposits in the city. All the financial documents and surety bonds were to be handed over to the *Safe Deposit & Co.*, a company specialising in the secure storage of valuable goods and in huge demand in Johannesburg.[64] The Exchange's two Afrikaner janitors offered to maintain the building during any potential hostilities and were to be immediately paid a salary advance by the JSE and the Estate Company for their loyalty.[65] With most JSE members having left Johannesburg, a small sub-committee was asked to stay behind to manage all simple administrative matters. Although the names of the four members who made up the sub-committee were not provided by the General Committee, the chairman, Mackie Niven, was to ensure the chosen members would sign the emergency operations agreement on the day war was declared.[66]

Niven, like most other committee members, left Johannesburg with his family on 1 October, and it was up to his deputy, Edward R Berlandina, to chair the final crisis meetings on 3 October. With only Colonel Rowland Bettington, G. C. K. Bennet, and Sep Edkins joining the meeting, it was unanimously agreed to close the Exchange at 6 pm that day.[67] All financial business in Johannesburg was put on hold and banks closed their doors after Pretoria stopped the supply of electricity to Johannesburg.[68] With

---

[63] Ibid.

[64] JSEA. *Minutes of an Ordinary Meeting of the Committee*, 1 September. 1899.

[65] JSEA. *Minutes of an Ordinary Meeting of the Committee*, 19 September 1899.
  See also: JSEA. *Minutes of an Ordinary Meeting of the Committee*, 3 October 1899.

[66] JSEA. *Minutes of an Ordinary Meeting of the Committee*, 20 September 1899.

[67] JSEA. *Minutes of an Ordinary Meeting of the Committee*, 3 October 1899.

[68] Ibid.

the support and consent of the Estate Company, the General Committee decided to offer the Exchange Hall to the ZAR government for use as a hospital for the duration of the war. All the offices inside the Exchange Hall were also offered to the Pretoria government as an act of political mediation, with the JSE continuing to pay the rent for the duration of the conflict.[69] By the evening of the same day, work on barricading all the windows was in full swing.[70]

INSTITUTIONAL SURVIVAL AND RECONSTRUCTION

Pretoria believed that the British government was delaying all diplomatic cooperation to allow for a greater mobilisation of troops on the Republic's borders.[71] On 10 October 1899 President Kruger's and Steyn's ultimatum to London was officially rejected.[72] Determined to take the first move, the ZAR and OFS declared war on Britain on 11 October and invaded the Natal Colony. The outbreak of the war cast a long shadow on the history of South Africa, Africa, and the British Empire. The economic and social impact the war would eventually have on all South Africans created the structural vacuum that led to a new political order, creating the divisive framework for the twentieth century, which would polarise South African society to levels never experienced before.

Initially the war did not mean an end to share trade in southern Africa. The day that significant fighting began with the Boer's siege of Mafeking in the Cape Colony, on 12 October 1899, there were still 19 transactions in JSE shares on the Cape Town Stock Exchange.[73] The Rhodesian exchange also continued to operate and their London-listed securities proved to be an adequate substitute for London investors during the war.[74] During the peak of the hostilities, in April 1900, there were 91 Rhodesian stocks traded on the London Exchange, the majority of which

---

[69] Minutes of an Ordinary Meeting of the Committee, 28 September 1899.

[70] JSEA. *Minutes of an Ordinary Meeting of the Committee*, 3 October 1899.

[71] Rosenthal, E. *Gold! Gold! Gold!* 1970. p. 329.

[72] Gilliomee, Hermann and Mbenga, Bernard, eds. *New History of South Africa*. 2007. pp. 209–210.

[73] Rosenthal, E. *On 'Change Through the Years; a History of Share Dealing in South Africa*. 1968. p. 197.

[74] See: "Bulawayo Stock Exchange." *The Financial Times*, 5 March 1900. p. 4.

were mining stocks with their primary market in Bulawayo.[75] Brokers in Bulawayo kept trading in small quantities of Rhodesian-listed stocks until food shortages towards the end of 1900 forced most colonial settlers to leave for Mozambique.[76]

The continuation of mining operations on the Rand was economically far more crucial and problematic. With the outbreak of the war in October, the offices of most mining groups were transferred to Cape Town. Except for small sections of the reefs being worked by the ZAR government, just about all private mining operations on the Rand were suspended for the duration of the war.[77] The great majority of gold mines in the ZAR were shut down due to the official expulsion of British subjects towards the end of November 1899.[78] Although some 10 000 people (7000 were *Uitlanders* with ZAR residence permits) who stayed behind on the Rand endured much suffering, no battles were fought in Johannesburg and neither did the Boer forces have enough time to confiscate all assets belonging to British subjects.[79] According to the interim Standard Bank Manager stationed in Johannesburg for the duration of the war, only three mines, the Robinson Mine, Bonanza Mine and the Ferreira Deep Mine were operated directly by the ZAR's government.[80] The only two mining groups, with understandably strong connections to the JSE that continued to operate with minimal political infringement were those of German and French investment houses, run by Adolf Goerz and George Farrar.[81] The case of German and French involvements confirmed that investors could bypass the politics of war if they could prove their non-political character to Kruger.[82] Many mines were nonetheless flooded after air compressors, engines, water pumps, boilers,

---

[75] Karekwaivenani, George. "A History of the Rhodesian Stock Exchange: The Formative Years, 1946–1952." (2003). p. 15.

[76] SBA. GMO 3/2/1/2, 8 August 1900. p. 52.

[77] Fraser, Maryna and Alan Jeeves. *All that Glittered: Selected Correspondence of Lionel Phillips, 1890–1924.* 1977. p. 100.

[78] SBA. GMO 3/2/1/2, 7 February 1900. p. 48.

[79] "War. The Mines at Ridk. 80 Years Johannesburg Special." *The Star*, 12 September 1976. p. 7.

[80] SBA. GMO 3/2/1/2, 7 February 1900. p. 48.

[81] "The Transvaal Mines and the War." *The Financial Times*, 17 October 1899. p. 3.

[82] Ibid.

and other critical mining machinery were either confiscated or vandalised by the Republican army.[83]

Although the headquarters of the Chamber of Mines were officially moved to Cape Town in February 1900, some members of the Chamber's committee remained in Johannesburg throughout the war.[84] From at least early May 1900, the Chamber was determined to send representatives back to the Rand to inspect the damage and restart the mines.[85] The plan collapsed after Milner was unable to secure a safe passage for mine workers back to the Rand, forcing the Chamber to employ men already in Johannesburg to begin work on pumping water out of the mine shafts.[86] According to the Chamber's War Report of 1902, some Chamber members even raised a small 'Mine Guard' in January 1901 to protect their operations from further Boer agitation and safeguard the passage of valuable mining equipment to and from the Rand.[87] Most importantly, the Chamber needed to establish a delegation of members on the Rand to assure a strong representation of the mining industry during the takeover of Johannesburg from the Pretoria Government, which to the Chamber was not a matter of certainty, but rather a matter of time.

At the international finance level, the outbreak of war in South Africa prompted the prohibition of gold exports from the ZAR by the government.[88] There were initially significant worries about London's gold supplies now that mines in the ZAR were being closed or at least in part nationalised by the Pretoria government.[89] British imports of bullion and specie from South Africa dropped from £ 15 041 631 in 1899 to just £ 378 626 in 1900.[90] William Gladstone's cousin, Samuel Steuart

[83] "The Rand Mines After the War." *The Economist*, 17 February 1900. pp. 226–227.

[84] "Transvaal Chamber of Mines." *The Financial Times*, 22 April 1902. p. 6.

[85] Cammack, Diana Rose. *The Rand at War, 1899–1902: The Witwatersrand and the Anglo-Boer War*. 1990. p. 182.

[86] Ibid.

[87] "Transvaal Chamber of Mines." *The Financial Times*, 22 April 1902. p. 6.

[88] Henry, J. A. *The First Hundred Years of the Standard Bank*. 1963. p. 137.

[89] "The Rand Mines After the War." *The Economist*, 17 February 1900. pp. 226–227.

[90] Van Helten, Jean Jacques. "Empire and High Finance: South Africa and the International Gold Standard, 1890–1914." *Journal of African History* 23, no. 4 (1982): 544.

Gladstone, the senior partner of the East Indian merchants Ogilvy, Gillanders & Co., was put in charge of the Bank of England for the duration of the war.[91] While the Bank of England's interest rate was raised to 6% in November in a climate of financial panic,[92] the rate was lowered to 4% in July 1900,[93] remaining at this level (with one quick drop to 3%) for the duration of the war.[94] The prevailing low-interest rate suggested that the Bank of England had little problems in maintaining its gold reserves, even if the gold did not come from the ZAR. French and German gold markets were the greatest beneficiaries of the South African War as their exports of gold to Britain increased from 12.9% in 1899 to 17.9% in 1900, in spite of the low-interest rate.[95] What is also very important to consider is that during the war the price of bullion on the London market declined,[96] further suggesting that the Bank of England had no difficulties in obtaining gold from alternative markets at moderate prices.[97]

There was no international financial intermediary that followed the course of South African War more closely than the London Stock Exchange. Since the solidarity the LSE showed by exerting its influence in the City to help reduce the heavy sentences passed upon the Reform Committee in April 1896, members remained heavily supportive of Johannesburg's financial and political autonomy in a polarised South Africa.[98] The LSE was also instrumental in galvanising imperial support

---

[91] Kynaston, David. *City of London: The History.* 2011. p. 183.

[92] "Bank Reserves and the Effect of High Money Rates on Banking Profits." *The Economist*, 13 January 1900. pp. 41–42.

[93] "Foreign Exchanges and Banks of Issue." *The Financial Times*, 11 June 1901. p. 5.

[94] Ally, Russell. *Gold and Empire: The Bank of England and South Africa's Gold Producers.* 1994. pp. 24–27.

[95] Van Helten, Jean Jacques. "Empire and High Finance: South Africa and the International Gold Standard, 1890–1914." *Journal of African history* 23, no. 4 (1982): 544.

[96] See Fig. 1: *Range of Prices Fixed by the Bank of England for One Kilogram of Pure Gold (in pounds).* In: Ugolini, Stefano. *The Bank of England as the World Gold Market-Maker During the Classical Gold Standard Era, 1889–1910.* No. 2012/15. Norges Bank (2012). p. 16.

[97] Ally, Russell. *Gold and Empire: The Bank of England and South Africa's Gold Producers.* 1994: pp. 22–23.

[98] "Message from the Johannesburg Exchange." *The Financial Times*, 30 April 1896. p. 5.

from other financial intermediaries in the City. The same could not be said about the state of trade on the London market. On 3 October 1899, a week before the outbreak of the war, the bank rate was raised from 3.5% to 4.5%, with British consol prices falling to 101¾ price index numbers, the lowest levels in five years.[99] Following significant losses in the final quarter of 1899 after international investors came to realise that the war was not going to be over quickly, trade on the LSE came close to a halt during the first weeks of 1900.[100] Furthermore, much to the LSE's surprise, the Chancellor of the Exchequer, Michael Hicks-Beach, decided against the Rothschild's offer, and floated a £ 10 million British war loan on the New York Stock Exchange.[101] The LSE's main worry remained the British government's heavy borrowing, putting the whole market under significant pressure.[102]

Even with the poor state of the market, the South African War had provoked regular public demonstrations and a general outpouring of British imperial patriotism in London's financial sector.[103] Apart from continued moral support, the LSE established its own relief fund for refugees leaving the ZAR for the Cape Colony. By the beginning of 1900, the LSE was able to raise £ 34 664 10s for the Transvaal Refugees Fund. The City's Lord Mayor Alfred J. Newton helped to coordinate the LSE's war relief efforts and used the financial community's support for the war to establish the City of London Imperial Volunteers.[104] Great scenes of celebration took place inside the Exchange Hall when the OFS was taken by the British on 3 March 1900. Two months later even greater displays of excitement were witnessed when news reached London that Mafikeng had been retaken from the Boers (Fig. 7.1).

[99] Duguid, Charles. *The Story of the Stock Exchange: Its History and Position.* 1901. p. 383.

See also: "Financial History for the Year 1899." *Investors Monthly Manual*, 30 December 1899. p. 672.

[100] Kynaston, David. *City of London: The History.* 2011. p. 183.

[101] Cassis, Youssef. *Capitals of Capital: The Rise and Fall of International Financial Centres 1780–2009.* 2010. p. 88.

[102] Kynaston, David. *City of London: The History.* 2011. p. 187.

[103] Duguid, Charles. *The Story of the Stock Exchange: Its History and Position.* 1901. pp. 384–385.

[104] Ibid. p. 388.

Fig. 7.1 London Stock Exchange after the news of General Piet Cronje's surrender of the Orange Free State to the British, 3 March 1900 (*Source London Illustrated News*, 3 March 1900. p. 287)

The war was still far from over with Boer Commandos under Jan Smuts and Koos de la Rey operating inside the Republic and northern parts of Natal, but British troops were about to push onwards into the ZAR and to Johannesburg. Even before the capture of Johannesburg, in March 1900 Joseph Chamberlain announced Britain's intentions to formally annex the ZAR and OFS.[105] As soon as Johannesburg was surrendered to British forces on 31 May 1900, JSE members residing in Natal and the Cape Colony requested permission to return to Johannesburg.[106] Although JSE members wasted no time in seeking permission to travel to the Rand, it would take another 18 months before they would be allowed to move

[105] "House Of Commons." *The Times*, 20 March 1900. p. 10.

[106] Cammack, Diana Rose. *The Rand at War, 1899–1902: The Witwatersrand and the Anglo-Boer War.* 1990. p. 182.

back to Johannesburg. Lord Horatio Herbert Kitchener, the second in command of the British forces in South Africa, retrospectively confirmed the importance of the financial sector for the war. After the takeover of Johannesburg, the mines were immediately sanctioned to open and Kitchener himself gave special permission for the rapid re-establishment of the JSE.[107] Kitchener, who visited the LSE in December 1898 just a few weeks after the Fashoda Incident, was an imperial hero of London's gentlemanly capitalists and would encourage the JSE to reorganise under much closer scrutiny of the City of London.[108] The JSE would honour Kitchener's commitment to opening up the Exchange before the end of the war with a celebratory dinner for him on 17 June 1902.[109]

The most direct link between imperial finance and its political strategy for the new South African colonies came with Lord Alfred Milner. Although it was Kitchener who worked closely with JSE members in the Cape Colony to reopen the JSE, it was Milner who personally intervened to speed up the recovery of Johannesburg's financial sector.[110] Milner had served as High Commissioner for South Africa since 5 May 1897, and from 4 January 1901 as the Governor of the Transvaal and the Orange River Colony. Milner's understanding of imperial finance was largely built up during his position as Under-Secretary of Finance in Egypt. Milner's colonial policies emphasised the role of stable financial institutions and strengthening links to the City of London.[111] It was also Milner who, already in 1898, asked the Colonial Office to intervene in the City of London's financial architecture to obstruct the ZAR's borrowing capacity on the international markets.[112]

After arriving in Johannesburg, Milner carefully examined the prospects of reopening the JSE with representatives of the Estate

---

[107] "We Have More Than Once Called Attention to the." *The Times*, 14 December 1901. p. 11.

[108] See: Dilley, Andrew. "'The Rules of the Game': London Finance, Australia, and Canada, c. 1900–14." *The Economic History Review* 63, no. 4 (2010): 1003–1031.

[109] See: Drew, Allison. *Between Empire and Revolution: A Life of Sidney Bunting, 1873–1936.* 2015. p. 57.

[110] "Lord Milner on the Finances of the New Colonies." *The Economist*, 2 May 1903. pp. 777–778.

[111] See: Milner, Alfred. *England in Egypt*. London: E. Arnold. 1903.

[112] Cain, Peter J., and Anthony G. Hopkins. *British Imperialism: 1688–2000.* 2002. p. 325.

Company and the JSE's General Committee throughout December 1901.[113] For Milner and his new colonial administration in Transvaal, Johannesburg was first and foremost an industrial capitalist city, and needed to be developed as the financial centre of sub-Saharan Africa.[114] Milner personally attended the first JSE meeting on 14 December 1901, mediating between the JSE and the Estate, and encouraging the General Committee to stay in the old Exchange building until significant political stability would be restored in the Transvaal.[115] Mackie Niven, who arrived back in Johannesburg at the beginning of December, tried to convince Milner to distribute more relocation permits to members of Johannesburg's financial community and allow them to return to Johannesburg.[116] Working from his headquarters in the north of Johannesburg, Milner laid out his plan for a new South African civil service, made up of Oxbridge graduates with strong links to the City of London and Johannesburg's financial sector, a group of loyal colonialists who came to be known as 'Milner's Kindergarten.'[117]

The war was not yet officially over and British troops were still fighting Boer commandos south of Pretoria, but Johannesburg's financial community was firmly focused on resuming business activities as soon as electricity and water supplies were restored.[118] All telephone and telegram communication was still down at the end of 1901, forcing the JSE to return to the pioneering methods of couriers delivering letters to telegram outposts beyond the Transvaal. Additionally, with Johannesburg on alert against continued Boer resistance and sabotage, all letters and communications directed to the Exchange would first have to be screened by the British forces in Johannesburg before being handed over to the General Committee.[119]

---

[113] JSEA. *Minutes of an Ordinary Meeting of the Committee*, 24 December 1901.

[114] Van Onselen, Charles. *Studies in the Social and Economic History of the Witwatersrand 1886–1914. New Babylon.* 1982. pp. 196–197.

[115] JSEA. *Minutes of an Ordinary Meeting of the Committee*, 24 December 1901.

[116] Ibid.

[117] Rosenthal, E. 1970. p. 339.

See also: Dubow, Saul. "Colonial Nationalism, the Milner Kindergarten and the Rise of 'South Africanism', 1902–10." *History Workshop Journal* 43 (1997): 53–85.

[118] SBA. GMO 3/2/1/2, 14 August 1901. p. 49.

[119] JSEA. *Minutes of an Ordinary Meeting of the Committee*, 28 January 1902.

The JSE eventually reopened on 23 December 1901, and according to *The Times*, was an indication of a new stable social and economic order in Johannesburg.[120] Although old memberships still needed to be verified, the reopening promoted a stream of new membership applications.[121] By the end of March 1902, a total of 507 new members had joined the Exchange and paid their subscription fees.[122] All stock exchanges in southern Africa were informed of the reopening of business and, despite Milner's advice to stay located in the Estate's old building, the JSE's plans for the purchase of the plot for the new building were confirmed.[123] Even if official trade was only started on 3 March,[124] by the end of January 1902, brokers were already gathering in front of the JSE building, in the area previously known as 'Between the Chains,' to trade various shares that were being delivered to Johannesburg from the Cape Colony on a daily basis.[125] According to an initial assessment of the reopening by Mackie Niven, Milner explicitly stipulated that no official and unofficial share trade be allowed outside the building when granting permission for the JSE to restart operations.[126] Unlike in the late 1880s, the General Committee followed a hard line on preventing the formation of an unofficial curb market with the British military police being asked to monitor the area outside the Exchange and in other parts of the city for illegal street dealing.[127]

With the JSE in operation and mining output picking up gradually, the London mining market was also waiting for the first signs of stability in Johannesburg. Most London financial commentators were convinced that once the war finished the Rand's mining and financial industries would thrive under the new colonial administration.[128] London

---

[120] JSEA. *Minutes of an Ordinary Meeting of the Committee*, 24 December 1901. "The War." *The Times*, 14 December 1901. p. 11.

[121] JSEA. *Minutes of an Ordinary Meeting of the Committee*, 24 December 1901.

[122] Official figures from JSEA. *JSE Members Roll Books for year ending 1902.*

[123] JSEA. *Minutes of an Ordinary Meeting of the Committee*, 24 December 1901.

[124] JSEA. *Minutes of an Ordinary Meeting of the Committee*, 3 March 1902.

[125] JSEA. *Minutes of an Ordinary Meeting of the Committee*, 28 January 1902.

[126] Ibid.

[127] JSEA. *Minutes of an Ordinary Meeting of the Committee*, 31 January 1902.

[128] "Rand Gold Mining Shares." *The Economist*, 17 August 1901. pp. 1243–1244.

investors believed that mining costs under British rule would be significantly reduced, but until the Transvaal Colony adopted a new commercial legal system, London's mining market was overshadowed by a new issue of various West Australian gold mining stocks.[129] In the short term, it remained unclear how the JSE would adapt its rules and regulations to the new British colonial legislature after the ending of martial law. For London's brokers, the South African War also had a particular personal connection. Many stock exchange members from London and Johannesburg had lost their lives fighting on both sides of the front. 5 members of the JSE and 23 members of the LSE had fought and died in the South African War.[130] A commemorative plaque was unveiled at the JSE shortly after the war, listing the names of members of both exchanges who served in the war.[131]

The military conflict in South Africa in general, and Johannesburg in particular, exposed the degree to which international finance became the critical element of power relations that developed between settler colonial societies and the metropole.[132] This imperial entanglement was also integral to the survival of the JSE and Johannesburg's financial class. Business had hardly started again when Cecil Rhodes died on 26 March 1902. Although he was never a member of the JSE, the Exchange was closed as a mark of respect on 1 April 1902, the day of his burial at the Matobo Hills in Rhodesia. The last occasion of imperial significance to be held at the old Exchange building was the visit of British Colonial Secretary, Joseph Chamberlain, on 15 January 1903.[133] Once again validating the JSE's political and economic significance for the new imperial system in South Africa, the foundation stone of the new Stock Exchange was laid by Lord Milner in May the same year.[134]

---

[129] "The Rise in Rand Gold Shares." *The Economist*, 1 February 1902. p. 164.
    See also: "Financial History of the Year 1902." *Investors Monthly Manual*, 31 December 1880. p. 679.

[130] Parkhouse, Valerie. *Memorializing the Anglo-Boer War of 1899–1902: Militarization of the Landscape, Monuments and Memorials in Britain.* Leicester: Matador. 2015. p. 294.

[131] Klein, Harry. *The Story of the Johannesburg Stock Exchange, 1887–1947.* 1948. p. 58.

[132] See: Attard, Bernard, and Andrew Dilley. "Finance, Empire and the British World." *The Journal of Imperial and Commonwealth History* 41, no. 1 (2013): 1–10.

[133] Rosenthal, Eric. *On 'Change Through the Years; a History of Share Dealing in South Africa.* 1968. p. 202.

[134] "Johannesburg Stock Exchange." *The Financial Times*, 4 May 1903. p. 1.

The last of the ZAR's Boer commandos surrendered in May 1902 and the South African War was officially ended with the signing of the Treaty of Vereeniging in Pretoria. The OFS and ZAR became crown colonies with the promise of eventual self-government in a union of southern African colonies.[135] The South African War severely disrupted the industrialisation of deep-level mining and caused estimated indirect losses of £ 25 million as the majority of the mining industry lay dormant.[136] The gradual exhaustion of the ore and its quality, forced mining companies into geologically more difficult and economically more costly reefs. For the recovery of the mining sector to be successful, the highly capitalised industry depended on a new pool of low-paid labourers.[137] After most African workers left Johannesburg during the war, there was only a small settler labour force available. According to *The Economist*, by March 1901 the Chamber of Mines was allowed to operate 350 of the total 6000 mining stamps in operation in October 1899.[138] Although African workers began to return gradually, by the end of 1902 there were still only 52 587 workers, compared to the 96 704 in October 1899.[139] Given the significant post-war labour constraints, the gradual expansion of the mining industry brought a wave of financial optimism to Johannesburg and European financial capitals eagerly awaiting the resurgence of South African securities. The initial 'Peace Boom' saw nearly 300 new companies floated on the Rand by the end of the year.[140]

Despite signs of revival, the JSE in the Transvaal Colony became a very different financial organisation from its rustic pioneering days. The Randlords and their antics on the markets of London, Paris, and Johannesburg

---

[135] See: Marks, Shula. "War and Union, 1899–1910." In: Ross, Robert, Anne Kelk Mager, and Bill Nasson, eds. *The Cambridge History of South Africa*. 2011. pp. 164–165.

[136] Van Onselen, Charles. *Studies in the Social and Economic History of the Witwatersrand 1886–1914. New Babylon*. 1982. p. 24.

[137] See: Denoon, Donald J. N. "The Transvaal Labour Crisis, 1901–1906." *The Journal of African History* 8, no. 3 (1967): 481–494.

[138] "The Working of the Rand Mines." *The Economist*, 16 March 1901. p. 405.

[139] Innes, Duncan. *Anglo: Anglo American and the Rise of modern South Africa*. 1984. p. 66.

[140] Innes, Duncan. *Anglo: Anglo American and the Rise of modern South Africa*. 1984. pp. 60–61.
Harries, Patrick. *Work, Culture, and Identity: Migrant Laborers in Mozambique and South Africa, c. 1860–1910*. 1994. p. 130.

were blamed for the sacrifices imposed upon the British public by the South African War.[141] The early speculative core of the JSE was slowly replaced by a more regulated approach to financing southern Africa's deep-level mines and the growing manufacturing sector. The move to the new building in Hollard Street in 1904 reflected the stabilisation of Johannesburg's political, social, and economic life. Although not central to the political identity of the city after the South African War, the financial organisation became a key financial component of a regional settler economy, serving an expanding colonial financial system between the Zambezi and the Cape Coast.

CONCLUSION

The outbreak of the South African War in October 1899 led to the largest military conquest of an African territory during the nineteenth-century Scramble for Africa. For Britain, the war proved to be the greatest military test since the Indian Mutiny of 1848 and turned into the most extensive military campaign of the Victorian and Edwardian era. The South African War was Britain's longest (lasting nearly three years), most expensive (costing over £200 million), and bloodiest (with about 25 000 Afrikaners, 22 000 British, and 12 000 Africans losing their lives) war between the Napoleonic Wars in 1815 and the outbreak of WWI in 1914.[142] More significantly for the study of South Africa's financial sector, the war paused twelve years of institutional development that took the JSE from a small tent in the original mining camp to the centre of Johannesburg's globalising financial industry.

This chapter exposed unique primary evidence on the economic, legal, and social concerns of Johannesburg's premier financial intermediary during the peak of Anglo-Afrikaner tensions in southern Africa. Analysing the rise and preference for Victorianism, the final two years of peace in Johannesburg were as testing for the JSE as they were for Afrikaner and British politicians. The General Committee navigated the JSE through an austere political climate that saw many members suspend or give up their memberships. Solomon's and later Mackie Niven's modernisation projects

[141] Kitzan, Laurence. *Victorian Writers and the Image of Empire: The Rose-colored Vision*. Westport: Greenwood Publishing Group. 2001. p. 60.

[142] See: Boer War. In: Raugh, Harold E. *The Victorians at War, 1815–1914: An Encyclopedia of British Military History*. Santa Barbara: Abc-Clio. 2004. pp. 51–53.

to overcome the technological and spatial constraints of the old Exchange building further revealed the divergence of interests between the General Committee and the JSE's members. With many members let down by the General Committee's lack of priorities during the financial and political crisis of 1898/9, the regular departures of JSE members were seen as evidence of the extreme political and economic difficulties facing the share trade in the ZAR.

The JSE was officially closed, the Exchange Hall cleared, and all windows boarded up on 3 October 1899. Despite measures taken to leave behind a small committee for the duration of the hostilities and maintain the building as a potential hospital, the formative years of the Exchange had come to an end with the outbreak of war on 11 October 1899. All other members left the ZAR for the Cape Colony and Natal. Even if Johannesburg's gold mining industry believed the conclusion of the war would bring numerous political and economic reforms, the evidence presented in the JSE's General Minutes points to great uncertainty and no outright support for a British invasion of the ZAR. Whether opportunistic or a sign of political goodwill, the decision to offer the offices inside the JSE to the Pretoria government for the duration of the conflict provides original insights into the Johannesburg financial sector's risk management during the South African War.

Although it was never the intention to debate the political causes and consequences of the South African War, a clear link to the complex entanglement of imperial finance was made using the JSE, and in part the LSE. As later demonstrated by Kitchener, Milner, and Chamberlain's post-war visits to the JSE, the reopening of the Exchange was seen as a notable sentiment to the significance of Johannesburg in the international financial system. Despite attempting to balance British financial interests with loyalty to Pretoria's republicanism before the war, the Exchange clearly sided with British commercial, political, and legal interests once its legitimacy among foreign investors was challenged. The importance of the JSE as a financial hub for the new Transvaal Colony cannot be overstated. With the explicit backing and support of the British administration for South Africa, the JSE would soon become the central capital market of a new settler colonial economy.

CHAPTER 8

Conclusions

The utter dependence upon financial "booms" and "slumps," conjoined with the strain and kaleidoscopic change of the political situation, has bred by selection and by education a type of man and of society which is different from that of Manchester as the latter is from the life of Hankow or Buenos Ayres.[1]
—John A. Hobson on Johannesburg

Southern Africa's mineral discoveries in the last quarter of the nineteenth century changed the nature of the region's society, economy, and political landscape in an increasingly imperial context. The growth of diamond mining in the late 1870s and the discovery of significant gold deposits in 1886 attracted European settlers, capital, and financial intermediaries in a process of imperial conquests, land dispossessions, and racial discrimination at a scale never before experienced on the African continent. The mineral revolutions facilitated South Africa's entry into an increasingly global financial system, but also exposed the region's political vulnerability and industrial resilience during the final stages of the imperial 'Scramble for southern Africa.' It was indeed international finance and its role in facilitating the exploitation of South Africa's human, physical, and

---

[1] Hobson, John Atkinson. *The War in South Africa: Its Causes and Effects.* 1900. p. 13.

© The Author(s), under exclusive license to Springer Nature   203
Switzerland AG 2024
M. Lukasiewicz, *Gold, Finance and Imperialism in South Africa,*
1887–1902, Cambridge Imperial and Post-Colonial Studies,
https://doi.org/10.1007/978-3-031-51947-5_8

political resources that subdued the African majority between the European settler minority's competing imperial and republican visions. It was however in Johannesburg, an industrialising city deep in the ZAR, where the institutions and intermediaries of finance set forth the clearest tangible manifestation of a fragmented settler society readying for war.

The increase in gold production in and around Johannesburg generated a simultaneous explosion of growth in local and foreign financial intermediaries such as banks, mining exploration companies and, most significantly for the arguments presented in this work, the Stock Exchange. This book examined the establishment, institutional development, and organisational expansion of the Johannesburg Stock Exchange and its industrial partners in a study that connected the local and global scale of its operations. By the outbreak of the South African War in October 1899, the JSE had become a modern financial intermediary in an industrialising regional economy and international mining market. Applying the stock exchange modality as an analytical lens into settler colonialism's relationships with private capital, British imperialism, and Boer republicanism, this book's main contribution lies in its critically examination of the internal contradictions of colonial South Africa's violent transformation by financial capitalism.

Building on the historiography of the South African War that has produced an immense wealth of social, economic, and political studies, the analytical isolation of the stock exchange modality exposes an undervalued component in South Africa's cauldron of capitalism. As maintained by Van der Poel, the social connections of Johannesburg's political mobilisation to the JSE are obscure, 'for the secrets of the share market are not easily uncovered.'[2] This book has revealed many of these secrets, as well as their consequences for British imperialism in Southern Africa. As an original historiographical contribution, this work also acts as a proof of concept, maintaining that the JSE and its partner organisations hold a unique value for the historical study of global finance and its interaction with imperialism in Africa. The reasons for the JSE's establishment and its financial objectives in colonial South Africa's political economy provide invaluable information on how financial market participants responded to international demands of mining finance and diverging settler colonial politics. This study was therefore not an isolated corporate history

---

[2] Van der Poel. *Jameson Raid*. 1951. p. 83.

of Africa's oldest existing and largest stock exchange, but a dynamic business, social, and political history of Johannesburg's capital market in a global financial system backed by gold. Testing the direct causality between the establishment of the JSE, the failed Jameson Raid and the outbreak of the South African War, this work concludes that the Exchange acted as a strategic financial and political intermediary that endorsed the British colonisation of the ZAR.

The main findings expose how the early development of the JSE's rules, regulations, and organisational microstructures was in many ways encouraged by South African mining securities' restricted access to the main trading floors of international capital markets in London and Paris. The JSE replicated and reinterpreted LSE rules and regulations to its benefit and shared cooperation at many financial and political levels throughout the 1890s. The early growth of the Exchange was not only a response to the barriers of international capital markets, but a reaction to the increased demand in global mining stocks and the internationalisation of nineteenth-century finance through the classical gold standard. Although initially only serving a small pool of European speculators in the ZAR, the higher capital demands of the deep-level mining revolution from 1890 elevated the JSE into a growing global network of stock exchanges, communicating with those in the Cape Colony, Natal, Rhodesia, London, and Paris. Considering the originality and extent of the JSE's official records, this work exposed new evidence on the establishment and corporate organisation of South Africa's financial sector. Along with primary material from the JSE's partner organisations, such as the Johannesburg Estate Company, the Chamber of Mines and the Standard Bank, the London Stock Exchange, and several Parisian banks, the work provided new insight into the local, regional, and global development of southern Africa's finance system during the first age of financial globalisation.

The JSE's close cooperation with the Chamber of Mines also needs to be viewed as a strategic industrial partnership in an assault on African labour. With the ZAR's agricultural sector under significant pressure from the political and fiscal consequences of droughts and the spread of rinderpest, the proletarianisation of local labour was replaced by the immigration of cheaper and more easily coercible labour from Portuguese Mozambique and India, in the process further exposing the transimperial connectedness of the mining industry's factors of production. Although the agency and voice of Africans in the development of the

ZAR's mining and financial industries are exposed, it is ultimately over-shadowed by the racialisation and explicit racism of the settler-dominated industrialising economy. Resistance to social and economic subordination through the adoption of strategies such as migration, economic diversi-fication, and non-industrial sector employment allowed many Africans to directly challenge republican and colonial policies.

The social analysis of Johannesburg's capital market and financial sector focused on explaining how the ZAR's major mining magnates, the Rand-lords, came to shape the corporate development of mining finance. By strategically using the JSE to restructure who owned and controlled the means of production in deep-level mining, the Randlords established and entrenched themselves in an increasingly international market for South African mining securities. Albu, Barnato, Beit, Eckstein, Farrar, Goerz, Rhodes, and Robinson expanded their networks from Kimberley to Johannesburg, Bulawayo, London, and Paris, using the JSE as a central financial intermediary for local and international capital. Barnato and his extended family were seen as the key to safeguarding the international reputation of the JSE and its listed securities as a legitimate and profitable organisation at the centre of the world's largest gold mining sector, estab-lishing the Exchange as a unique and unlikely organisational component of South Africa's international mining finance. Though not 'gentle-manly capitalists,' Johannesburg's frontier financiers were nonetheless closely connected to Victorian financial institutions, corporate cultures, and colonial ideology. These connections and values were clearly ampli-fied when Johannesburg's financial sector was confronted by Pretoria's anti-British republicanism. Furthermore, and in a manner that was very much indicative of Johannesburg's early social development, the produc-tion, and preservation of these contested identities transpired within a hyper-masculine organisational space.

The economic and political dynamics around financial speculation on the international market for South African mining shares have revisited Hobson's insights, despite their many shortcomings, into Johannesburg's diverging society. Through applying the stock exchange modality to the reorganisation of the deep-level mining initiative, the operations on the JSE exposed the Rand's global financial fragility in rampant risk-taking, short-term speculation, and capital misallocation. Even when Johan-nesburg's financial speculation was deemed both acceptable and highly profitable, it was ultimately speculation on the political divergence from Pretoria that took the heaviest toll on South Africa's divided societies.

Although Hobson's grand theories about the economic and financial origins of imperialism have been debated continuously since their publication in the early twentieth century, this book has been able to deconstruct the global web of the JSE's social architecture to confirm his assertion of the stock exchange as a major tool in the political organisation of Johannesburg's foreign capitalists.

The dynamic study of the JSE's entanglement in a globalising financial system also revealed the participation of new social networks in established capital markets such as London and Paris. The analysis of Johannesburg's financial class and its interaction with the JSE exposed new evidence on the Randlords' international ambitions. More importantly for the relationship between finance and territorial imperialism in Africa, the study confirmed previous research on Johannesburg's capitalist class, using the JSE to reveal certain members' direct links to the 'Scramble for southern Africa.' The sequence of events that led up to the South African War begins with the Jameson Raid which had its origins in Parisian trade in South African mining stocks towards the end of 1895. Most significantly for this work's contribution to imperial history, the JSE anticipated the coming of the war and prepared accordingly. After measures were taken to leave behind a small four-member committee for the duration of the hostilities and maintain the building as a potential hospital, most members left the ZAR for the Cape Colony and Natal. Even if Johannesburg's gold mining industry believed the conclusion of the war would bring political and economic reforms, the JSE did not show outright support for the British invasion of the ZAR. Despite attempting to balance British financial interests with loyalty to Pretoria's republicanism before the war, the Exchange clearly sided with British commercial, political, and legal interests after Johannesburg was occupied by the British forces. As demonstrated immediately after the British occupation of Johannesburg, Kitchener, Milner, and Chamberlain's visits to the Exchange prioritised the significance of the JSE as a financial hub for the new Transvaal colony. With the explicit backing and support of the new colonial administration in South Africa, the JSE was poised to become the main capital market of new settler economy. Moreover, it was precisely during the JSE's post-war institutional reconstruction that the intricate connections between London's gentlemanly capitalism and the British colonial empire were revealed.

As the results presented in this book show, the early corporate organisation of the Rand's mineral-energy complex exposes the regional dependence on financial capitalism and its implications for political power in modern South Africa. Three decades after the dismantling of apartheid, South Africa remains deeply segregated. If apartheid is taken as not just an ideology of racism and racial segregation, but also a system of economic exploitation, it becomes difficult to argue that it has meaningfully ended. South Africa's capital market and its international exposure have in many ways been at the centre of current discourse on monopoly capitalism and the government's inability to reduce the staggering economic inequality which continues to divide South Africans along racial lines. It is hoped, therefore, that the findings of this book will provide important historical insights into the forces of international finance and South Africa's continued socioeconomic disparities.

BIBLIOGRAPHY

Archives diplomatiques du ministère des Affaires étrangères. Paris, France
Afrique Australe. 1862–1887
Correspondance Commerciale Pretoria 1887–1895

Banque de Paris et des Pays-Bas Archives. Paris, France
Paribas Transvaal papers
Banque française d'Afrique du Sud papers

Barloworld Archives. Barloworld Limited. Johannesburg
Corner House papers
Jules Porges & Co. papers
London Letters of Wernher, Beit & Co.

Basler Afrika Bibliographien. Basel, Switzerland
Argus Photographic Collection
Bodleian Archives and Manuscripts Collection. Oxford, United Kingdom
Papers of Cecil John Rhodes
Brenthurst Archives. Houghton, Johannesburg
Archives of the Johannesburg Estate Company
British South Africa Company collection
Rhodes letters

Guildhall Manuscripts. London Metropolitan Archives. London
LSE company filles
LSE company annual reports
LSE Minute Meetings

© The Editor(s) (if applicable) and The Author(s), under exclusive
license to Springer Nature Switzerland AG 2024
M. Lukasiewicz, *Gold, Finance and Imperialism in South Africa,
1887–1902*, Cambridge Imperial and Post-Colonial Studies,
https://doi.org/10.1007/978-3-031-51947-5

LSE Mining Reports 1886–1888

The National Archives. London.
Transvaal under British occupation.

National Archives Repository of South Africa. Pretoria, South Africa
Public Records of former Transvaal Province and its predecessors

South African Chamber of Mines Archives. Marshalltown, Johannesburg
Annual Reports

Standard Bank of South Africa Archives. Standard Bank. Johannesburg
Inspection Reports
Branch Reports
Annual Reports (London, Cape Town, Port Elizabeth)

Johannesburg Stock Exchange Archives. Sandton, Johannesburg
Minutes of Meetings
Members' Roll

Wits Historical Papers. University of Witwatersrand. Johannesburg
Rhodes Papers
Early Johannesburg collection
Archives of the *Committee into the discovery of gold on the Witwatersrand*

NEWSPAPERS

The Economist
The Cape Argus
The Daily Mail
Le Figaro
The Financial Times
Frankfurter Zeitung
The Journal (Graham's Town)
Leselinyana La Lesutho
Libération
London Illustrated News
The Investors Monthly Manual
New York Times
North China Herald
Revue Sud-Africaine
The Rhodesia Herald
The Spectator
The Star
The Statist

The Standard and Diggers' News
The Telegraph
The Times of London

CONTEMPORARY WORKS (PUBLISHED BEFORE 1910)

Abraham, Felix. *The Excesses of the Witwatersrand Gold Shares Speculation of 1894.* London: Published by author. 1895.

de Bremont, Comtesse Anna. *The Gentlemen Digger.* London: Greening and Co. 1899.

Compagnie des agents de change. *Règlement intérieur de la Compagnie des agents de change de Paris.* Paris: Chambre syndicale des agents de change. 1891.

Curle, James Herbert. *The Gold Mines of the World: Containing Concise and Practical Advice for Investors Gathered from a Personal Inspection of the Mines of the Transvaal, India, West Australia, Queensland, New Zealand, British Columbia, and Rhodesia.* London: Waterlow and Sons Limited. 1899.

Duguid, Charles. *The Story of the Stock Exchange: Its History and Position.* London: G. Richards. 1901.

Dupont, Henry. *Les mines d'or de l'Afrique du Sud.* Paris: Lemaire & Dupont. 1893.

Glanville, Ernest. *The South African Goldfields.* London: Swan Sonnenschein & Company. 1888.

Goldman, Charles Sydney. *The Financial, Statistical, and General History of the Gold & Other Companies of Witwatersrand, South Africa.* London: E. Wilson and Co. 1892.

Haggard, Henry Rider. *King Solomon's Mines.* London: Cassell and Co. 1885.

Hatch, Frederick and John Alexander Chalmers. *The Gold Mines of the Rand.* London: Macmillan and Co. 1895.

Hobson, John Atkinson. *Capitalism and Imperialism in South Africa.* Evansville: Tucker Publishing Company. 1900

Hobson, John Atkinson. *The War in South Africa: Its Causes and Effects.* London: James Nisbet & Co. 1900.

Hobson, John Atkinson. *Imperialism: A Study.* London: J. Pott. 1902.

Jeppe, Fred. *Jeppe's Transvaal Almanac and Directory for 1889.* Cape Town: Argus Printing and Publishing Co. 1889.

Kennedy, E. E. *Waiting for the Boom.* London: Effingham Wilson and Co. 1890.

King, James. *Dr. Jameson's Raid: Its Causes and Consequences.* London: Routledge. 1896.

Kipling, Rudyard. *Rewards and Fairies.* London: Macmillan and Co. 1910.

Krout, Mary Hannah. *A Looker on in London.* New York: Dodd, Mead and Company. 1899.

Lamy, Charles. *Annuaire Français des Mines D'Or: Transvaal, Sudafrique.* Paris: Charles Lamy. 1896.

Levien, Francis. *Rules and Regulations for the Conduct of Business on the Stock Exchange.* London: Committee for General Purposes. London Stock Exchange. 1888.

Melsheimer, Rudolph Eyre and Walter Laurence. *The Law and Customs of the London Stock Exchange.* London: Sweet Law Publications. 1879.

Michelet, Jacques. *Annuaire des mines d'or pour 1896. Renseignements généraux sur les mines d'or et de métaux précieux du monde entier.* Paris: Boullay. 1896.

Milner, Alfred Milner. *England in Egypt.* London: E. Arnold. 1903.

Vidal, Emmanuel. *The history and Methods of the Paris Bourse.* Vol. 573. Washington: US Government Printing Office. 1910.

Wills, Walter H. and R. J. Barrett. *The Anglo-African Who's Who and Biographical Sketch-book.* London: George Routledge & Sons Limited. 1907.

JOURNAL ARTICLES, BOOKS AND UNPUBLISHED DISSERTATIONS

Accominotti, Olivier, Marc Flandreau, Riad Rezzik, and Frederic Zumer. 'Black Man's Burden, White Man's Welfare: Control, Devolution and Development in the British Empire, 1880–1914.' *European Review of Economic History.* 14. 1 (2010). pp. 47–70.

Acemoglu, Daron, and James A. Robinson. 'The Rise and Decline of General Laws of Capitalism.' *The Journal of Economic Perspectives.* 29. 1 (2015). pp. 16–19.

Aghion, Philippe and Steven N. Durlauf, eds. *Handbook of Economic Growth.* Vol. 1. Amsterdam: Elsevier. 2005.

Akita, Shigeru, ed. *Gentlemanly Capitalism, Imperialism and Global History.* Springer, 2002.

Allen, Franklin, and Douglas Gale. *Comparing Financial Systems.* Cambridge: MIT Press Books. 2001.

Ally, Russell. *Gold and Empire: The Bank of England and South Africa's Gold Producers.* Johannesburg: Witwatersrand University Press. 1994.

Anievas, Alexander, Nivi Manchanda and Robbie Robbie Shilliam, eds. *Race and Racism in International Relations: Confronting the Global Colour Line.* Abingdon: Routledge. 2014.

Ansari, Shaukat. 'The Neo-Liberal Incentive Structure and the Absence of the Developmental State in Post-Apartheid South Africa.' Forthcoming in *African Affairs* (2017). https://doi.org/10.1093/afraf/adw074

Appiah, Anthony and Henry Louis Gates. *Encyclopedia of Africa.* Vol. 1. Oxford: Oxford University Press. 2010.

Arestis, Philip, Panicos O. Demetriades and Kul B. Luintel. 'Financial Development and Economic Growth: The Role of Stock Markets.' *Journal of Money Credit and Banking*. 33. 1 (2001). pp. 16–41.

Arcand, Jean Louis, Enrico Berkes and Ugo Panizza. 'Too Much Finance?' *Journal of Economic Growth*. 20. 2 (2015). pp. 105–148.

Arndt, Ernst Heinrich Daniel. *Banking and Currency Development in South Africa (1652–1927)*. Cape Town: Juta. 1928.

Attard, Bernard. 'From Free-Trade Imperialism to Structural Power: New Zealand and the Capital Market, 1856–68.' *The Journal of Imperial and Commonwealth History*. 35. 4 (2007). pp. 505–527.

Attard, Bernard and Andrew Dilley. 'Finance, Empire and the British World.' *The Journal of Imperial and Commonwealth History*. 41. 1 (2013). pp. 1–10.

Aubert, Victor-Stéphane. *Exposition universelle de 1889 à Paris. La République Sud-Africaine, situation économique et commerciale en 1889*. Paris: V.-S. Aubert. 1889.

Auchterlonie, Paul. 'A Turk of the West: Sir Edgar Vincent's Career in Egypt and the Ottoman Empire.' *British Journal of Middle Eastern Studies*. 27. 1 (2000). pp. 49–68.

Austin, Gareth and Stephen Broadberry. 'Introduction: The Renaissance of African Economic History.' *The Economic History Review*. 67. 4 (2014). pp. 893–906.

Bach, Daniel C. ed. *La France et l'Afrique du Sud. Histoire, Mythes et Enjeux Contemporains*. Paris: Karthala. 1990.

Baldasty, G. J. 1992. *The Commercialization of News in the Nineteenth Century*. University of Wisconsin Press.

Baltzer, Markus. 'Cross-listed stocks as an information vehicle of speculation: evidence from European cross-listings in the early 1870s.' *European Review of Economic History*. 10. 3 (2006). pp. 301–327

Barber, Sydney Hilton. *Transvaal Gold Law. Translation into English of Law No. 15 of 1898*. Cape Town: T. Maskew Miller. 1904.

Barker, H. A. F. *The Principles and Practice of Banking in South Africa*. 3rd Ed. Cape Town: Juta & Co. 1952.

Bagehot, Walter. *Lombard Street: A Description of the Money Market*. London: C. Kegan Paul. 1878.

Baskin, Jonathan. B. 'The Development of Corporate Financial Markets in Britain and the United States, 1600–1914: Overcoming Asymmetric Information.' *Business History Review*. 62. 2 (1988). pp. 199–237.

Beauchamp, Ken. *History of Telegraphy*. History of Technology Series No. 26. London: The Institution of Engineering and Technology. 2001.

Beavon, K. S. O. 'The Role of Transport in the Rise and Decline of the Johannesburg CBD, 1886–2001.' Unpublished conference paper. *Proceedings of the*

Southern African Transport Conference (SATC 2001), Pretoria. 2001. http://www.cursoaprovacao.com.br/scasat/arquivos/20100519194812_5b4.pdf

Beck, Thorsten, Asli Demirgüç-Kunt and Ross Levine. 'A New Database on the Structure and Development of the Financial Sector.' *The World Bank Economic Review.* 14. 3. (2000). pp. 597–605

Becker, Chris. *A Short History of the South African Monetary System.* Mises Institute South Africa. 14 December 2011. http://www.mises.co.za/2011/12/a-short-history-of-gold-in-the-south-african-monetary-system/

Beinart, William and Saul Dubow, eds. *Segregation and Apartheid in Twentieth-Century South Africa.* London: Routledge. 1995.

Bekaert, Geert and Campbell R. Harvey. 'Time-varying World Market Integration.' *The Journal of Finance.* 50. 2 (1995). pp. 403–444.

Berghoff, Hartmut and Uwe Spiekermann. 'Shady Business: On the History of White-collar Crime.' *Business History.* 60. 3 (2018). pp. 289–304.

Bennett, Cheltenham. *Dictionary of Insurance.* London: Pearson Education. 2004

Bhorat, H. and S. Goga. 'Occupational Shifts and Shortages: Skills Challenges Facing the South African Economy.' *Labour Market Intelligence Partnership.* 2013.

Bignon, Vincent and Marc Flandreau. 'The Economics of Badmouthing: Libel Law and the Underworld of the Financial Press in France before World War I.' *The Journal of Economic History.* 71. 3 (2011). pp. 616–653.

Bignon, Vincent and Antonio Miscio. 'Media Bias in Financial Newspapers: Evidence from Early Twentieth-Century France.' *European Review of Economic History.* 14. 3 (2010). pp. 383–432.

Blainey, Geoffrey. 'Lost Causes of the Jameson Raid.' *The Economic History Review.* 18. 2 (1965). pp. 350–366.

Boahen, Albert Adu, ed. *General History of Africa: Vol. VII Africa Under Colonialism 1880–1935.* Paris: UNESCO. 1990

Bond, Patrick. 'Debt, Uneven Development and Capitalist Crisis in South Africa: from Moody's Macroeconomic Monitoring to Marikana Microfinance Mashonisas.' *Third World Quarterly.* 34. 4 (2013). pp. 569–592.

Bond, Patrick. 'Bankrupt Africa: Imperialism, Sub-imperialism and the Politics of Finance.' *Historical Materialism* 12. 4 (2004). pp. 145–172.

Bond, Patrick. *Elite Transition: From Apartheid to Neoliberalism in South Africa.* London: Pluto Press. 2000.

Bordo, Michael D. and Anna J. Schwartz, eds. *A retrospective on the Classical Gold Standard, 1821–1931.* Chicago: University of Chicago Press. 2009.

Bordo, Michael D., Alan M. Taylor and Jeffrey G. Williamson, eds. *Globalization in Historical Perspective.* Chicago: University of Chicago Press. 2007.

Bowen, Huw V. 'Gentlemanly Capitalism and the Making of a Global British Empire: Some Connections and Contexts, 1688–1815.' In: Akita, Shigeru, ed. *Gentlemanly Capitalism, Imperialism and Global History.* Springer, 2002.

Bowen, Huw V. "The Pests of Human Society": Stockbrokers, Jobbers and Speculators in Mid-eighteenth-century Britain.' *History.* 78. 252 (1993). pp. 38–53.

Breckenridge, Keith. 'Money with Dignity: Migrants, Minelords and the Cultural Politics of the South African Gold Standard Crisis, 1920–33.' *The Journal of African History.* 36. 2 (1995). pp. 271–304.

Brenthurst Press. *The Jameson Raid: A Centennial Retrospective.* Johannesburg: Brenthurst Press. 1996.

Brodie, Nechama. *The Joburg Book: A Guide to the City's History, People & Places.* Johannesburg: Pan Macmillan and Sharp Sharp Media. 2008.

Bussière, Eric and Youssef Cassis. *London and Paris as International Financial Centres in the Twentieth Century.* Oxford: Oxford University Press. 2005.

Bonin, Hubert. '"Blue Angels," "Venture Capital," and "Whales": Networks Financing the Takeoff of the Second Industrial Revolution in France, 1890s–1920s.' *Business and Economic History On-Line.* 2004. pp. 1–49. https://the bhc.org/sites/default/files/Bonin_0.pdf

Bryant, Margot. *Taking Stock: Johannesburg Stock Exchange, the First 100 Years.* Johannesburg: Jonathan Ball Publishers. 1987.

Bundy, Collin. *The Rise and Fall of African Peasantry.* Berkeley: University of California Press. 1979.

Burdett, Henry. *Burdett's Official Intelligence.* London: Committee of the Stock Exchange. Editions 1886–1889.

Butler, Jeffrey. *The Liberal Party and the Jameson Raid.* Oxford: Oxford University Press. 1968.

Burt, Roger. 'Segmented Capital Markets and Patterns of Investment in Late Victorian Britain: Evidence from the Non-ferrous Mining Industry.' *Economic History Review.* 51. 4 (1998). pp. 709–733.

Burt, Roger. 'The London Mining Exchange 1850–1900.' *Business History.* 14. 2 (1972). pp. 124–143.

Cain, Peter J. 'Capitalism, Aristocracy and Empire: Some 'Classical' Theories of Imperialism Revisited.' *The Journal of Imperial and Commonwealth History.* 35. 1 (2007). pp. 25–47.

Cain, Peter J. and Anthony G. Hopkins. *British Imperialism: 1688–2000.* London: Pearson Education. 2002.

Cain, Peter. 'JA Hobson, Financial Capitalism and Imperialism in Late Victorian and Edwardian England.' *The Journal of Imperial and Commonwealth History.* 13. 3 (1985). pp. 1–27.

Cammack, Diana Rose. *The Rand at War, 1899–1902: The Witwatersrand and the Anglo-Boer War.* Berkeley: University of California Press. 1990.

Cammack, Diana. 'The Politics of Discontent: The Grievances of the Uitlander Refugees, 1899–1902.' *Journal of Southern African Studies*. 8. 2 (1982). pp. 243–270.

Cartwright, Alan Patrick. *Gold Paved the Way: The Story of the Gold Fields Group of Companies*. London: Macmillan. 1967.

Cartwright, Alan Patrick. *The Story of 'Johnnies', 1889–1964: A History of the Johannesburg Consolidated Investment Co. Ltd*. Johannesburg: JCI. 1965.

Cartwright, Alan Patrick. *The Corner House: The Early History of Johannesburg*. London: McDonald. 1965.

Cassim, Fuad. *Growth, crisis and Change in the South African Economy*. University of York, Centre for Southern African Studies. 1986.

Cassis, Youssef, Ricahrd S. Grossman and Catherine R. Schenk, eds. *The Oxford Handbook of Banking and Financial History*. Oxford University Press. 2016.

Cassis, Youssef. *Capitals of Capital: The Rise and Fall of International Financial Centres 1780–2009*. Cambridge University Press. 2010.

Cassis, Youssef, ed. *Finance and Financiers in European History, 1880–1960*. Cambridge University Press. 2002.

Cassis, Youssef. 'Financial Elites in Three European Centres: London, Paris, Berlin, 1880s–1930s.' *Business History*. 33. 3 (1991). pp. 53–71.

Cassis, Youssef. 'Bankers in English Society in the Late Nineteenth Century.' *The Economic History Review*. 38. 2 (1985). pp. 210–229.

Cetina, Karin Knorr and Urs Bruegger. 'Global Microstructures: The Virtual Societies of Financial Markets.' *American Journal of Sociology*. 107. 4. (2002). pp. 905–950.

Chambers, David and Rui Esteves. 'The First Global Emerging Markets Investor: Foreign & Colonial Investment Trust 1880–1913.' *Explorations in Economic History*. 52 (April 2014). pp. 1–21.

Churchill, Lord Randolph Henry Spencer. *Men, Mines and Animals in South Africa*. London: S. Low, Marston. 1895.

Cleveland, Todd. *Stones of Contention: A History of Africa's Diamonds*. Athens: Ohio University Press. 2014

Coetzee, J. H. and J. de W. Keyter. *Verarming en oorheersing*. Pretoria: Nasionale Pers Bpk. 1942

Coleman, William Oliver. 'Anti-semitism in Anti-economics.' *History of Political Economy*. 35. 4 (2003). pp. 759–777.

Comaroff, John L. and Brian Willan. *The Mafeking Diary of Sol T. Plaatje*. London: James Currey Publishers. 1999.

Cooper, John. *The Unexpected Story of Nathaniel Rothschild*. London: Bloomsbury Publishing. 2015.

Cottrell, Philip L., Monika Pohle Fraser and Iain L. Fraser, eds. *East meets West: Banking, Commerce and Investment in the Ottoman Empire*. London: Ashgate Publishing, Ltd. 2008.

Coulson, Michael. *The History of Mining: The Events, Technology and People Involved in the Industry that Forged the Modern World.* Petersfields: Harriman House Limited. 2012.

Cowen, Michael, and Robert W. Shenton. *Doctrines of Development.* Abingdon: Taylor & Francis, 1996.

Crush, Jonathan, Alan Jeeves and David Yudelman. *South Africa's Labor Empire: A History of Black Migrancy to the Gold Mines.* Cape Time: Westview Press Cape Town. 1991.

Darwin, John. *The Empire Project: The Rise and Fall of the British World-system, 1830–1970.* Cambridge: Cambridge University Press. 2009.

Darwin, John. 'Imperialism and the Victorians: The Dynamics of Territorial Expansion.' *The English Historical Review* 112. 447 (1997). pp. 614–642.

Davenport-Hines, Richard Peter Treadwell. ed. *Speculators and Patriots: Essays in Business Biography.* London: Routledge. 2005.

Davenport-Hines, R. P. T. and Jean-Jacques Van Helten. 'Edgar Vincent, Viscount D'Abernon, and the Eastern Investment Company in London, Constantinople and Johannesburg.' *Business History.* 28. 1 (1986). pp. 35–61.

Davidson, Jim. 'Also Under the Southern Cross: Federation Australia and South Africa—The Boer War and Other Interactions. The 2011 Russel Ward Annual Lecture.' *Journal of Australian Colonial History.* 14 (2012). pp. 183–204.

Davis, Lance, Larry Neal and Eugene N. White. 'How it all began: the rise of Listing Requirements on the London, Berlin, Paris, and New York Stock Exchanges.' *The International Journal of Accounting.* 38. 2 (2003). pp. 117–143.

Davis, Lance and Larry Neal. 'Micro Rules and Macro Outcomes: The Impact of Micro Structure on the Efficiency of Security Exchanges, London, New York, and Paris, 1800–1914.' *American Economic Review.* 88. 2 (1998). pp. 40–45.

Davis, Lance Edvin and Robert A. Huttenback. *Mammon and the Pursuit of Empire: The Political Economy of British Imperialism, 1860–1912.* Cambridge: Cambridge University Press. 1986.

De Beer, Jesse, Nico Keyser and Ivan Van der Merwe. 'The Johannesburg Stock Exchange (JSE) Returns, Political Development and Economic Forces: A Historical Perspective.' *Journal for Contemporary History.* 40. 2 (2015). pp. 1–24.

De Bruijn, Mirjam and van Dijk, Rijk, eds. *The Social Life of Connectivity in Africa.* New York: Palgrave Macmillan US. 2012.

De Cecco, Marcello. *Money and Empire: The International Gold Standard, 1890–1914.* Lanham: Rowman and Littlefield. 1975.

De Jongh T. W. *An Analysis of Banking Statistics in the Union of South Africa, 1910–1945.* Pretoria: JL van Schaik Ltd. 1947.

De Kiewiet, Cornelius William. *A History of South Africa: Social & Economic.* Oxford: The Clarendon Press. 1942.

De Kock, G. *A History of the South African Reserve Bank, 1920–1952.* Pretoria: JL van Schaik Ltd. 1954.

De Kock, Michiel Hendrik. *Selected Subjects in the Economic History of South Africa.* Cape Town: Juta. 1924.

Denoon, Donald. 'Capital and Capitalists in the Transvaal in the 1890s and 1900s.' *The Historical Journal.* 23. 1 (1980). pp. 111–132.

Denoon, Donald J. N. 'The Transvaal Labour Crisis, 1901–6.' *The Journal of African History.* 8. 3 (1967). pp. 481–494.

Denzel, Markus A. *Handbook of World Exchange Rates, 1590–1914.* Farnham: Ashgate Publishing, Ltd. 2010.

Dilley, Andrew. 'The Rules of the Game': London Finance, Australia, and Canada, c. 1900–14.' *The Economic History Review.* 63. 4 (2010). pp. 1003–1031

Donaldson, Peter. *Remembering the South African War: Britain and the Memory of the Anglo-Boer War, from 1899 to the Present.* Oxford: Oxford University Press. 2013.

Drew, Allison. *Between Empire and Revolution: A Life of Sidney Bunting, 1873–1936.* London: Routledge. 2015.

Drus, Ethel. 'The Question of Imperial Complicity in the Jameson Raid.' *English Historical Review.* 68. 269 (1953). pp. 582–593.

Du Bois, Duncan. 'The "Coolie Curse": The Evolution of White Colonial Attitudes Towards the Indian Question, 1860–1900.' *Historia.* 57. 2 (2012). pp. 37–67.

Dubow, Saul. 'How British was the British World? The Case of South Africa.' *Journal of Imperial and Commonwealth History.* 37. 1 (2009). pp. 1–27.

Dubow, Saul. 'Colonial Nationalism, the Milner Kindergarten and the Rise of "South Africanism", 1902–10.' *History Workshop Journal.* 43 (1997). pp. 53-85

Duke, Maurice and Edward N. Coffman. 'Writing an accounting or business history: notes toward a methodology.' *The Accounting Historians Journal.* 20. 2 (1993). pp. 217–235.

Dumett, Raymond E. 'Introduction: Exploring the Cain/Hopkins Paradigm: Issues for Debate; Critique and Topics for New Research.' In: Dumett, Raymond E., ed. *Gentlemanly Capitalism and British Imperialism: The New Debate on Empire.* Routledge. 2014. pp. 1–43.

Du Toit, André. 'No Chosen People: The Myth of the Calvinist Origins of Afrikaner Nationalism and Racial Ideology.' *The American Historical Review.* 88. 4 (1983). pp. 920–952.

Du Toit, Darcy. *Capital and Labour in South Africa: Class Struggle in the 1970s.* London: Routledge. 1981.

Eatwell, John, Murray Milgate and Peter Newman. *The New Palgrave: A Dictionary of Economics.* New York: Palgrave Macmillan. 1987.

Edelstein, Michael. *Overseas Investment in the Age of High Imperialism: The United Kingdom, 1850–1914*. London: Taylor & Francis. 1982.

Eichengreen, Barry and Marc Flandreau. *The Gold Standard in Theory and History*. London: Routledge. 1997.

El-Dean, Bahaa Ali. *Privatisation and the Creation of a Market-based Legal System: The Case of Egypt*. Vol. 82. Boston: Brill. 2002.

Eldredge, Elizabeth A. 'Sources of Conflict in Southern Africa, c. 1800–30: The 'Mfecane' Reconsidered.' *The Journal of African History*. 33. 1 (1992). pp. 1–35.

Emden, Paul Herman. *Randlords*. London: Hodder & Stoughton. 1935.

Engerman, Stanley L., et al., eds. *Finance, Intermediaries, and Economic Development*. Cambridge: Cambridge University Press. 2003.

Etherington, Norman. 'A Tempest in a Teapot? Nineteenth-Century Contests for Land in South Africa's Caledon Valley and the Invention of the Mfecane.' *The Journal of African History*. 45. 2 (2004). pp. 203–219.

Etherington, Norman. 'Theories of Imperialism in Southern Africa Revisited.' *African Affairs*. 81. 234 (1982). pp. 385–407.

Esteves, Rui. 'The Belle Epoque of International Finance: French Capital Exports, 1880–1914.' University of Oxford Department of Economics Discussion Paper Series. Nr. 534. November 2011.

Farnie, Douglas Anthony. 'The Mineral Revolution in South Africa.' *South African Journal of Economics* 24. 2 (1956). pp. 125–134.

Feingold, Ellen, Johan Fourie, and Leigh Gardner. 'A Tale of Paper and Gold: The Material History of Money in South Africa.' *Economic History of Developing Regions*. 36. 2 (2021). pp. 264–281.

Feinstein, Charles H. *An Economic History of South Africa: Conquest, Discrimination, and Development*. Cambridge: Cambridge University Press. 2005.

Feldman, Gerald D. and Peter Hertner, eds. *Finance and Modernization*. London: Ashgate. 2008.

Ferguson, Niall. *The Ascent of Money: A Financial History of the World*. London: Penguin. 2008.

Ferguson, Niall. *Empire: The Rise and Demise of the British World Order and the Lessons for Global Power*. New York: Basic Books. 2003.

Fetherling, George. *The Gold Crusades: A Social History of Gold Rushes, 1849–1929*. Toronto: University of Toronto Press. 1997.

Fine, Ben and Zavareh Rustomjee. *The Political Economy of South Africa: From Minerals-energy Complex to Industrialisation*. London: C. Hurst & Co. Publishers. 1996.

First, Ruth. 'The Gold of Migrant Labour.' *Review of African Political Economy*. 9. 25 (1982). pp. 5–21.

Fitzpatrick, Percy. *The Transvaal from Within: A Private Record of Public Affairs*. London: W. Briggs. 1900.

Flandreau, Marc. *Anthropologists in the Stock Exchange.* Chicago: Chicago University Press. 2016

Flandreau Marc and Vincent Bignon. 'The Price of Media Capture and the Debasement of the French Newspaper's Industry During the Interwar.' *The Journal of Economic History.* 74. 3 (2014). pp. 799–830.

Flandreau, Marc and Zumer Frédéric. *Development Centre Studies the Making of Global Finance 1880–1913.* Paris: OECD Publishing. 2009.

Flandreau, Marc. 'The French Crime of 1873: An Essay on the Emergence of the International Gold Standard, 1870–1880.' *The Journal of Economic History.* 56. 4 (1996). pp. 862–897.

Fourie, Johan and Christie Swanepoel. 'Impending Ruin' or 'Remarkable Wealth'? The Role of Private Credit Markets in the 18th-Century Cape Colony.' *Journal of Southern African Studies.* 44. 1 (2018). pp. 7–25.

Frankel, Philip. *Between the Rainbows and the Rain: Marikana, Migration, Mining and the Crisis of Modern South Africa.* Oxford: African Books Collective. 2013.

Frankel, Sally Herbert. *Investment and the Return to Equity Capital in the South African Gold Mining Industry, 1887–1965: An International Comparison.* Oxford: Blackwell. 1967.

Frankel, Sally Herbert. *Capital Investment in Africa: Its Course and Effects.* Oxford University Press. 1938.

Fraser, Maryna. *Johannesburg Pioneer Journals, 1888–1909.* Cape Town: Van Riebeeck Society. 1985.

Fraser, Maryna. 'International Archives in South Africa.' *Business and Economic History.* Vol. 16. Papers presented at the thirty-third annual meeting of the Business History Conference. 1987. pp. 163–173.

Fraser, Maryna. 'Profile of a South African Company Archive.' *Archivaria.* 1. 7 (1978). pp. 95–102.

Fraser, Maryna and Alan Jeeves. *All that glittered: Selected Correspondence of Lionel Phillips, 1890–1924.* Cape Town: Oxford University Press. 1977.

Fraser, Maryna. *Inventory of the Archives of H. Eckstein & Co. 1887–1910.* Johannesburg: Barlow Rand Limited. 1975.

Freund, Bill. 'The Significance of the Minerals-energy Complex in the Light of South African Economic Historiography.' *Transformation: Critical Perspectives on Southern Africa.* 71. 1 (2010). pp. 3–25.

Fröhlich, Michael. *Imperialismus. Deutsche Kolonial- und Weltpolitik 1880–1914.* Munich: Deutscher Taschenbuch Verlag. 1994.

Galbraith, John S. *Crown and Charter: The Early Years of the British South Africa Company.* Vol. 14. University of California Press. 1974.

Gale, William D. 'The Rhodesian Press.' Salisbury: *Rhodesian Printing and Publishing* Company. 1962.

Gallagher, John and Ronald Robinson. 'The Imperialism of Free Trade.' *The Economic History Review*. 6. 1 (1953). pp. 1–15.

Gann, Lewis H. and Peter Duignan. *Colonialism in Africa 1870–1960*. Vol. 4. Cambridge: Cambridge University Press. 1975.

Geisler Mesevage, Gabriel F. *The Industrial Organization of Asymmetric Information. Industrial Decline and the British Financial Press, 1870–1914*. Unpublished M.A. Thesis. Graduate Institute of International and Development Studies. 2011.

Gelbard, Enrique and Sé Leite. *Measuring Financial Development in Sub-Saharan Africa*. Working Paper 99/105. Washington: International Monetary Fund. 1999.

Gerhard-Mark Van der Waal. *From Mining Camp to Metropolis: The Buildings of Johannesburg, 1886–1940*. Chris van Rensburg Publishing: Johannesburg. 1987.

Guy, Jeff and Motlatsi Thabane. 'Technology, Ethnicity and Ideology: Basotho Miners and Shaft-sinking on the South African Gold Mines.' *Journal of Southern African Studies*. 14. 2 (1988). pp. 257–278.

Giliomee, Hermann Buhr and Bernard Mbenga. *New History of South Africa*. Cape Town: Tafelberg. 2007.

Goodfellow, David Martin. *A Modern Economic History of South Africa*. London: Routledge & Sons. 1931.

Graham, Wayne. *The Randlord's Bubble 1894–6: South African Goldmines and Stock Market Manipulation*. Discussion Papers in Economic and Social History. Paper 10. University of Oxford. 1996. http://www.nuff.ox.ac.uk/economics/history/Paper10/10graham.pdf

Gwaindepi, Abel. 'State Building in the Colonial Era: Public Revenue, Expenditure and Borrowing Patterns in the Cape Colony, 1820–1910.' PhD diss., Stellenbosch: Stellenbosch University, 2018.

Haber, Stephen H., Douglass Cecil North and Barry R. Weingast, eds. *Political Institutions and Financial Development*. Palo Alto: Stanford University Press. 2008.

Hafer, Rik W. and Scott E. Hein. *The Stock Market*. Westport: Greenwood Publishing Group. 2007.

Hammond, John Hays and Alleyne Ireland. *The Truth about the Jameson Raid*. Boston: Marshall Jones Company. 1918.

Hannah, Leslie. 'The London Stock Exchange, 1869–1929: New Statistics for Old?' *The Economic History Review*. 71. 4 (2018). pp. 1349–1356.

Hanson, Samuel G., Anil K. Kashyap and Jeremy C. Stein. 'A Macroprudential Approach to Financial Regulation.' *The Journal of Economic Perspectives*. 25. 1 (2011). pp. 3–28.

Harris, Larry. *Trading and Exchanges: Market Microstructure for Practitioners*. Oxford: Oxford University Press. 2002.

Harris, Verne. 'The Archival Sliver: Power, Memory, and Archives in South Africa.' *Archival Science*. 2. 1 (2002). pp. 63v86.

Harries, Patrick. 'Capital, State, and Labour on the 19th Century Witwatersrand: A Reassessment.' *South African Historical Journal*. 8. 1 (1986). pp. 25–45.

Harris, Robert. *South Africa: Illustrated by a Series of One Hundred and Four Permanent Photographs*. Port Elizabeth: Robert Harris. 1888.

Harrison, Philip and Tanya Zack. 'The Power of Mining: The Fall of Gold and Rise of Johannesburg.' *Journal of Contemporary African Studies*. 30. 4 (2012). pp. 551–570.

Hart, Gillian. *Rethinking the South African Crisis: Nationalism, Populism, Hegemony*. Vol. 20. Athens: University of Georgia Press. 2014.

Hart, Keith and Vishnu Padayachee. 'A History of South African Capitalism in National and Global Perspective.' *Transformation: Critical Perspectives on Southern Africa*. 81. 1 (2013). pp. 55–85.

Hautcoeur, Pierre-Cyrille, Amir Rezaee, and Angelo Riva. 'Competition Between Securities Markets: Stock Exchange Industry Regulation in the Paris Financial Center at the Turn of the Twentieth Century.' *Cliometrica* (2022). pp. 1–39.

Hautcoeur, Pierre-Cyrille, Angelo Riva and Eugene N. White. 'Floating a "Lifeboat": The Banque de France and the Crisis of 1889.' *Journal of Monetary Economics*. 65 (July 2014). pp. 104–119.

Hautcoeur, Pierre-Cyrille, Amir Rezaee and Angelo Riva. *Stock Exchange Industry Regulation The Paris Bourse, 1893–1898*. Working Paper, Paris School of Economics. 2010. http://federation.ens.fr/ydepot/semin/texte1 112/RIV2012STO.pdf

Henry, J. A. *The First Hundred Years of the Standard Bank*. Oxford: Oxford University Press. 1963.

Hermes, Niels and Robert Lensink. *Financial Development and Economic Growth: Theory and Experiences from Developing Countries*. London: Routledge. 2013.

Herranz-Loncán, Alfonso, and Johan Fourie. '"For the public benefit"? Railways in the British Cape Colony.' *European Review of Economic History*. 22. 1 (2018). pp. 73–100.

Hickson, Charles R. and John D. Turner. 'Free Banking Gone Awry: The Australian Banking Crisis of 1893.' *Financial History Review*. 9. 2 (2002). pp. 147–167.

Hilferding, Rudolf. *Das finanzkapital: eine studie über die jüngste Entwicklung, des Kapitalismus*. Wien: Ignaz Brand Verlag. 1910.

Hitchens, Christopher. *Blood, Class, and Empire: The Enduring Anglo-American Relationship*. New York: Nation Books. 1990.

Hirshfield, Claire. 'The British Left and the "Jewish Conspiracy": A Case Study of Modern Antisemitism.' *Jewish Social Studies*. 43. 2 (1981). pp. 95–112.

Hobsbawm, Eric J. and Chris Wrigley. *Industry and Empire: From 1750 to the Present Day*. New York: The New Press. 1999.

Hobsbawm, Eric J. *The Age of Empire: 1875–1914*. London: Abacus (Time Warner Books UK). 1987.

Hochfelder, David. 'Partners in Crime: The Telegraph Industry, Finance Capitalism, and Organized Gambling, 1870–1920.' IEEE History Center. Rutgers University. (unpublished paper) 2001. http://ieeeghn.org/wiki/images/5/5b/Hochfelder.pdf

Hodgson, Geoffrey M. 'What are Institutions?' *Journal of Economic Issues*. 40. 1 (2006). pp. 1–25.

Houghton, Hobart. *The South African Economy*. Oxford: Oxford University Press. 1973.

Hopkins, A. G. 'Gentlemanly Capitalism in New Zealand.' *Australian Economic History Review*. 43. 3 (2003). pp. 287–297.

Howe, Anthony C. 'Bimetallism, c. 1880–1898: A Controversy Re-Opened?' *The English Historical Review*. 105. 415 (1990). pp. 377–391.

Humby, Tracy-Lynn. 'Redressing Mining Legacies: The Case of the South African Mining Industry.' *Journal of Business Ethics* (2016). pp. 1–12.

Iliffe, John. *Africans: The History of a Continent*. 2nd Ed. Cambridge: Cambridge University Press. 2007.

Iliffe, John. 'The South African Economy, 1652–1997.' *The Economic History Review*. 52. 1 (1999). pp. 87–103.

Innes, Duncan. *Anglo: Anglo American and the rise of Modern South Africa*. Johannesburg: Raven Press. 1984.

Itzkowitz, David C. 'Fair Enterprise or Extravagant Speculation: Investment, Speculation, and Gambling in Victorian England.' *Victorian Studies*. 45. 1 (2002). pp. 121–147.

Jeeves, Alan. 'The Rand Capitalists and the Coming of the South African War 1896–1899.' *South African Journal of Economic History*. 11. 2 (1996). pp. 55–81.

Jeeves, Alan. *Migrant Labour in South Africa's Mining Economy: The Struggle for the Gold Mines' Labour Supply, 1890–1920*. Montreal: McGill-Queen's University Press. 1985

Jeeves, Alan. 'Aftermath of Rebellion—The Randlords and Kruger's Republic After the Jameson Raid.' *South African Historical Journal*. 10. 1 (1978). pp. 102–116.

Jeeves, Alan. 'The Control of Migratory Labour on the South African Gold Mines in the Era of Kruger and Milner.' *Journal of Southern African Studies*. 2. 1 (1975). pp. 3–29.

Jeppe, Carl Wilhelm Biccard. *Gold Mining in South Africa*. Johannesburg: Chamber of Mines. 1948.

Johannesburg Consolidated Investment Company. *The Story of 'Johnnies', 1889–1964: A History of the Johannesburg Consolidated Investment Co. Ltd.* JCI: Johannesburg. 1965.

Johnson, Paul. *Making the Market: Victorian Origins of Corporate Capitalism.* Cambridge: Cambridge University Press. 2010.

Johnson, R. W. *How Long Will South Africa Survive? The Looming Crisis.* Johannesburg: Jonathan Ball Publishers. 2015.

Jones, Geoffrey and Jonathan Zeitlin. *The Oxford Handbook of Business History.* Oxford: Oxford University Press. 2008.

Jones, Stuart. *The Great Imperial Banks in South Africa. A Study of the Business of Standard Bank and Barclays Bank 1861–1961.* Pretoria: UNISA. 1996.

Jones, Stuart and André Müller. *The South African Economy: 1910–1990.* London: Macmillan. 1992.

Karekwaivenani, George. 'A History of the Rhodesian Stock Exchange: The Formative Years, 1946–1952.' *Zambezia: The Journal of Humanities of the University of Zimbabwe.* 30. 1 (2003). pp. 9–34.

Katz, Elaine. 'The Role of American Mining Technology and American Mining Engineers in the Witwatersrand Gold Mining Industry 1890–1910.' *South African Journal of Economic History.* 20. 2 (2005). pp. 48–82.

Katz, Elaine. 'Revisiting the Origins of the Industrial Colour Bar in the Witwatersrand Gold Mining Industry, 1891–1899.' *Journal of Southern African Studies.* 25. 1 (1999). pp. 73–97.

Katz, Elaine. 'Outcrop and Deep Level Mining in South Africa Before the Anglo-Boer War: Re-examining the Blainey Thesis.' *The Economic History Review.* 48. 2 (1995). pp. 304–328.

Katzen, Leo. *Gold and the South African Economy.* Rotterdam: Balkema. 1964.

Katzenellenbogen, Simon E. *South Africa and Southern Mozambique: Labour, Railways, and Trade in the Making of a Relationship.* Manchester: Manchester University Press. 1982.

Karatasli, Sahan Savas, and Sefika Kumral. 'Financialization and International (Dis) Order: A Comparative Analysis of the Perspectives of Karl Polanyi and John Hobson.' *Berkeley Journal of Sociology* (2013). pp. 40–73.

Kindleberger, Charles and Robert Z. Aliber. *Manias, Panics and Crashes: A History of Financial Crises.* London: Palgrave Macmillan. 2011.

Kindleberger, Charles. *A Financial History of Western Europe.* New York: Taylor & Francis US. 1984.

Kitzan, Laurence. *Victorian Writers and the Image of Empire: The Rose-colored Vision.* Vol. 104. Westport. Greenwood Publishing Group. 2001.

Klein, Harry. *The Story of the Johannesburg Stock Exchange: 1887–1947.* Johannesburg: The Committee of the Johannesburg Stock Exchange. 1948.

Knorr Cetina, Karin and Alex Preda. *The Sociology of Financial Markets.* Oxford University Press. 2004.

Knorr-Cetina, Karin and Urs Bruegger. 'Global Microstructures: The Virtual Societies of Financial Markets.' *American Journal of Sociology*. 107. 4 (2002). pp. 905–950.

Knowles, Lilian Charlotte Anne and Charles Matthew Knowles. *The Economic Development of the British Overseas Empire: The Union of South Africa*. Vol. 3. London: Taylor & Francis. 1964.

Konczacki, Zbigniew A., Jane L. Parpart and Timothy M. Shaw, eds. *Studies in the Economic History of South Africa: The Front-Line States*. Vol. 1. London: Taylor & Francis. 1990.

Konczacki, Zbigniew A., Jane L. Parpart and Timothy M. Shaw, eds. *Studies in the Economic History of South Africa: South Africa, Lesotho and Swaziland*. Vol. II. London: Taylor & Francis. 1991.

Kubicek, Robert V. *Economic Imperialism in Theory and Practice: The Case of South African Gold Mining Finance 1886–1914*. Durham. Duke University Press. 1979.

Kubicek, Robert V. 'The Randlords in 1895: A Reassessment.' *The Journal of British Studies*. 11. 2 (1972). pp. 84–103.

Kubicek, Robert. 'Finance Capital and South African Goldmining 1886–1914.' *The Journal of Imperial and Commonwealth History*. 3. 3 (1975). pp. 386–395.

Kwasitsu, Lishi. 'Promoting Commercial Activities in Cape Town Newspapers, 1876–1901.' *Social Dynamics*. 30. 1 (2004). pp. 170–192.

Kynaston, David. *City of London: The History*. London: Random House. 2011.

Kynaston, David. *The Financial Times: A Centenary History*. London: Viking Publishing 1988.

Kynaston, David Thomas Anthony. *The London Stock Exchange, 1870–1914: An Institutional History*. Unpublished Dissertation. London School of Economics and Political Science (University of London). 1983.

Laband, John. *The Transvaal Rebellion: The First Boer War, 1880–1881*. London: Routledge. 2014.

Lampe, Markus and Florian Ploeckl. 'Spanning the Globe: The Rise of Global Communications Systems and the First Globalisation.' *Australian Economic History Review*. 54. 3(2014). pp. 242–261.

Landes, David S. *Bankers and Pashas: International Finance and Economic Imperialism in Egypt*. Cambridge: Harvard University Press. 1958.

Lang, Jonathan. *Bullion Johannesburg: Men, Mines, and the Challenge of Conflict* Johannesburg: Jonathan Ball. 1986.

Leasor, James. *Rhodes & Barnato: The Premier and the Prancer*. London: Leo Cooper. 1997.

Lehmann, Paul-Jacques. *Histoire de la Bourse de Paris*. Paris: Presses Universitaires de France. 1997.

Lesger, Clé. *The rise of the Amsterdam Market and Information Exchange: Merchants, Commercial Expansion, and Change in the Spatial Economy of the Low Countries*, c. 1550–1630, Burlington, VT: Ashgate. 2006.

Leys, Roger. 'South African Gold Mining in 1974: "The Gold of Migrant Labour".' *African Affairs*. 74. 295 (1975). pp. 196–208.

Levine, Ross. 'Financial Development and Economic Growth: Views and Agenda.' *Journal of Economic Literature*. 35. 2 (1997). pp. 688–726.

Levine, Ross, Norman Loayza and Thorsten Beck. 'Financial Intermediation and Growth: Causality and Causes.' *Journal of monetary Economics*. 46. 1 (2000). pp. 31–77.

Levy, N. *The Foundations of the South African Cheap Labour System*. Vol. 12. Taylor & Francis. 2022.

Lipton, Marle. *Capitalism and Apartheid: South Africa, 1910–1986*. Cape Town: New Africa Books. 1986.

Henry Longland. *The Golden Transvaal, an Illustrated Review, Descriptive, Historical, etc.* London: Simpkin, Marshall, Hamilton, Kento & Co. 1896.

Louis, William Roger. *Ends of British Imperialism: The Scramble for Empire, Suez, and Decolonization*. London: I B Tauris. 2006

Louis, William Roger, ed. *Imperialism: The Robinson and Gallagher Controversy*. London: Franklin Watts. 1976.

Lowry, Donal, ed. *The South African War Reappraised*. New York: Manchester University Press. 2000.

Lowry, Donal. '"The Play of Forces World-Wide in their Scope and Revolutionary in their Operation [JA Hobson]": The South African War as an International Event.' *South African Historical Journal*. 41. 1 (1999). pp. 83–105.

Lukasiewicz, Mariusz. 'Bourses, Banks, and Boers: Johannesburg's French Connections and the Paris Krach of 1895.' *Economic History of Developing Regions*. 36. 2 (2021). pp. 124–148.

Lukasiewicz, Mariusz. 'Early Regulation and Social Organisation on the Johannesburg Stock Exchange, 1887–1892.' *Business History*. 63. 4 (2021). pp. 686–704.

Lukasiewicz, Mariusz. 'From Diamonds to Gold: The Making of the Johannesburg Stock Exchange, 1880–1890.' *Journal of Southern African Studies*. 43. 4 (2017). pp. 715–732.

Lukasiewicz, Mariusz. *Gold, Finance and Speculation*. Doctoral Dissertation. Graduate Institute of International and Development Studies, 2017.

Lumby, Anthony. 'Industrial History in South Africa: Past Trends and Future Needs.' *South African Journal of Economic History*. 10. 1 (1995). pp. 74–88.

Lumby, Anthony B. *Economic History of South Africa*. Preoria: HAUM. 1983.

Luxemburg, Rosa. *Die Akkumulation des Kapitals. Ein Beitrag zur ökonomischen Erklärung des Imperialismus*. Berlin: Paul Singer. 1913.

Mabin A and Conradie B, eds. *The Confidence of the Whole Country, Standard Bank Reports on Economic Conditions in Southern Africa.* Johannesburg: Standard Bank Investment Corporation. 1987.

Maddison, E. C. *The Paris Bourse and the London Stock Exchange: A Comparison of the Course of Business on Each Exchange.* London: Effingham Wilson. 1877.

Magee, Gary B., Lorraine Greyling and Grietjie Verhoef. 'South Africa in the Australian Mirror: Per Capita Real GDP in the Cape Colony, Natal, Victoria, and New South Wales, 1861–1909.' *The Economic History Review.* 69. 3 (2016). pp. 893–914.

Magee, Gary B. and Andrew S. Thompson. *Empire and Globalisation: Networks of People, Goods and Capital in the British World, c. 1850–1914.* Cambridge: Cambridge University Press. 2010.

Magubane, Bernard. *The Making of a Racist State: British Imperialism and the Union of South Africa, 1875–1910.* Trenton: Africa World Press. 1996.

Marais, Hein. *South Africa: Limits to Change: The Political Economy of Transition.* London: Palgrave Macmillan. 2001.

Marais, Johannes Stephanus. *The Fall of Kruger's Republic.* Oxford: Clarendon Press. 1961.

Marks, Shula and S. Trapido. 'Lord Milner and the South African State.' *History Workshop Journal.* 8. 1 (1979). pp. 50–80.

Marks, Shula and Richard Rathbone. *Industrialisation and Social Change in South Africa: African Class Formation, Culture, and Consciousness, 1870–1930.* New York: Longman. 1982.

Marks, Steven G. *The Information Nexus: Global Capitalism from the Renaissance to the Present.* Cambridge University Press, 2016.

McCulloch, Jock. *South Africa's Gold Mines and the Politics of Silicosis.* Woodbridge: Boydell & Brewer Ltd. 2012.

Mendelsohn, Richard. 'Blainey and the Jameson Raid: The Debate Renewed.' *Journal of Southern African Studies.* 6. 2 (1980). pp. 157–170.

Meredith, Martin. *Diamonds, Gold, and War: The Making of South Africa.* London: Simon & Schuster. 2008.

Meredith, Hubert A. *The Drama of Money Making: Tragedy and Comedy of the London Stock Exchange.* London: S. Low, Marston & Company Limited. 1931.

Michie, Ranald C. *Guilty Money: The City of London in Victorian and Edwardian Culture, 1815–1914.* London: Routledge. 2016.

Michie, Ranald. *The Global Securities Market: A History.* Oxford: Oxford University Press. 2007.

Michie, Ranald. *The London Stock Exchange: A History.* Oxford: Oxford University Press. 1999.

Michie, Ranald. *The London and New York Stock Exchanges, 1850–1914.* London: Allen & Unwin. 1987.

Michie, Ranald. 'The London and New York Stock Exchanges, 1850–1914.' *Journal of Economic History.* 46. 1 (1986). pp. 171–187.

Michie, Ranald. 'The London Stock Exchange and the British Securities Market 1850–1914.' *The Economic History Review.* 38. 1 (1985). pp. 61–82.

Miller, Carman. *Painting the Map Red: Canada and the South African War, 1899–1902.* Montreal: McGill-Queen''s Press. 1998.

Mills, Greg and Jeffrey Herbst. *How South Africa Works: And Must Do Better.* London: Hurst. 2014

Mishkin, Frederic S. *Asymmetric information and financial crises: a historical perspective.* NBER Working Paper No. 3400. Cambridge: National Bureau of Economic Research. 1991. http://www.nber.org/papers/w3400.

Mitchener, Kris James, and Marc D. Weidenmier. 'The Baring Crisis and the Great Latin American Meltdown of the 1890s.' *Journal of Economic History.* 68. 2 (2008). pp. 462–500.

Mokyr, Joel. *The Gifts of Athena: Historical Origins of the Knowledge Economy.* Princeton University Press. 2002.

Mommsen, Wolfgang J. *Theories of Imperialism.* Chicago: University of Chicago Press. 1980.

Moll, Terence. 'Did the Apartheid Economy 'Fail'?' *Journal of Southern African Studies.* 17. 2 (1991). pp. 271–291.

Moos, Ferdinand. 'Ursprung, Entwickelung und Zusammenbruch der Spekulation in Goldaktien. (Nach statistischen Quellen.).' *Jahrbücher für Nationalökonomie und Statistik/Journal of Economics and Statistics.* 10. 6 (1895). pp. 901–918.

Morris, Jan. *Heaven's Command.* London: Faber & Faber. 2010.

Moss, Todd J. *Adventure Capitalism: Globalization and the Political Economy of Stock Markets in Africa.* New York: Palgrave Macmillan. 2003.

Müller, André L., ed. *Die Ekonomiese Ontwikkeling van Suid-Afrika.* Pretoria and Cape Town: H&R Academica (Pty) Ltd. 1978.

Muller, Cornelis Hermanus Muller. *Policing the Witwatersrand: A History of the South African Republic Police, 1886–1899.* Unpublished Dissertation. Bloemfontein: University of the Free State. 2016.

Murray, Martin J. *City of Extremes: The Spatial Politics of Johannesburg.* Durham: Duke University Press. 2011.

Musiker, Naomi and Reuben Musiker. *A Concise Historical Dictionary of Greater Johannesburg.* Johannesburg: Francolin Publishers. 2000.

Nasson, Bill. 'Commemorating the Anglo-Boer War in Post-Apartheid South Africa.' *Radical History Review.* 78 (2000). pp. 149–165.

Nasson, Bill. *The South African War 1899–1902.* New York: Bloomsbury Press USA. 1999.

Nathan, Manfred. *The South African Commonwealth.* Cape Town: Speciality Press of South Africa Limited. 1919.

Nattrass, Jill. *The South African Economy: Its Growth and Change.* Cape Town: Oxford University Press. 1981.

Nattrass, Nicoli. 'Controversies about Capitalism and Apartheid in South Africa: An Economic Perspective.' *Journal of Southern African Studies.* 17. 4 (1991). pp. 654–677.

Neal, Larry and Jeffrey Williamson. *Cambridge History of Capitalism. Vol. 2. The Spread of Capitalism: From 1848 to the Present.* Cambridge University Press. 2014.

Neal, Larry and Lance Davis. 'The Evolution of the Structure and Performance of the London Stock Exchange in the First Global Financial Market, 1812–1914.' *European Review of Economic History.* 10. 3 (2006). pp. 279–300.

Neal, Larry. 'How It All Began: The Monetary and Financial Architecture of Europe During the First Global Capital Markets, 1648–1815.' *Financial History Review.* 7. 2 (2000). pp. 117–140.

Neal, Larry. *The Rise of Financial Capitalism: International Capital Markets in the Age of Reason.* Cambridge: Cambridge University Press. 1993.

Nel, Etienne. 'South Africa Pushed to the Limit: The Political Economy of Change.' *African Affairs.* 112. 446 (2013). pp. 165–167.

Ness, Immanuel and Zak Cope, eds. *The Palgrave Encyclopedia of Imperialism and Anti-imperialism.* Vol.1 New York: Palgrave Macmillan. 2016.

Newbury, Colin. 'The Origins and Function of the London Diamond Syndicate, 1889–1914.' *Business History.* 29. 1 (1987). pp. 5–26.

Newbury, Colin. 'Technology, Capital, and Consolidation: The Performance of De Beers Mining Company Limited, 1880–1889.' *Business History Review* 61. 1 (1987). pp. 1–42.

Noer, Thomas J. *Briton, Boer, and Yankee: The United States and South Africa, 1870–1914.* Kent: Kent State University Press. 1978.

Norcliffe, Glen. *Critical Geographies of Cycling: History, Political Economy and Culture.* London: Routledge. 2016.

Noyes, Alexander D. 'Stock Exchange Clearing Houses.' *Political Science Quarterly.* 8. 2 (1893). pp. 252–267.

Ntim, Collins G. 'Why African Stock Markets Should Formally Harmonise and Integrate their Operations.' *African Review of Economics and Finance.* 4. 1 (2012). pp. 53–72.

Nyamunda, Tinashe. 'Gold, Currency and Stamps: The Rejected Plans for a State and Public Bank in Early Colonial Zimbabwe (1896–1907).' In: Pallaver, Karin, ed. *Monetary Transitions: Currencies, Colonialism and African Societies.* Palgrave Macmillan, 2022.

O'Brien, Patrick. 'Historiographical Traditions and Modern Imperatives for the Restoration of Global History.' *Journal of Global History* 1. 1 (2006). pp. 3–39.

Obstfeld, Maurice and Alan M. Taylor. *Global Capital Markets: Integration, Crisis, and Growth*. Cambridge: Cambridge University Press. 2004.

Olivier Feiertag and Michel Margairaz, eds. *Politiques et pratiques des banques d'émission en Europe*. Paris: Albin Michel. 2003.

Oppenheimer, Harry. 'The Orange Free State Gold Fields.' *South African Journal of Economics*. 18. 2 (1950). pp. 148–156.

Orhangazi, Özgür. 'Finance, Finance Capital, Financialisation.' In: Ness, Immanuel, and Zak Cope, eds. *The Palgrave Encyclopedia of Imperialism and Anti-imperialism*. Vol.1 New York: Palgrave Macmillan. 2016.

O'Rourke Kevin H. *Why Economics Needs Economic History*. VOXEU. 24 July 2013. http://www.voxeu.org/article/why-economics-needs-economic-history.

O'Rourke, Kevin and Jeffrey G. Williamson. 'Late Nineteenth-Century Anglo-American Factor-price Convergence: Were Heckscher and Ohlin Right?' *The Journal of Economic History*. 54. 4 (1994). pp. 892–916.

O'Rourke, Kevin H. and Jeffrey Gale Williamson. *Globalization and History: The Evolution of a Nineteenth Century Atlantic Economy*. Cambridge: MIT Press. 1999.

Ory, Pascal. *L'Expo universelle, 1889*. Vol. 210. Paris: Editions Complexe. 1989.

Osterhammel, Jürgen. *Die Verwandlung der Welt: eine Geschichte des 19. Jahrhunderts*. München: CH Beck. 2010.

O'Sullivan, Mary A. 'Yankee Doodle Went to London: Anglo-American Breweries and the London Securities Market, 1888–92.' *The Economic History Review*. 68. 4 (2015).pp. 1365–1387.

Pakenham, Thomas. *The Boer War*. London: Weidenfeld and Nicolson. 1979.

Parker, Robert Henry. 'Regulating British Corporate Financial Reporting in the Late Nineteenth Century.' *Accounting, Business & Financial History*. 1. 1 (1990). pp. 51–71.

Parkhouse, Valerie. *Memorializing the Anglo-Boer War of 1899–1902: Militarization of the Landscape, Monuments and Memorials in Britain*. Kibworth Beauchamp: Matador. 2015.

Paterson, Michael. *Winston Churchill: Personal Accounts of the Great Leader at War*. London: David & Charles. 2005.

Petterson, Donald R. 'The Witwatersrand a Unique Gold Mining Community.' *Economic Geography*. 27. 3 (1951). pp. 209–221.

Patteson, Richard F. 'King Solomon's Mines: Imperialism and Narrative Structure.' *The Journal of Narrative Technique*. 8. 2 (1978). pp. 112–123.

Philippon, Daniel J., J. A. Pullen and Arthur G. Enock. 'Mark Twain in South Africa. Day by Day.' *Mark Twain Journal*. 40. 1 (2002). pp. 14–24.

Phimister, Ian. 'Markets, Mines, and Magnates: Finance and the Coming of War in South Africa, 1894–1899.' *Africa: Rivista semestrale di studi e ricerche*. 2. 2 (2020). pp. 5–22.

Phimister, Ian. 'Late Nineteenth-Century Globalization: London and Lomagundi Perspectives on Mining Speculation in southern Africa, 1894–1904.' *Journal of Global History*. 10. 1 (2015). pp. 27–52.

Phimister, Ian and Stanley Trapido. 'Introduction to "Imperialism, Settler Identities and Colonial Capitalism": The Hundred Year Origins of the 1899 South African War.' *Historia*. 53. 1 (2008). pp. 45–75.

Phimister, Ian and Jeremy Mouat. 'Mining, Engineers and Risk Management: British Overseas Investment, 1894–1914.' *South African Historical Journal*. 49. 1 (2003). pp. 1–26.

Phimister, I. Speculation and Exploitation: The Southern Rhodesian Mining Industry in the Company Era. *Historia*. 48. 2 (2003). pp. 88–97.

Phimister, Ian. 'Empire, Imperialism and the Partition of Africa.' In: Akita, Shigeru, ed. *Gentlemanly Capitalism, Imperialism and Global History*. Springer. 2002.

Phimister, Ian R. *An Economic and Social History of Zimbabwe, 1890–1948: Capital Accumulation and Class Struggle*. Harlow: Longman Ltd. 1988

Phimister, Ian R. 'Rhodes, Rhodesia and the Rand.' *Journal of Southern African Studies*. 1. 1 (1974). pp. 74–90.

Pierson, Paul. *Politics in Time: History, Institutions, and Social Analysis*. Princeton: Princeton University Press. 2004.

Piketty, Thomas. *Capital in the Twenty-First Century*. Cambridge: Harvard University Press. 2014.

Poitras, Geoffrey, ed. *Handbook of Research on Stock Market Globalization*. Cheltenham: Edward Elgar Publishing. 2012.

Porter, Andrew. 'Britain, the Cape Colony, and Natal, 1870–1914: Capital, Shipping, and the Imperial Connexion.' *The Economic History Review*. 34. 4 (1981). pp. 554–577.

Porter, A. 'Gentlemanly Capitalism' and Empire: The British Experience Since 1750?' *The Journal of Imperial and Commonwealth History*. 18. 3 (1990). pp. 265–295.

Porter, Andrew. 'Religion and Empire: British Expansion in the Long Nineteenth Century, 1780–1914.' *The Journal of Imperial and Commonwealth History*. 20. 3 (1992). pp. 370–390.

Porter, Andrew. 'The South African War and the Historians.' *African Affairs*. 99. 397 (2000). pp. 633–648.

Porter, Dilwyn. 'A Trusted Guide of the Investing Public': Harry Marks and the Financial News 1884–1916.' *Business History*. 28. 1 (1986). pp. 1–17.

Potter, Elaine. *The Press as Opposition: The Political Role of South African Newspapers*. London: Chatto & Windus. 1975.

Platt, D. C. M. *Finance, Trade, and Politics in British Foreign Policy, 1815–1914*. Oxford: Clarendon Press. 1968.

Plug, C. Early Scientific and Professional Societies in the Transvaal: Barberton 1887–1889. *South African Journal of Cultural History*. 4. 3 (1990). pp. 190–199.

Preda, Alex. 'The Rise of the Popular Investor: Financial Knowledge and Investing in England and France, 1840–1880.' *The Sociological Quarterly*. 42. 2 (2001). pp. 205–232.

Preda, Alex. 'The Sociological Approach to Financial Markets.' *Journal of Economic Surveys*. 21. 3 (2007). pp. 506–533.

Previts, Gary John, Peter Walton and P. W. Wolnizer. *A Global History of Accounting, Financial Reporting and Public Policy: Europe*. Sydney: Emerald Group Publishing. 2010.

Rhoodie, Denys O. *Conspirators in Conflict: A Study of the Johannesburg Reform Committee and Its Role in the Conspiracy Against the South African Republic*. Cape Town: Tafelberg-uitgewers. 1967.

Radford, Dennis. 'The Early History of the Tall Building in the South African City.' *Construction History*. 14 (1998). pp. 41-58.

Ranger, Terence O. *Bulawayo Burning: The Social History of a Southern African City, 1893–1960*. Woodbridge: Boydell & Brewer. 2010.

Ranger, Terence O. *Revolt in Southern Rhodesia, 1896–7: A Study in African Resistance*. London: Heinemann. 1967.

Raugh, Harold E. *The Victorians at War, 1815–1914: An Encyclopedia of British Military History*. Santa Barbara: Abc-Clio. 2004.

Reese, Trevor R. *The History of the Royal Commonwealth Society 1868–1968*. London: Oxford University Press. 1968.

Renfrew, Christie. *Electricity, Industry and Class in South Africa*. Albany: State University of New York Press. 1984.

Richards, Cecil Sydney. 'The Report of the Company Law Amendment Enquiry Commission.' *South African Journal of Economics*. 17. 3 (1949). pp. 229–251.

Richards, Cecil Sydney. 'Stock Exchange Facilities in the Union–The Open Call Exchange.' *South African Journal of Economics*. 1. 4 (1933). pp. 511–518.

Riva, Angelo and Eugene N. White. 'Danger on the Exchange: How Counterparty Risk was Managed on the Paris Exchange in the Nineteenth Century.' *Explorations in Economic History*. 48. 4 (2011). pp. 478–493.

Roberts, A. D. 'The Earlier Historiography of Colonial Africa.' *History in Africa*. 5 (1978). pp. 153–167.

Rodney, Robert M. *Mark Twain Overseas: A Biographical Account of his Voyages, Travels, and Reception in Foreign Lands, 1866–1910*. No. 5. Washington D.C.: Three Continents Press. 1993.

Robinson, Cynthia A. *The Power Behind the Press. English Newspapers in The Transvaal, 1870–1899*. Unpublished Dissertation. University of British Columbia. 1989.

Robinson Ronald, James Gallagher and Alice Denny. *Africa and the Victorians: The Official Mind of Imperialism*. London: Macmillan. 1981

Rosenthal, Eric. *The Rand Rush: 1886–1911, Johannesburg's First 25 Years in Pictures*. Johannesburg: A. Donker Publising. 1974.

Rosenthal, Eric. *Gold ! Gold ! Gold !* New York: Macmillan. 1970.

Rosenthal, Eric. *On 'Change Through the Years; a History of Share Dealing in South Africa*. Cape Town: Flesch Financial Publications. 1968

Rosenthal, Eric. *Other Men's Millions*. Cape Town: Howard Timmins. 1965.

Rosenthal, Eric. *Gold Bricks and Mortar: 60 Years of Johannesburg History*. Johannesburg: Printing House. 1946.

Ross, Robert, Anne Kelk Mager and Bill Nasson, eds. *The Cambridge History of South Africa. Vol: 2: 1885–1994*. Cambridge: Cambridge University Press. 2011.

Ross, Robert. *A Concise History of South Africa*. 2nd Ed. Cambridge: Cambridge University Press. 2008.

Rossouw, Jannie and Vishnu Padayachee. 'Reflecting on Ninety Years of Intermittent Success: The Experience of the South African Reserve Bank with Inflation Since 1921.' *Economic History of Developing Regions*. 26. 1 (2011). pp. 53–72

Rönnbäck, Klas, and Oskar Broberg. *Capital and Colonialism: The Return on British Investments in Africa 1869–1969*. Springer. 2019.

Rubinstein, David. 'Cycling in the 1890s.' *Victorian Studies* 21. 1 (1977). pp. 47–71.

Rubinstein, William D. *The Palgrave Dictionary of Anglo-Jewish History*. London: Palgrave Macmillan. 2011.

Scharnhorst, Gary. *Twain in His Own Time: A Biographical Chronicle of His Life, Drawn from Recollections, Interviews, and Memoirs by Family, Friends, and Associates*. Iowa City: University of Iowa Press. 2010.

Scharnhorst, Gary. *Mark Twain: The Complete Interviews*. Tuscaloosa: University of Alabama Press. 2006.

Scheidegger, Ursula. *Transformation from Below? White Suburbia in the Transformation of Apartheid South Africa to Democracy*. Vol. 9. Basel: Basler Afrika Bibliographien. 2015.

Schirmer, Stefan. 'The Contribution of Entrepreneurs to the Emergence of Manufacturing in South Africa Before 1948.' *South African Journal of Economic History* 23. 2 (2008). pp. 184–215.

Schmitt, Cannon, Nancy Henry and Anjali Arondekar. 'Introduction: Victorian Investments.' *Victorian Studies*. 45. 1 (2002). pp. 7–16.

Schneidermann, Harry. 'Necrology.' *The American Jewish Year Book*. 36 (1935). pp. 277–298.

Schreuder, Deryck and Jeffrey Butler, eds. *Sir Graham Bower's The History of the Jameson Raid and the South African Crisis, 1895–1902*. No. 33. Cape Town: The Van Riebeeck Society. 2002.

Schreuder, Deryck Marshall. *The Scramble for southern Africa, 1877–1895: The Politics of Partition Reappraised.* Vol. 11. Cambridge: Cambridge University Press. 1980.

Schumpeter, Joseph. *Theorie der wirtschaftlichen Entwicklung.* Berlin: Duncker & Humblot. 1911.

Shillington, Kevin, ed. *Encyclopedia of African History 3-Volume Set.* London: Routledge. 2013.

Shorten, John R. *The Johannesburg Saga.* Johannesburg: John R. Shorten (Proprietary) ltd.1970.

Seekings, Jeremy and Nicoli Nattrass. *Class, Race, and Inequality in South Africa.* New Haven: Yale University Press. 2008.

Simonson, Peter, Janice Peck, Robert T Craig and John Jackson. *The Handbook of Communication History.* London: Routledge. 2013.

Slater, Henry. 'Land, Labour and Capital in Natal: The Natal Land and Colonisation Company 1860–19481.' *The Journal of African History* 16, no. 2 (1975): 257-283.

Smith, Iain R. 'Jan Smuts and the South African War.' *South African Historical Journal.* 41. 1 (1999). pp. 172–195.

Southall, Roger. *New Black Middle Class in South Africa.* London: James Currey. 2016.

Standage, Tom. *The Victorian Internet: The Remarkable Story of the Telegraph and the Nineteenth Century's Online Pioneers.* London: Weidenfeld & Nicolson. 1998.

Stevenson, Michael. *Old Masters and Aspirations: The Randlords, Art and South Africa.* Unpublished Dissertation. University of Cape Town. 1997.

The Star. *Like it Was: The Star 100 Years in Johannesburg.* Johannesburg: The Star Publishing. 1987.

Stephens, John. *Fuelling the Empire: South Africa's Road to War.* London: John Wiley & Sons. 2003.

Stiglitz, Joseph E. 'Capital Market Liberalization, Economic Growth, and Instability.' *World Development.* 28. 6 (2000). pp. 1075–1086.

Stoler, Ann Laura. *Along the Archival Grain: Epistemic Anxieties and Colonial Common Sense.* Princeton: Princeton University Press. 2010.

Stone, Irving. *The Global Export of Capital from Great Britain, 1865–1914: A Statistical Survey.* London: Macmillan. 1999.

Strydom, Nicolaas Tjaart. *Stock Exchange Legitimacy: The Case of the Johannesburg Stock Exchange, 1887–1945.* Doctoral Dissertation. University of Johannesburg (South Africa). 2021.

Swanson, Maynard W. 'The Asiatic Menace: Creating Segregation in Durban, 1870–1900.' *International Journal of African Historical Studies.* 13. 3 (1983). pp. 401–421.

Tamarkin, Mordechai. *Cecil Rhodes and the Cape Afrikaners: The Imperial Colossus and the Colonial Parish Pump*. London: Frank Cass and Co. 1996

Teisch, Jessica B. *Engineering Nature: Water, Development, and the Global Spread of American Environmental Expertise*. Chapel Hill: Univ of North Carolina Press. 2011.

Teisch, Jessica. "Home is Not So Very Far Away': Californian Engineers in South Africa, 1868–1915.' *Australian Economic History Review*. 45. 2 (2005). pp. 139–160.

Terreblanche, Sampie. *Politieke ekonomie en sosiale welvaart: met'n toepassing op Suid-Afrika*. Cape Town: Academica. 1986.

Thompson, Leonard Monteath. *A History of South Africa*. New Haven: Yale University Press. 2014.

Trapido, Stanley. 'Landlord and Tenant in a Colonial Economy: The Transvaal 1880–1910.' *Journal of Southern African Studies*. 5. 1 (1978). pp. 26–58

Trapido, Stanley. 'The South African Republic: Class Formation and the State, 1850–1900.' *Collected Seminar Papers*. *Institute of Commonwealth Studies*. Vol. 16. London: Institute of Commonwealth Studies. 1973.

Trapido, Stanley. 'South Africa in a Comparative Study of Industrialization.' *The Journal of Development Studies*. 7. 3 (1971). pp. 309–320.

Tuffnell, Stephen. 'Engineering Inter-imperialism: American Miners and the Transformation of Global Mining, 1871–1910.' *Journal of Global History*. 10. 1 (2015). pp. 53–76.

Turrell, Robert Vicat. *Capital and Labour on the Kimberley Diamond Fields, 1871–1890*. Cambridge: Cambridge University Press. 1987.

Turrell, Robert Vicat. 'Review Article: 'Finance... the Governor of the Imperial Engine': Hobson and the Case of Rothschild and Rhodes.' *Journal of Southern African Studies* 13. 3 (1987). pp. 417–432.

Turrell, Robert Vicat and Jean-Jacques Van Helten. 'The Rothschilds, the Exploration Company and Mining Finance.' *Business History*. 28. 2 (1986). pp. 181–205.

Ugolini, Stefano. *The Bank of England as the World Gold Market-Maker During the Classical Gold Standard Era, 1889–1910*. Norges Bank. No. 2012/15. https://hal.inria.fr/hal-01293932/document

van den Bersselaar, Dmitri 'Business Records as Sources for African History' in Thomas Spear, ed., *The Oxford Encyclopedia of African Historiography: Methods and Sources Vol 1* (New York: Oxford University Press, 2019.

Van der Poel, Jean. *The Jameson Raid*. Oxford: Oxford University Press. 1951.

Van Helten Jean Jacques and Youssef Cassis. *Capitalism in a Mature Economy: Financial Institutions, Capital Exports and British Industry, 1870–1939*. London: Edward Edgar Publishing. 1990.

Van Helten, Jean Jacques. 'Empire and High Finance: South Africa and the International Gold Standard, 1890–1914.' *Journal of African history* 23. 4 (1982). pp. 529–548.

Van Helten, Jean Jacques. *British and European Economic Investment in the Transvaal: With Specific Reference to the Witwatersrand Gold Fields and District, 1886–1910.* Unpublished Dissertation. University of London. 1981.

Van Helten, Jean Jacques. 'Mining and Imperialism.' *Journal of Southern African Studies.* 6. 2 (1980). pp. 230–235.

Van Helten, Jean Jacques. 'German Capital, the Netherlands Railway Company and the Political Economy of the Transvaal, 1886-1900.' *Journal of African history.* 19. 3 (1978). pp. 369–390.

Van Helten, Jean Jacques. 'British Capital, the British State and Economic Investment in South Africa 1886–1914.' *University of London, Institute of Commonwealth Studies, Collected Seminar Papers, The Societies of Southern Africa in the 19th and 20th Centuries.* 9. 24 (1977). http://sas-space.sas. ac.uk/4066/1/J_J_van_Helten_-_British_capital,_the_British_state_and_eco nomic_investment_in_South_African_1886-1914.pdf

Van Onselen, Charles. *Studies in the Social and Economic History of the Witwatersrand 1886–1914: New Babylon.* London: Addison-Wesley Longman Ltd. 1982

Van Onselen, Charles. 'Reactions to Rinderpest in southern Africa 1896–97.' *The Journal of African History.* 13. 3 (1972). pp. 473–488.

Van der Waal, G-M. *From Mining Camp to Metropolis: The Buildings of Johannesburg, 1886–1940.* Pretoria: Chris van Rensburg for the Human Sciences Research Council. Pretoria. 1987.

Verhoef, Grietjie, Lorraine Greyling and John Mwamba. 'Savings and Economic Growth: A Historical Analysis of the Relationship Between Savings and Economic Growth in the CAPE Colony Economy, 1850–1909.' *MPRA Working Paper No.* 47819. 2013. https://mpra.ub.uni-muenchen.de/ 47819/1/MPRA_paper_47819.pdf

Verhoef, Grietjie. 'Mutuality and Regulation: The Transition from Mutual to Public in the South African Long-term Insurance Industry.' *Journal of Economic and Financial Sciences.* 5. 2 (2012). pp. 567–590.

Verhoef, Grietjie. 'Informal Financial Service Institutions for Survival: African Women and Stokvels in Urban South Africa, 1930–1998.' *Enterprise and Society.* 2. 2 (2001). pp. 259–296.

Verhoef, Grietjie. 'The Role of Women in the South African Economy.' *South African Journal of Economics.* 64. 3 (1996). pp. 178–187.

Verhoef, Grietjie. *Die geskiedenis van Nedbank, 1945–1973.* PhD Dissertation. Johannesburg: Randse Afrikaanse Universiteit. 1987.

Visser, Wessel. 'Trends in South African Historiography and the Present State of Historical Research.' *Nordic Africa Institute, Uppsala*. Working Paper 23. 2004.

Walker, Donald A. 'A Factual Account of the Functioning of the Nineteenth-Century Paris Bourse.' *European Journal of the History of Economic Thought*. 8. 2 (2001). pp. 186–207.

Walker, Eric Anderson. *The Cambridge History of the British Empire*. Cambridge: Cambridge University Press Archive. 1963.

Warwick, Peter. *Black People and the South African War 1899–1902*. Cambridge: Cambridge University Press. 1983.

Warwick, Peter. *The South African War: The Anglo-Boer War, 1899–1902*. London: Addison-Wesley Longman Ltd. 1980.

Warwick, Peter. 'African Labour During the South African War, 1899–1902.' *Collected Seminar Papers. Institute of Commonwealth Studies*. Vol. 21. London: Institute of Commonwealth Studies. 1977. http://sas-space.sas.ac.uk/4048/1/Peter_Warwick_-_African_labour_during_the_South_African_war,_1899-1902.pdf

Webb, Arthur. 'Blainey and Early Witwatersrand Profitability Some Thoughts on Financial Management and Capital Constraints Facing the Gold Mining Industry 1886–1894.' *South African Journal of Economic History*. 12. 1 (1997). pp. 128–152.

Webb, Arthur. *The Roots of the Tree. A Study in Early South African Banking: The Predecessors of the First National Bank, 1838–1926*. Cape Town: First National Bank of Southern Africa Ltd. 1992.

Webb, Arthur. 'The Early History of the Witwatersrand Gold Mining Company.' *South African Journal of Economics*. 48. 2 (1980). pp. 95–109.

Weber, Max. *Boersenwesen: Schriften und Reden: 1893–1898. Halbband 1*. Vol. 5. Tübingen: Mohr Siebeck. 2000

Wessels, André. *The Anglo-Boer War 1889–1902: White Man's War, Black Man's War, Traumatic War*. Stellenbosch: African Sun Media. 2011.

Wheatcroft, Geoffrey. *The Randlords*. London: Simon & Schuster. 1987.

White, Eugene N. *The Crash of 1882, Counterparty Risk, and the Bailout of the Paris Bourse*. No. w12933. National Bureau of Economic Research. 2007.

Wilburn, Kenneth. 'The Nature of the Rothschild Loan: International Capital and South African Railway Diplomacy, Politics, and Construction 1891–1892.' *South African Journal of Economic History*. 3. 1 (1988). pp. 4–19.

Wilson, Bobby M. *America's Johannesburg: Industrialization and Racial Transformation in Birmingham*. Rowman & Littlefield. 2000.

Winseck, Dwayne R. and Robert M. Pike. *Communication and Empire: Media, Markets, and Globalization, 1860–1930*. Durham: Duke University Press. 2007.

Wood, Geoffrey, Terence Mills and Nicholas Crafts, eds. *Monetary and Banking History: Essays in Honour of Forrest Capie*. London: Taylor & Francis. 2011.

Woods, Ngaire and Leonardo Martinez-Diaz, eds. *Networks of Influence? Developing Countries in a Networked Global Order*. Oxford: Oxford University Press. 2009.

Wolpe, Harold. 'Capitalism and Cheap Labour-power in South Africa: From Segregation to Apartheid.' *Economy and Society*. 1. 4 (1972). pp. 425–456.

Wragg, Thomas Walter and Henry Ernest Bulwer. *Report of the Indian Immigrants Commission: 1885–1887*. Natal Colonial Office: Pietermaritzburg. 1887. http://scnc.ukzn.ac.za/doc/INDENTURE/Reports/Report_indian_immigrants_commission_1885_7_Wragg_Commission.pdf

Wright, Robert E. *The First Wall Street: Chestnut Street, Philadelphia, and the Birth of American Finance*. Chicago: University of Chicago Press. 2010.

Zeleza, Tiyambe. *A Modern Economic History of Africa: The Nineteenth Century*. Vol. 1. Nairobi: East African Publishers. 1997.

Index

Printed by Printforce, United Kingdom